Virtues and Vices
and Other Essays
in Moral Philosophy

Virtues and Vices
and Other Essays
in Moral Philosophy

PHILIPPA FOOT

CLARENDON PRESS · OXFORD

OXFORD
UNIVERSITY PRESS

Great Clarendon Street, Oxford OX2 6DP

Oxford University Press is a department of the University of Oxford.
It furthers the University's objective of excellence in research, scholarship,
and education by publishing worldwide in

Oxford New York

Auckland Bangkok Buenos Aires Cape Town Chennai
Dar es Salaam Delhi Hong Kong Istanbul Karachi Kolkata
Kuala Lumpur Madrid Melbourne Mexico City Mumbai Nairobi
São Paulo Shanghai Singapore Taipei Tokyo Toronto

with an associated company in Berlin

Oxford is a registered trade mark of Oxford University Press
in the UK and in certain other countries

Published in the United States
by Oxford University Press Inc., New York

© in this edition, Philippa Foot 2002

The moral rights of the author have been asserted
Database right Oxford University Press (maker)

First published 1978 by Blackwell Publishers and University of California Press

First published by Oxford University Press 2002

All rights reserved. No part of this publication may be reproduced,
stored in a retrieval system, or transmitted, in any form or by any means,
without the prior permission in writing of Oxford University Press,
or as expressly permitted by law, or under terms agreed with the appropriate
reprographics rights organization. Enquiries concerning reproduction
outside the scope of the above should be sent to the Rights Department,
Oxford University Press, at the address above

You must not circulate this book in any other binding or cover
and you must impose this same condition on any acquirer

British Library Cataloguing in Publication Data

Data available

Library of Congress Cataloging in Publication Data

Foot, Philippa.
Virtues and vices and other essays in moral philosophy/Philippa Foot.
p. cm.
Originally published: Berkeley: University of California Press, 1978. With new pref.
and index.
Includes bibliographical references and index.
Contents: Virtues and vices—The problem of abortion and the doctrine of the double
effect—Euthanasia—Free will as involving determinism—Hume on moral judgement—
Nietzsche, the revaluation of values—Moral arguments—Moral beliefs—Goodness
and choice—Reasons for action and desires—Morality as a system of hypothetical
imperatives—A reply to Professor Frankena—Are moral considerations overriding?—
Approval and disapproval.
1. Ethics. I. Title.
BJ1012.F57 2002   170—dc21   2002025813

ISBN 0-19-925285-8
ISBN 0-19-925286-6 (pbk.)

1 3 5 7 9 10 8 6 4 2

Printed in Great Britain
on acid-free paper by
Biddles Ltd.,
Guildford & King's Lynn

TO
THE MEMORY OF
IRIS MURDOCH

Contents

Preface to 2002 Edition

These essays, originally published between 1958 and 1977, were written at a time when emotivist and prescriptivist views reigned in analytic moral philosophy, and when individual virtues and vices were still given relatively little attention. Things have changed since then, and I am conscious that some of the papers have dated at least in their idiom, given that at the time they appeared 'man' was taken to mean 'human being' rather than 'male person', so that the intrusively corrective 'she' or the cumbrous 'he or she' were considered unnecessary. But I believe that the path that I was taking in most of the papers towards an objectivist theory of ethics is still serviceable today, while other essays such as the one on euthanasia are fairly constantly in demand.

In general I still agree with what I wrote in younger days. But I can claim little consistency over the years in respect of one crucial problem in moral philosophy: that of the relation between practical rationality and moral virtue. The problem is to see how for every person and in every case it can be rational to follow moral edicts—in particular the demands of justice and charity—when these seem to clash with self-interest or desire. We want to be able to say that to act as justice or charity demands is to act rationally in every case, even in the tight corner. But how is this possible?

Ever preoccupied by this problem, I have tried now this now that way out of the difficulty. In 'Moral Beliefs' I argued that only the coincidence of virtue and self-interest could give the desired rationality to each and every person whatever his or her contingent desires. Later, when writing 'Morality as a System of Hypothetical Imperatives', the problem of the 'tight corner' made me dissatisfied with this supposed solution, after which, in a despairing mood, I was even ready to deny that for everyone, always, it *would* be rational to act morally. This was often identified as 'Foot's position', long after I myself had abandoned it and was working my way around, very slowly, to the quite different position that I first took up in the eighties and have held ever since.

In a 1995 lecture called 'Does Moral Subjectivism Rest on a Mistake?', which is substantially Chapter I of my 2001 book *Natural Goodness*, as well as in Chapter 4 of that book, I argued that the whole direction of my earlier efforts (and of those of many others) had been mistaken. We had tried to reconcile the demands of virtue with an independently determined canon of practical rationality such as conduciveness to the fulfilment of desire or to rational self-interest. *And that was a mistake.* A tip-off from my UCLA colleague the late Warren Quinn had allowed me to see that the very concept of practical rationality might not be independent of that of practical *goodness* as describable in a really general account of the virtues: indeed that it might have to fit in with them rather than them with it.[1] Therefore, the appearance of a clash between the requirements of moral virtue and practical rationality should put in question not charity or justice but rather the theory of reasons for action that gave that result. I am only sad that Quinn did not have time to develop this idea himself.

P.R.F.
December 2001

---

[1] See 'Putting Rationality in its Place', in Warren Quinn, *Morality and Action*, (Cambridge University Press, 1993).

Preface

It is hard to thank all those who have helped me with my work over the years in which these essays were written. I owe most, perhaps, to Donald MacKinnon who first taught me moral philosophy, but also much to Somerville College where I was supported most generously through many unproductive years. I was most fortunate to have Elizabeth Anscombe as my colleague at Somerville, and I know that some of the ideas for these essays came out of our lunchtime discussions in the Senior Common Room.

More recently I have been helped, in different but always important ways, by Rogers Albritton, John Giuliano, Rosalind Hursthouse, Jerrold Katz, John McDowell, Warren Quinn, David Sachs, Barry Stroud, and Michael Sukale, while special thanks must go to Derek Parfit who has worked on drafts of my papers with a speed and skill that amaze me, and a kindness to warm the heart. I am also most grateful to the Philosophy Department at the University of California at Los Angeles, and to the efficient and generous office staff, with Louise Nunnink as its guiding spirit.

P.R.F.
November 1977

Introduction
(1977)

Two of the papers in this volume, 'Virtues and Vices' and 'Are Moral Considerations Overriding?', are published here for the first time. The others were written between 1957 and 1976, and are mostly reprinted as they originally appeared. I have, however, added footnotes here and there; and as well as a short Postscript to 'Reasons for Action and Desires' there is a long footnote to 'Morality as a System of Hypothetical Imperatives' containing material from an earlier version of that essay. Furthermore I have made some changes in the paper called 'Approval and Disapproval' which originally appeared as part of the Festschrift for Herbert Hart. I included this last essay after some hesitation, and I hope it may be read not as a finished product but rather as an indication of the direction in which I should like to go after the publication of the present volume. I am sad that even after much work I did not have something more complete to offer for the Festschrift.

The volume falls into two parts. Papers I–VI are on various topics and authors, and not presented here in the order in which they were written. Papers VII–XIV do, however, represent the development of a certain line of thought on the theory of moral judgement, and the General Editor of this series has suggested that I should say something here about the way in which my views changed over the period of time in which these papers were written. Two themes run through many of the essays: opposition to emotivism and prescriptivism, and the thought that a sound moral philosophy should start from a theory of the virtues and vices. It was reading Aquinas on the individual virtues that first made me suspicious of contemporary theories about the relation between 'fact' and 'value'; and I have thought about virtues and vices on and off for the last twenty years. Meanwhile I was moving, a step at a time, away from the theories of philosophers such as C. L. Stevenson and R. M. Hare.

When I wrote 'Moral Arguments' I was still very much under the influence of these theories, and supposed, even if only for the sake of the argument, that my opponents were right in thinking that evaluations involved emotions, attitudes, the acceptance of first person imperatives, the recognition of reason for action or something of the sort. What I argued was that no such 'evaluative element' could explain the *whole* meaning of moral terms such as 'right' and 'wrong', and that there were in fact logical limits to the considerations that could be used to back up moral judgements. In my opponents' terminology, which I never found perspicuous, I was saying not just that moral terms must have some 'descriptive' meaning but that they had a more or less determinate 'descriptive' meaning. I was not prepared to say just what this meaning should be, but I was sure that it would not do to suppose that, for instance, someone might have a *morality* in whose ultimate principle was that it was wrong to run round trees right handed or to look at hedgehogs in the light of the moon. And if there were limits to the considerations that could be used to support a moral judgement, it followed that my emotivist and prescriptivist opponents were wrong in their account of moral argument. For they thought they could see, without enquiring into the details, that moral arguments 'might always break down', because there were invulnerable positions to which each side might retreat in case of need. I argued that no such general account of moral disputes could be given, and that for all we knew there might be a quite determinate starting point provided by the concept of morality. I supposed that moral considerations were necessarily related in some way to human good and harm, though I did not at any time accept a utilitarian theory of ethics, and have argued against it in some of the essays on substantial moral problems reprinted here.

In 'Moral Beliefs' I took up a position more radically opposed to the emotivists and prescriptivists. There I queried the existence of a separate 'evaluative element' in the meaning of ethical terms, logically unrelated to the descriptive element in moral judgement; and I argued that the facts are such as to provide all the connexion required between moral judgement and the will. In the actual conditions of human life—the conditions shared by all men—anyone has reason to cultivate the virtues. I thought it was necessary for me to show this, because at that stage it had simply not occurred to me to question the often repeated dictum that moral judgements necessarily give reasons for acting to each and every man. Nor was it too hard to argue that any man has reason to choose the virtues of courage, wisdom and temperance; since courage, wisdom and temperance are necessary for a man's well being whatever his particular interests and desires. And as self-interest seemed to me to be though not indeed the only reason for acting the only one that could be appealed to universally, I tried to show that there was a necessary connexion between virtues and self-interest. Where I came to grief was, predictably, over justice. It seems obvious that a man who acts justly must on occasion be ready to go against his own interests; but so determined was I to think that every man must have reason to act morally that I was prepared to doubt that justice is a virtue rather than give up that idea.

By the time I came to write 'Goodness and Choice' a few years later it had come to seem important that in non-moral contexts a predication of goodness was not necessarily related to the choices of the individual speaker. It was possible for someone who did not share standard desires to have no reason to choose the good cars or the good knives, or to choose to be a good rider, a good patient and all the rest. Might it not be the same with good actions and good character traits? In 'Morality as a System of Hypothetical Imperatives' I argued this explicitly, finally getting away from the presuppositions of emotivism and prescriptivism, and also from the widely accepted neo-Kantian supposition that immoral action must somehow be irrational. This argument seems to me to be undoubtedly correct; but whether I was wise to adopt the Kantian terminology of categorical and hypothetical imperatives is another matter. If a categorical imperative is understood as one that any man must automatically have reason to obey, then moral judgements are in my opinion not categorical imperatives. But I do not suppose that the means–ends model of Kant's hypothetical imperatives fits all cases of reasons, and I now wish that I had attacked Kant without taking over his terminology.

To sum up. The essays discussed in this introductory note are ones in which I was making a painfully slow journey, upward or downward according to your opinion, away from theories that located the special character of evaluations in each speaker's attitudes, feelings, or recognition of reason for acting. So far as I know the earlier essays are incomplete rather than mistaken, except for the arguments about virtue and self-interest in the second part of 'Moral Beliefs'. It is to this that the footnote on pp. 130–131 of this volume relates, and I explain there my change of mind about the necessary relation between virtue and happiness: it is not that I have given up thinking that there is a close connexion between the two, but that I no longer have to say that justice and advantage coincide, because I no longer think that each man, whatever his desires and whatever his situation, necessarily has reason to be just.

I should add that while some people take my position to be inimical to morality I myself do not. Considerations of justice, charity and the like have a strange and powerful appeal to the human heart, and we do not need bad arguments to show that no one could be indifferent to morality without error. If I am right that cannot be shown, but morality may be stronger rather than weaker if we look this fact in the face.

Acknowledgements

The author and publisher wish the thank the original publishers for permission to reprint the following essays: 'The Problem of Abortion and the Doctrine of the Double Effect', from the *Oxford Review*, No. 5 (1967); 'Euthanasia', from *Philosophy and Public Affairs*, Vol. 6, No. 2 (Winter 1977); 'Free Will as Involving Determinism', from *The Philosophical Review*, LXVI, No. 4 (October 1957); 'Hume on Moral Judgement', from David Pears (ed.), *David Hume* (London, Macmillan, 1963); 'Nietzsche: The Revaluation of Values', from R. C. Solomon (ed.), *Nietzsche, A Collection of Critical Essays* (New York, Doubleday, 1973); 'Moral Arguments', from *Mind*, 67 (1958); 'Moral Beliefs', from *Proceedings of the Aristotelian Society*, Vol. 59 (1958–1959); 'Goodness and Choice', from *The Aristotelian Society Supplementary Volume* 1961; 'Reasons for Actions and Desires', from *The Aristotelian Society Supplementary Volume* 1972; 'Morality as a System of Hypothetical Imperatives', from *The Philosophical Review*, Vol. 81, No. 3 (July 1972); 'A Reply to Professor Frankena', from *Philosophy*, 50 (1975); and 'Approval and Disapproval', from P. M. S. Hacker (ed.), *Law, Morality, and Society: Essays in Honour of H. L. A. Hart*, (Oxford: Clarendon Press, 1977).

I

Virtues and Vices

I

For many years the subject of the virtues and vices was strangely neglected by moralists working within the school of analytic philosophy. The tacitly accepted opinion was that a study of the topic would form no part of the fundamental work of ethics; and since this opinion was apparently shared by philosophers such as Kant, Mill, G. E. Moore, W. D. Ross, and H. A. Prichard, from whom contemporary moral philosophy has mostly been derived, perhaps the neglect was not so surprising after all. However that may be, things have recently been changing. During the past ten or fifteen years several philosophers have turned their attention to the subject; notably G. H. von Wright and Peter Geach. Von Wright devoted a not at all perfunctory chapter to the virtues in his book *The Varieties of Goodness*[1] published in 1963, and Peter Geach's book called *The Virtues*[2] appeared in 1977. Meanwhile a number of interesting articles on the topic have come out in the journals.

In spite of this recent work, it is best when considering the virtues and vices to go back to Aristotle and Aquinas. I myself have found Plato less helpful, because the individual virtues and vices are not so clearly or consistently distinguished in his work. It is certain, in any case, that the most systematic account is found in Aristotle, and in the blending of Aristotelian and Christian philosophy found in St. Thomas. By and large Aquinas followed Aristotle—sometimes even heroically—where Aristotle gave an opinion, and where St. Thomas is on his own, as in developing the doctrine of the theological virtues of faith, hope and charity, and in his theocentric doctrine of happiness, he still uses an Aristotelian framework where he can: as for instance in speaking of happiness as man's last end. However, there are different emphases and new elements in Aquinas's ethics: often he works things out in far more detail than Aristotle did, and it is possible to learn a great deal from Aquinas that one could not have got from Aristotle. It is my opinion that the *Summa Theologica* is one of the best sources we have for moral philosophy, and moreover that St. Thomas's ethical writings are as useful to the atheist as to the Catholic or other Christian believer.

There is, however, one minor obstacle to be overcome when one goes back to Aristotle and Aquinas for help in constructing a theory of virtues, namely a lack of coincidence between their terminology and our own. For when we talk about the virtues we are not taking as our subject everything to which Aristotle gave the name *aretē* or Aquinas *virtus*, and consequently not everything called a virtue in translations of these authors. 'The virtues' to us are the moral virtues whereas *aretē* and *virtus* refer also to arts, and even to excellences of the speculative intellect whose domain is theory rather than practice. And to make things more confusing we find some dispositions called moral virtues in translations from the Greek and Latin, although the class of virtues that Aristotle calls *aretai ēthikai* and Aquinas *virtutes morales* does not exactly correspond with our class of moral virtues. For us there are four cardinal moral virtues: courage, temperance, wisdom and justice. But Aristotle and Aquinas call only three of these virtues moral virtues; practical wisdom (Aristotle's *phronēsis* and Aquinas's *prudentia*) they class with the intellectual virtues, though they point out the close connexions between practical wisdom and what they call moral virtues; and sometimes they even use *aretē* and *virtus* very much as we use 'virtue'.

I will come back to Aristotle and Aquinas, and shall indeed refer to them frequently in this paper. But I want to start by making some remarks, admittedly fragmentary, about the concept of a moral virtue as we understand the idea.

First of all it seems clear that virtues are, in some general way, beneficial. Human beings do not get on well without them. Nobody can get on well if he lacks courage, and does not have some measure of temperance and wisdom, while communities where justice and charity are lacking are apt to be wretched places to live, as Russia was under the Stalinist terror, or Sicily under the Mafia. But now we must ask to whom the benefit goes, whether to the man who has the virtue or rather to those who have to do with him? In the case of some of the virtues the answer seems clear. Courage, temperance and wisdom benefit both the man who has these dispositions and other people as well; and moral failings such as pride, vanity, worldliness, and avarice harm both their possessor and others, though chiefly perhaps the former. But what about the virtues of charity and justice? These are directly concerned with the welfare of others, and with what is owed to them; and since each may require sacrifice of interest on the part of the virtuous man both may seem to be deleterious to their possessor and beneficial to others. Whether in fact it is so has, of course, been a matter of controversy since Plato's time or earlier. It is a reasonable opinion that on the whole a man is better off for being charitable and just, but this is not to say that circumstances may not arise in which he will have to sacrifice everything for charity or justice.

Nor is this the only problem about the relation between virtue and human good. For one very difficult question concerns the relation between justice and the common good. Justice, in the wide sense in which it is understood in discussions of the cardinal virtues, and in this paper, has to do with that to which someone has a right—that which he is owed in respect of non-interference and positive service—and rights may stand in the way of the pursuit of the common good. Or so at least it seems to those who reject utilitarian doctrines. This dispute cannot be settled here, but I shall treat justice as a virtue independent of charity, and standing as a possible limit on the scope of that virtue.

Let us say then, leaving unsolved problems behind us, that virtues are in general beneficial characteristics, and indeed ones that a human being needs to have, for his own sake and that of his fellows. This will not, however, take us far towards a definition of a virtue, since there are many other qualities of a man that may be similarly beneficial, as for instance bodily characteristics such as health and physical strength, and mental powers such as those of memory and concentration.

What is it, we must ask, that differentiates virtues from such things?

As a first approximation to an answer we might say that while health and strength are excellences of the body, and memory and concentration of the mind, it is the will that is good in a man of virtue. But this suggestion is worth only as much as the explanation that follows it. What might we mean by saying that virtue belongs to the will?

In the first place we observe that it is primarily by his intentions that a man's moral dispositions are judged. If he does something unintentionally this is usually irrelevant to our estimate of his virtue. But of course this thesis must be qualified, because failures in performance rather than intention may show a lack of virtue. This will be so when, for instance, one man brings harm to another without realising he is doing it, but where his ignorance is itself culpable. Sometimes in such cases there will be a previous act or omission to which we can point as the source of the ignorance. Charity requires that we take care to find out how to render assistance where we are likely to be called on to do so, and thus, for example, it is contrary to charity to fail to find out about elementary first aid. But in an interesting class of cases in which it seems again to be performance rather than intention that counts in judging a man's virtue there is no possibility of shifting the judgement to previous intentions. For sometimes one man succeeds where another fails not because there is some specific difference in their previous conduct but rather because his heart lies in a different place; and the disposition of the heart is part of virtue.

Thus it seems right to attribute a kind of moral failing to some deeply discouraging and debilitating people who say, without lying, that they mean to be helpful; and on the other side to see virtue *par excellence* in one who is prompt and resourceful in doing good. In his novel *A Single Pebble* John Hersey describes such a man, speaking of a rescue in a swift flowing river:

It was the head tracker's marvellous swift response that captured my admiration at first, his split second solicitousness when he heard a cry of pain, his finding in mid-air, as it were, the only way to save the injured boy. But there was more to it than that. His action, which could not have been mulled over in his mind, showed a deep,

instinctive love of life, a compassion, an optimism, which made me
feel very good . . .

What this suggests is that a man's virtue may be judged by his
innermost desires as well as by his intentions; and this fits with
our idea that a virtue such as generosity lies as much in someone's attitudes as in his actions. Pleasure in the good fortune of
others is, one thinks, the sign of a generous spirit; and small
reactions of pleasure and displeasure often the surest signs of a
man's moral disposition.

None of this shows that it is wrong to think of virtues as
belonging to the will; what it does show is that 'will' must here
be understood in its widest sense, to cover what is wished for
as well as what is sought.

A different set of considerations will, however, force us to
give up any simple statement about the relation between virtue and will, and these considerations have to do with the
virtue of wisdom. Practical wisdom, we said, was counted by
Aristotle among the intellectual virtues, and while our *wisdom*
is not quite the same as *phronēsis* or *prudentia* it too might seem
to belong to the intellect rather than the will. Is not wisdom a
matter of knowledge, and how can knowledge be a matter of
intention or desire? The answer is that it isn't, so that there is
good reason for thinking of wisdom as an intellectual virtue.
But on the other hand wisdom has special connexions with the
will, meeting it at more than one point.

In order to get this rather complex picture in focus we must
pause for a little and ask what it is that we ourselves understand
by wisdom: what the wise man knows and what he does.
Wisdom, as I see it, has two parts. In the first place the wise
man knows the means to certain good ends; and secondly he
knows how much particular ends are worth. Wisdom in its
first part is relatively easy to understand. It seems that there are
some ends belonging to human life in general rather than to
particular skills such as medicine or boatbuilding, ends having
to do with such matters as friendship, marriage, the bringing
up of children, or the choice of ways of life; and it seems that
knowledge of how to act well in these matters belongs to some
people but not to others. We call those who have this knowledge wise, while those who do not have it are seen as lacking

wisdom. So, as both Aristotle and Aquinas insisted, wisdom is to be contrasted with cleverness because cleverness is the ability to take the right steps to any end, whereas wisdom is related only to good ends, and to human life in general rather than to the ends of particular arts.

Moreover, we should add, there belongs to wisdom only that part of knowledge which is within the reach of any ordinary adult human being: knowledge that can be acquired only by someone who is clever or who has access to special training is not counted as part of wisdom, and would not be so counted even if it could serve the ends that wisdom serves. It is therefore quite wrong to suggest that wisdom cannot be a moral virtue because virtue must be within the reach of anyone who really wants it and some people are too stupid to be anything but ignorant even about the most fundamental matters of human life. Some people are wise without being at all clever or well informed: they make good decisions and they know, as we say, 'what's what'.

In short wisdom, in what we called its first part, is connected with the will in the following ways. To begin with it presupposes good ends: the man who is wise does not merely know *how* to do good things such as looking after his children well, or strengthening someone in trouble, but must also want to do them. And then wisdom, in so far as it consists of knowledge which anyone can gain in the course of an ordinary life, is available to anyone who really wants it. As Aquinas put it, it belongs 'to a power under the direction of the will'.[3]

The second part of wisdom, which has to do with values, is much harder to describe, because here we meet ideas which are curiously elusive, such as the thought that some pursuits are more worthwhile than others, and some matters trivial and some important in human life. Since it makes good sense to say that most men waste a lot of their lives in ardent pursuit of what is trivial and unimportant it is not possible to explain the important and the trivial in terms of the amount of attention given to different subjects by the average man. But I have never seen, or been able to think out, a true account of this matter, and I believe that a complete account of wisdom, and of certain other virtues and vices must wait until this gap can be filled. What we can see is that one of the things a wise man knows and a foolish man does not is that such things as social position, and wealth, and the good opinion of the world, are too dearly bought at the cost of health or friendship or family ties. So we may say that a man who lacks wisdom 'has false values', and that vices such as vanity and worldliness and avarice are contrary to wisdom in a special way. There is always an element of false judgement about these vices, since the man who is vain for instance sees admiration as more important than it is, while the worldly man is apt to see the good life as one of wealth and power. Adapting Aristotle's distinction between the weak-willed man (the akratēs) who follows pleasure though he knows, in some sense, that he should not, and the licentious man (the akolastos) who sees the life of pleasure as the good life,[4] we may say that moral failings such as these are never purely 'akratic'. It is true that a man may criticise himself for his worldliness or vanity or love of money, but then it is his values that are the subject of his criticism.

Wisdom in this second part is, therefore, partly to be described in terms of apprehension, and even judgement, but since it has to do with a man's attachments it also characterises his will.

The idea that virtues belong to the will, and that this helps to distinguish them from such things as bodily strength or intellectual ability has, then, survived the consideration of the virtue of wisdom, albeit in a fairly complex and slightly attenuated form. And we shall find this idea useful again if we turn to another important distinction that must be made, namely that between virtues and other practical excellences such as arts and skills.

Aristotle has sometimes been accused, for instance by von Wright, of failing to see how different virtues are from arts or skills;[5] but in fact one finds, among the many things that Aristotle and Aquinas say about this difference, the observation that seems to go the heart of the matter. In the matter of arts and skills, they say, voluntary error is preferable to involuntary error, while in the matter of virtues (what we call virtues) it is the reverse.[6] The last part of the thesis is actually rather hard to interpret, because it is not clear what is meant by the idea of involuntary viciousness. But we can leave this aside and still have all we need in order to distinguish arts or skills from virtues. If we think, for instance, of someone who deliberately makes a spelling mistake (perhaps when writing on the blackboard in order to explain this particular point) we see that this does not in any way count against his skill as a speller: 'I did it deliberately' rebuts an accusation of this kind. And what we can say without running into any difficulties is that there is no comparable rebuttal in the case of an accusation relating to lack of virtue. If a man acts unjustly or uncharitably, or in a cowardly or intemperate manner, 'I did it deliberately' cannot on any interpretation lead to exculpation. So, we may say, a virtue is not, like a skill or an art, a mere capacity: it must actually engage the will.

II

I shall now turn to another thesis about the virtues, which I might express by saying that they are *corrective*, each one standing at a point at which there is some temptation to be resisted or deficiency of motivation to be made good. As Aristotle put it, virtues are about what is difficult for men, and I want to see in what sense this is true, and then to consider a problem in Kant's moral philosophy in the light of what has been said.

Let us first think about courage and temperance. Aristotle and Aquinas contrasted these virtues with justice in the following respect. Justice was concerned with operations, and courage and temperance with passions.[7] What they meant by this seems to have been, primarily, that the man of courage does not fear immoderately nor the man of temperance have immoderate desires for pleasure, and that there was no corresponding moderation of a passion implied in the idea of justice. This particular account of courage and temperance might be disputed on the ground that a man's courage is measured by his action and not by anything as uncontrollable as fear; and similarly that the temperate man who must on occasion refuse pleasures need not *desire* them any less than the intemperate man. Be that as it may (and something will be said about it later) it is obviously true that courage and temperance have to do with particular springs of action as justice does not. Almost any desire can lead a man to act unjustly, not even excluding the desire to help a friend or to save a life, whereas a cowardly act must be motivated by fear or a desire for safety, and an act of intemperance by a desire for pleasure, perhaps even for a particular range of pleasures such as those of eating or drinking or sex. And now, going back to the idea of virtues as correctives, one may say that it is only because fear and the desire for pleasure often operate as temptations that courage and temperance exist as virtues at all. As things are we often want to run away not only where that is the right thing to do but also where we should stand firm; and we want pleasure not only where we should seek pleasure but also where we should not. If human nature had been different there would have been no need of a corrective disposition in either place, as fear and pleasure would have been good guides to conduct throughout life. So Aquinas says, about the passions

They may incite us to something against reason, and so we need a curb, which we name *temperance*. Or they may make us shirk a course of action dictated by reason, through fear of dangers or hardships. Then a person needs to be steadfast and not run away from what is right; and for this *courage* is named.[8]

As with courage and temperance so with many other virtues: there is, for instance, a virtue of industriousness only because idleness is a temptation; and of humility only because men tend to think too well of themselves. Hope is a virtue because despair too is a temptation; it might have been that no one cried that all was lost except where he could really see it to be so, and in this case there would have been no virtue of hope.

With virtues such as justice and charity it is a little different, because they correspond not to any particular desire or tendency that has to be kept in check but rather to a deficiency of motivation; and it is this that they must make good. If people were as much attached to the good of others as they are to their own good there would no more be a general virtue of benevolence than there is a general virtue of self-love. And if people cared about the rights of others as they care about their own rights no virtue of justice would be needed to look after the matter, and rules about such things as contracts and promises would only need to be made public, like the rules of a game that everyone was eager to play.

On this view of the virtues and vices everything is seen to depend on what human nature is like, and the traditional catalogue of the two kinds of dispositions is not hard to understand. Nevertheless it may be defective, and anyone who accepts the thesis that I am putting forward will feel free to ask himself where the temptations and deficiencies that need correcting are really to be found. It is possible, for example, that the theory of human nature lying behind the traditional list of the virtues and vices puts too much emphasis on hedonistic and sensual impulses, and does not sufficiently take account of less straightforward inclinations such as the desire to be put upon and dissatisfied, or the unwillingness to accept good things as they come along.

It should now be clear why I said that virtues should be seen as correctives; and part of what is meant by saying that virtue is about things that are difficult for men should also have appeared. The further application of this idea is, however, controversial, and the following difficulty presents itself: that we both are and are not inclined to think that the harder a man finds it to act virtuously the more virtue he shows if he does act well. For on the one hand great virtue is needed where it is particularly hard to act virtuously; yet on the other it could be argued that difficulty in acting virtuously shows that the agent is imperfect in virtue: according to Aristotle, to take pleasure in virtuous action is the mark of true virtue, with the self-mastery of the one who finds virtue difficult only a second best. How then is this conflict to be decided? Who shows most courage, the one who wants to run away but does not, or the one who does not even want to run away? Who shows most charity, the one who finds it easy to make the good of others his object, or the one who finds it hard?

What is certain is that the thought that virtues are corrective does not constrain us to relate virtue to difficulty in each individual man. Since men in general find it hard to face great dangers or evils, and even small ones, we may count as courageous those few who without blindness or indifference are nevertheless fearless even in terrible circumstances. And when someone has a natural charity or generosity it is at least part of the virtue that he has; if natural virtue cannot be the whole of virtue this is because a kindly or fearless disposition could be disastrous without justice and wisdom, and because these virtues have to be learned, not because natural virtue is too easily acquired. I have argued that the virtues can be seen as correctives in relation to human nature in general but not that each virtue must present a difficulty to each and every man.

Nevertheless many people feel strongly inclined to say that it is for moral effort that moral praise is to be bestowed, and that in proportion as a man finds it easy to be virtuous so much the less is he to be morally admired for his good actions. The dilemma can be resolved only when we stop talking about difficulties standing in the way of virtuous action as if they were of only one kind. The fact is that some kinds of difficulties do indeed provide an occasion for much virtue, but that others rather show that virtue is incomplete.

To illustrate this point I shall first consider an example of honest action. We may suppose for instance that a man has an opportunity to steal, in circumstances where stealing is not morally permissible, but that he refrains. And now let us ask our old question. For one man it is hard to refrain from stealing and for another man it is not: which shows the greater virtue in acting as he should? It is not difficult to see in this case that it makes all the difference whether the difficulty comes from circumstances, as that a man is poor, or that his theft is unlikely to be detected, or whether it comes from something that belongs to his own character. The fact that a man is *tempted* to steal is something about him that shows a certain lack of honesty: of the thoroughly honest man we say that it 'never entered his head', meaning that it was never a real possibility for him. But the fact that he is poor is something that makes the occasion more *tempting*, and difficulties of this kind make honest action all the more virtuous.

A similar distinction can be made between different obstacles standing in the way of charitable action. Some circumstances, as that great sacrifice is needed, or that the one to be helped is a rival, give an occasion on which a man's charity is severely tested. Yet in given circumstances of this kind it is the man who acts easily rather than the one who finds it hard who shows the most charity. Charity is a virtue of attachment, and that sympathy for others which makes it easier to help them is part of the virtue itself.

These are fairly simple cases, but I am not supposing that it is always easy to say where the relevant distinction is to be drawn. What, for instance, should we say about the emotion of fear as an obstacle to action? Is a man more courageous if he fears much and nevertheless acts, or if he is relatively fearless? Several things must be said about this. In the first place it seems that the emotion of fear is not a necessary condition for the display of courage; in face of a great evil such as death or injury a man may show courage even if he does not tremble. On the other hand even irrational fears may give an occasion for courage: if someone suffers from claustrophobia or a dread of heights he may require courage to do that which would not be a courageous action for others. But not all fears belong from this point of view to the circumstances rather than to a man's character. For while we do not think of claustrophobia or a dread of heights as features of character, a general timorousness may be. Thus, although pathological fears are not the result of a man's choices and values some fears may be. The fears that count against a man's courage are those that we think he could overcome, and among them, in a special class, those that reflect the fact that he values safety too much.

In spite of problems such as these, which have certainly not all been solved, both the distinction between different kinds of obstacles to virtuous action and the general idea that virtues are correctives will be useful in resolving a difficulty in Kant's moral philosophy closely related to the issues discussed in the preceding paragraphs. In a passage in the first section of the *Groundwork of the Metaphysics of Morals* Kant notoriously tied himself into a knot in trying to give an account of those actions which have as he put it 'positive moral worth'. Arguing that only actions done out of a sense of duty have this worth he contrasts a philanthropist who 'takes pleasure in spreading happiness around him' with one who acts out of respect for duty, saying that the actions of the latter but not the former have moral worth. Much scorn has been poured on Kant for this curious doctrine, and indeed it does seem that something has gone wrong, but perhaps we are not in a position to scoff unless we can give our own account of the idea on which Kant is working. After all it does seem that he is right in saying that some actions are in accordance with duty, and even required by duty, without being the subjects of moral praise, like those of the honest trader who deals honestly in a situation in which it is in his interest to do so.

It was this kind of example that drove Kant to his strange conclusion. He added another example, however, in discussing acts of self-preservation; these he said, while they normally have no positive moral worth, may have it when a man preserves his life not from inclination but without inclination and from a sense of duty. Is he not right in saying that acts of self-preservation normally have no moral significance but that they may have it, and how do we ourselves explain this fact?

To anyone who approaches this topic from a consideration of the virtues the solution readily suggests itself. Some actions are in accordance with virtue without requiring virtue for their performance, whereas others are both in accordance with virtue and such as to show possession of a virtue. So Kant's trader was dealing honestly in a situation in which the virtue of honesty is not required for honest dealing, and it is for this reason that his action did not have 'positive moral worth'. Similarly, the care that one ordinarily takes for one's life, as for instance on some ordinary morning in eating one's breakfast and keeping out of the way of a car on the road, is something for which no virtue is required. As we said earlier there is no general virtue of self-love as there is a virtue of benevolence or charity, because men are generally attached sufficiently to their own good. Nevertheless in special circumstances virtues such as temperance, courage, fortitude, and hope may be needed if someone is to preserve his life. Are these circumstances in which the preservation of one's own life is a duty? Sometimes it is so, for sometimes it is what is owed to others that should keep a man from destroying himself, and then he may act out of a sense of duty. But not all cases in which acts of self-preservation show virtue are like this. For a man may display each of the virtues just listed even where he does not do any harm to others if he kills himself or fails to preserve his life. And it is this that explains why there may be a moral aspect to suicide which does not depend on possible injury to other people. It is not that suicide is 'always wrong', whatever

that would mean, but that suicide is *sometimes* contrary to
virtues such as courage and hope.

Let us now return to Kant's philanthropists, with the
thought that it is action that is in accordance with virtue and
also displays a virtue that has moral worth. We see at once that
Kant's difficulties are avoided, and the happy philanthropist
reinstated in the position which belongs to him. For charity is,
as we said, a virtue of attachment as well as action, and the
sympathy that makes it easier to act with charity is part of the
virtue. The man who acts charitably out of a sense of duty is
not to be undervalued, but it is the other who most shows
virtue and therefore to the other that most moral worth is
attributed. Only a detail of Kant's presentation of the case of
the dutiful philanthropist tells on the other side. For what he
actually said was that this man felt no sympathy and took no
pleasure in the good of others because 'his mind was clouded
by some sorrow of his own', and this is the kind of circumstance that increases the virtue that is needed if a man is to
act well.

III

It was suggested above that an action with 'positive moral
worth', or as we might say a positively good action, was to be
seen as one which was in accordance with virtue, by which I
mean contrary to no virtue, and moreover one for which a
virtue was required. Nothing has so far been said about
another case, excluded by the formula, in which it might seem
that an act displaying one virtue was nevertheless contrary to
another. In giving this last description I am thinking not of
two virtues with competing claims, as if what were required
by justice could nevertheless be demanded by charity, or
something of that kind, but rather of the possibility that a
virtue such as courage or temperance or industry which over-
comes a special temptation, might be displayed in an act of
folly or villainy. Is this something that we must allow for, or is
it only good or innocent actions which can be acts of these
virtues? Aquinas, in his definition of virtue, said that virtues
can produce only good actions, and that they are dispositions

'of which no one can make bad use',[9] except when they are
treated as objects, as in being the subject of hatred or pride.
The common opinion nowadays is, however, quite different.
With the notable exception of Peter Geach hardly anyone sees
any difficulty in the thought that virtues may sometimes be
displayed in bad actions. Von Wright, for instance, speaks of
the courage of the villain as if this were a quite unproblematic
idea, and most people take it for granted that the virtues of
courage and temperance may aid a bad man in his evil work. It
is also supposed that charity may lead a man to act badly, as
when someone does what he has no right to do, but does it for
the sake of a friend.

There are, however, reasons for thinking that the matter is
not so simple as this. If a man who is willing to do an act of
injustice to help a friend, or for the common good, is supposed
to act out of charity, and he so acts where a just man will not,
it should be said that the unjust man has more charity than
the just man. But do we not think that someone not ready to
act unjustly may yet be perfect in charity, the virtue having
done its whole work in prompting him to do the acts that are
permissible? And is there not more difficulty than might
appear in the idea of an act of injustice which is nevertheless an
act of courage? Suppose for instance that a sordid murder were
in question, say a murder done for gain or to get an inconve-
nient person out of the way, but that this murder had to be
done in alarming circumstances or in the face of real danger;
should we be happy to say that such an action was an act of
courage or a courageous act? Did the murderer, who certainly
acted boldly, or with intrepidity, if he did the murder, also act
courageously? Some people insist that they are ready to say
this, but I have noticed that they like to move over to a murder
for the sake of conscience, or to some other act done in the
course of a villainous enterprise but whose immediate end is
innocent or positively good. On their hypothesis, which is
that bad acts can easily be seen as courageous acts or acts of
courage, my original example should be just as good.

What are we to say about this difficult matter? There is no
doubt that the murderer who murdered for gain was *not a
coward*: he did not have a second moral defect which another
villain might have had. There is no difficulty about this

because it is clear that one defect may neutralise another. As Aquinas remarked, it is better for a blind horse if it is slow.[10] It does not follow, however, that an act of villainy can be courageous; we are inclined to say that it 'took courage', and yet it seems wrong to think of courage as equally connected with good actions and bad.

One way out of this difficulty might be to say that the man who is ready to pursue bad ends does indeed have courage, and shows courage in his action, but that in him courage is not a virtue. Later I shall consider some cases in which this might be the right thing to say, but in this instance it does not seem to be. For unless the murderer consistently pursues bad ends his courage will often result in good; it may enable him to do many innocent or positively good things for himself or for his family and friends. On the strength of an individual bad action we can hardly say that in him courage is not a virtue. Nevertheless there is something to be said even about the individual action to distinguish it from one that would readily be called an act of courage or a courageous act. Perhaps the following analogy may help us to see what it is. We might think of words such as 'courage' as naming characteristics of human beings in respect of a certain power, as words such as 'poison' and 'solvent' and 'corrosive' so name the properties of physical things. The power to which virtue-words are so related is the power of producing good action, and good desires. But just as poisons, solvents and corrosives do not always operate characteristically, so it could be with virtues. If P (say arsenic) is a poison it does not follow that P acts as a poison wherever it is found. It is quite natural to say on occasion 'P does not act as a poison here' though P is a poison and it is P that is acting here. Similarly courage is not operating as a virtue when the murderer turns his courage, which is a virtue, to bad ends. Not surprisingly the resistance that some of us registered was not to the expression 'the courage of the murderer' or to the assertion that what he did 'took courage' but rather to the description of that action as an act of courage or a courageous act. It is not that the action *could* not be so described, but that the fact that courage does not here have its characteristic operation is a reason for finding the description strange.

In this example we were considering an action in which courage was not operating as a virtue, without suggesting that in that agent it generally failed to do so. But the latter is also a possibility. If someone is both wicked and foolhardy this may be the case with courage, and it is even easier to find examples of a general connexion with evil rather than good in the case of some other virtues. Suppose, for instance, that we think of someone who is over-industrious, or too ready to refuse pleasure, and this is characteristic of him rather than something we find on one particular occasion. In this case the virtue of industry, or the virtue of temperance, has a systematic connexion with defective action rather than good action; and it might be said in either case that the virtue did not operate as a virtue in this man. Just as we might say in a certain setting 'P is not a poison here' though P is a poison and P is here, so we might say that industriousness, or temperance, is not a virtue in some. Similarly in a man habitually given to wishful thinking, who clings to false hopes, hope does not operate as a virtue and we may say that it is not a virtue in him.

The thought developed in the last paragraph, to the effect that not every man who has a virtue has something that is a virtue in him, may help to explain a certain discomfort that one may feel when discussing the virtues. It is not easy to put one's finger on what is wrong, but it has something to do with a disparity between the moral ideals that may seem to be implied in our talk about the virtues, and the moral judgements that we actually make. Someone reading the foregoing pages might, for instance, think that the author of this paper always admired most those people who had all the virtues, being wise and temperate as well as courageous, charitable, and just. And indeed it is sometimes so. There are some people who do possess all these virtues and who are loved and admired by all the world, as Pope John XXIII was loved and admired. Yet the fact is that many of us look up to some people whose chaotic lives contain rather little of wisdom or temperance, rather than to some others who possess these virtues. And while it may be that this is just romantic nonsense I suspect that it is not. For while wisdom always operates as a virtue, its close relation prudence does not, and it is prudence rather than wisdom that inspires many a careful life. Prudence is not a virtue in everyone, any more than industriousness is, for in some it is rather an over-anxious concern for safety and propriety, and a determination to keep away from people or situations which are apt to bring trouble with them; and by such defensiveness much good is lost. It is the same with temperance. Intemperance can be an appalling thing, as it was with Henry VIII of whom Wolsey remarked that

rather than he will either miss or want any part of his will or appetite, he will put the loss of one half of his realm in danger.

Nevertheless in some people temperance is not a virtue, but is rather connected with timidity or with a grudging attitude to the acceptance of good things. Of course what is best is to live boldly yet without imprudence or intemperance, but the fact is that rather few can manage that.

NOTES

I am indebted to friends in many universities for their help in forming my views on this subject; and particularly to John Giuliano of UCLA, whose unpublished work on the unity of the virtues I have consulted with profit, and to Rosalind Hursthouse who commented on a draft of the middle period.

[1] G. H. von Wright *The Varieties of Goodness* (London, 1963).

[2] Peter Geach, *The Virtues* (Cambridge, 1977).

[3] Aquinas, *Summa Theologica*, 1a2ae Q.56 a.3.

[4] Aristotle, *Nicomachean Ethics*, especially bk. VII.

[5] von Wright op. cit. chapter VIII.

[6] Aristotle op. cit. 1140 b 22–25. Aquinas op. cit. 1a2ae Q.57 a.4.

[7] Aristotle op. cit. 1106 b 15 and 1129 a.4 have this implication; but Aquinas is more explicit in op. cit. 1a2ae Q.60 a.2.

[8] Aquinas op. cit. 1a2ae Q.61 a.3.

[9] Aquinas op. cit. 1a2ae Q.56 a.5.

[10] Aquinas op. cit. 1a2ae Q.58 a.4.

II

The Problem of Abortion and the Doctrine of the Double Effect*

One of the reasons why most of us feel puzzled about the problem of abortion is that we want, and do not want, to allow to the unborn child the rights that belong to adults and children. When we think of a baby about to be born it seems absurd to think that the next few minutes or even hours could make so radical a difference to its status; yet as we go back in the life of the foetus we are more and more reluctant to say that this is a human being and must be treated as such. No doubt this is the deepest source of our dilemma, but it is not the only one. For we are also confused about the general question of what we may and may not do where the interests of human beings conflict. We have strong intuitions about certain cases; saying, for instance, that it is all right to raise the level of education in our country, though statistics allow us to predict that a rise in the suicide rate will follow, while it is not all right to kill the feeble-minded to aid cancer research. It is not easy, however, to see the principles involved, and one way of throwing light on the abortion issue will be by setting up parallels involving adults or children once born. So we will be able to isolate the 'equal rights' issue and should be able to make some advance.

I shall not, of course, discuss all the principles that may be used in deciding how to act where the interests or rights of human beings conflict. What I want to do is to look at one particular theory, known as the 'doctrine of the double effect' which is invoked by Catholics in support of their views on abortion but supposed by them to apply elsewhere. As used in the abortion argument this doctrine has often seemed to non-Catholics to be a piece of complete sophistry. In the last number of the *Oxford Review* it was given short shrift by Professor Hart.[1] And yet this principle has seemed to some non-Catholics as well as to Catholics to stand as the only defence against decisions on other issues that are quite unacceptable. It will help us in our difficulty about abortion if this conflict can be resolved.

The doctrine of the double effect is based on a distinction between what a man foresees as a result of his voluntary action and what, in the strict sense, he intends. He intends in the strictest sense both those things that he aims at as ends and those that he aims at as means to his ends. The latter may be regretted in themselves but nevertheless desired for the sake of the end, as we may intend to keep dangerous lunatics confined for the sake of our safety. By contrast a man is said not strictly, or directly, to intend the foreseen consequences of his voluntary actions where these are neither the end at which he is aiming nor the means to this end. Whether the word 'intention' should be applied in both cases is not of course what matters: Bentham spoke of '*oblique intention*', contrasting it with the '*direct intention*' of ends and means, and we may as well follow his terminology. Everyone must recognise that some such distinction can be made, though it may be made in a number of different ways, and it is the distinction that is crucial to the doctrine of the double effect. The words 'double effect' refer to the two effects that an action may produce: the one aimed at, and the one foreseen but in no way desired. By 'the doctrine of the double effect' I mean the thesis that it is sometimes permissible to bring about by oblique intention what one may not directly intend. Thus the distinction is held to be relevant to moral decision in certain difficult cases. It is said for instance that the operation of hysterectomy involves the death of the foetus as the foreseen but not strictly or directly intended consequence of the surgeon's act, while other operations kill the child and count as the direct intention of taking an innocent life, a distinction that has evoked particularly bitter reactions on the part of non-Catholics. If you are permitted to bring about the death of the child, what does it matter how it is done? The doctrine of the double effect is also used to show why in another case, where a woman in labour will die unless a craniotomy operation is performed, the intervention is not to be condoned. There, it is said, we may not operate but must let the mother die. We foresee her death but do not directly intend it, whereas to crush the skull of the child would count as direct intention of its death.[2]

This last application of the doctrine has been queried by Professor Hart on the ground that the child's death is not strictly a means to saving the mother's life and should logically be treated as an unwanted but foreseen consequence by those who make use of the distinction between direct and oblique intention. To interpret the doctrine in this way is perfectly reasonable given the language that has been used; it would, however, make nonsense of it from the beginning. A certain event may be desired under one of its descriptions, unwanted under another, but we cannot treat these as two different events, one of which is aimed at and the other not. And even if it be argued that there are here two different events—the crushing of the child's skull and its death—the two are obviously much too close for an application of the doctrine of the double effect. To see how odd it would be to apply the principle like this we may consider the story, well known to philosophers, of the fat man stuck in the mouth of the cave. A party of potholers have imprudently allowed the fat man to lead them as they make their way out of the cave, and he gets stuck, trapping the others behind him. Obviously the right thing to do is to sit down and wait until the fat man grows thin; but philosophers have arranged that flood waters should be rising within the cave. Luckily (luckily?) the trapped party have with them a stick of dynamite with which they can blast the fat man out of the mouth of the cave. Either they use the dynamite or they drown. In one version the fat man, whose head is *in* the cave, will drown with them; in the other he will be rescued in due course.[3] Problem: may they use the dynamite or not? Later we shall find parallels to this example. Here it is introduced for light relief and because it will serve to show how ridiculous one version of the doctrine of the double effect would be. For suppose that the trapped explorers were to argue that the death of the fat man might be taken as a merely foreseen consequence of the act of blowing him up. ('We didn't want to kill him. . .only to blow him into small pieces' or even '. . . only to blast him out of the cave.') I believe that those who use the doctrine of the double effect would rightly reject such a suggestion, though they will, of course, have considerable difficulty in explaining where the line is to be drawn. What is to be the criterion of 'closeness' if we say that anything very close to what we are literally aiming at counts as if part of our aim?

Let us leave this difficulty aside and return to the arguments for and against the doctrine, supposing it to be formulated in the way considered most effective by its supporters, and ourselves bypassing the trouble by taking what must on any reasonable definition be clear cases of 'direct' or 'oblique' intention.

The first point that should be made clear, in fairness to the theory, is that no one is suggesting that it does not matter what you bring about as long as you merely foresee and do not strictly intend the evil that follows. We might think, for instance, of the (actual) case of wicked merchants selling, for cooking, oil they knew to be poisonous and thereby killing a number of innocent people, comparing and contrasting it with that of some unemployed gravediggers, desperate for custom, who got hold of this same oil and sold it (or perhaps *they* secretly gave it away) in order to create orders for graves. They strictly (directly) intend the deaths they cause, while the merchants could say that it was not part of their *plan* that anyone should die. In morality, as in law, the merchants, like the gravediggers, would be considered as murderers; nor are the supporters of the doctrine of the double effect bound to say that there is the least difference between them in respect of moral turpitude. What they are committed to is the thesis that *sometimes* it makes a difference to the permissibility of an action involving harm to others that this harm, although foreseen, is not part of the agent's direct intention. An end such as earning one's living is clearly not such as to justify *either* the direct or oblique intention of the death of innocent people, but in certain cases one is justified in bringing about knowingly what one could not directly intend.

It is now time to say why this doctrine should be taken seriously in spite of the fact that it sounds rather odd, that there are difficulties about the distinction on which it depends, and that it seemed to yield one sophistical conclusion when applied to the problem of abortion. The reason for its appeal is that its opponents have often *seemed* to be committed to quite indefensible views. Thus the controversy has raged around examples such as the following. Suppose that a judge or magistrate is faced with rioters demanding that a culprit be found for a certain crime and threatening otherwise to take their own bloody revenge on a particular section of the community. The real culprit being unknown, the judge sees himself as able to prevent the bloodshed only by framing some innocent person and having him executed. Beside this example is placed another in which a pilot whose aeroplane is about to crash is deciding whether to steer from a more to a less inhabited area. To make the parallel as close as possible it may rather be supposed that he is the driver of a runaway tram which he can only steer from one narrow track on to another; five men are working on one track and one man on the other; anyone on the track he enters is bound to be killed. In the case of the riots the mob have five hostages, so that in both the exchange is supposed to be one man's life for the lives of five. The question is why we should say, without hesitation, that the driver should steer for the less occupied track, while most of us would be appalled at the idea that the innocent man could be framed. It may be suggested that the special feature of the latter case is that it involves the corruption of justice, and this is, of course, very important indeed. But if we remove that special feature, supposing that some private individual is to kill an innocent person and pass him off as the criminal we still find ourselves horrified by the idea. The doctrine of double effect offers us a way out of the difficulty, insisting that it is one thing to steer towards someone foreseeing that you will kill him and another to aim at his death as part of your plan. Moreover there is one very important element of good in what is here insisted. In real life it would hardly ever be certain that the man on the narrow track would be killed. Perhaps he might find a foothold on the side of the tunnel and cling on as the vehicle hurtled by. The driver of the tram does *not* then leap off and brain him with a crowbar. The judge, however, needs the death of the innocent man for his (good) purposes. If the victim proves hard to hang he must see to it that he dies another way. To choose to execute him is to choose that this evil *shall come about*, and this must therefore count as a *certainty* in weighing up the good and evil involved. The distinction between direct and oblique intention is crucial here, and is of great importance in an uncertain world. Nevertheless this is no way to defend the doctrine of double effect. For the question is whether the difference between aiming at something and obliquely intending it is *in itself* relevant to moral decisions; not whether it is important when correlated with a difference of certainty in the balance of good and evil. Moreover we are particularly interested in the application of the doctrine of the double effect to the question of abortion, and no one can deny that in medicine there are sometimes certainties so complete that it would be a mere quibble to speak of the 'probable outcome' of this course of action or that. It is not, therefore, with a merely philosophical interest that we should put aside the uncertainty and scrutinise the examples to test the doctrine of the double effect. Why can we not argue from the case of the steering driver to that of the judge?

Another pair of examples poses a similar problem. We are about to give a patient who needs it to save his life a massive dose of a certain drug in short supply. There arrive, however, five other patients each of whom could be saved by one-fifth of that dose. We say with regret that we cannot spare our whole supply of the drug for a single patient, just as we should say that we could not spare the whole resources of a ward for one dangerously ill individual when ambulances arrive bringing in victims of a multiple crash. We feel bound to let one man die rather than many if that is our only choice. Why then do we not feel justified in killing people in the interests of cancer research or to obtain, let us say, spare parts for grafting on to those who need them? We can suppose, similarly, that several dangerously ill people can be saved only if we kill a certain individual and make a serum from his dead body. (These examples are not over-fanciful considering present controversies about prolonging the life of mortally ill patients whose eyes or kidneys are to be used for others.) Why cannot we argue from the case of the scarce drug to that of the body needed for medical purposes? Once again the doctrine of the double effect comes up with an explanation. In one kind of case but not the other we aim at the death of an innocent man.

A further argument suggests that if the doctrine of the double effect is rejected this has the consequences of putting us hopelessly in the power of bad men. Suppose for example that some tyrant should threaten to torture five men if we ourselves would not torture one. Would it be our duty to do so, supposing we believed him, because this would be no different from choosing to rescue five men from his torturers rather than one? If so, anyone who wants us to do something we think wrong has only to threaten that otherwise he himself will do something we think worse. A mad murderer, known to keep his promises, could thus make it our duty to kill some innocent citizen to prevent him from killing two. From this conclusion we are again rescued by the doctrine of the double effect. If we refuse, we foresee that the greater number will be killed but we do not intend it: it is he who intends (that is strictly or directly intends) the death of innocent persons; we do not.

At one time I thought that these arguments in favour of the doctrine of the double effect were conclusive, but I now believe that the conflict should be solved in another way. The clue that we should follow is that the strength of the doctrine seems to lie in the distinction it makes between what we *do* (equated with direct intention) and what we allow (thought of as obliquely intended). Indeed it is interesting that the disputants tend to argue about whether we are to be held responsible for what we allow as we are for what we do.[4] Yet it is not obvious that this is what they should be discussing, since the distinction between what one does and what one allows to happen is not the same as that between direct and oblique intention. To see this one has only to consider that it is possible *deliberately* to allow something to happen, aiming at it either for its own sake or as part of one's plan for obtaining something else. So one person might want another person dead and deliberately allow him to die. And again one may be said to *do* things that one does not aim at, as the steering driver would kill the man on the track. Moreover there is a large class of things said to be brought about rather than either done or allowed where either kind of intention is possible. So it is possible to *bring about* a man's death by getting him to sea in a leaky boat, and the intention of his death may be either direct or oblique.

Whatever it may, or may not, have to do with the doctrine of the double effect, the idea of *allowing* is worth looking into in this context. I shall leave aside the special case of giving permission, which involves the idea of authority, and consider the two main divisions into which cases of allowing seem to fall. There is firstly the allowing which is forbearing to prevent. For this we need a sequence thought of as somehow already in train, and something that an agent could do to intervene. (The agent must be able to intervene, but does not do so.) So, for instance, he could warn someone, but *allows* him to walk into a trap. He could feed an animal but *allows* it to die for lack of food. He could stop a leaking tap but *allows* the water to go on flowing. This is the case of allowing with which we shall be concerned, but the other should be mentioned. It is the kind of allowing which is roughly equivalent to *enabling*; the root idea being the removal of some obstacle which is, as it were, holding back a train of events. So someone may remove a plug and *allow* water to flow; open a door and *allow* an animal to get out; or give someone money and *allow* him to get back on his feet.

The first kind of allowing requires an omission, but there is no other general correlation between omission and allowing, commission and bringing about or doing. An actor who fails to turn up for a performance will generally spoil it rather than allow it to be spoiled. I mention the distinction between omission and commission only to set it aside.

Thinking of the first kind of allowing (forbearing to prevent), we should ask whether there is any difference, from the moral point of view, between what one does or causes and what one merely allows. It seems clear that on occasions one is just as bad as the other, as is recognised in both morality and law. A man may murder his child or his aged relatives by allowing them to die of starvation as by giving poison; he may also be convicted of murder on either account. In another case we would, however, make a distinction. Most of us allow people to die of starvation in India and Africa, and there is surely something wrong with us that we do; it would be nonsense, however, to pretend that it is only in law that we make the distinction between allowing people in the underdeveloped countries to die of starvation and sending them poisoned food. There is worked into our moral system a distinction between what we owe people in the form of aid and what we owe them in the way of non-interference. Salmond, in his *Jurisprudence*, expressed as follows the distinction between the two.

A positive right corresponds to a positive duty, and is a right that he on whom the duty lies shall do some positive act on behalf of the person entitled. A negative right corresponds to a negative duty, and is a right that the person bound shall refrain from some act which would operate to the prejudice of the person entitled. The former is a right to be positively benefited; the latter is merely a right not to be harmed.[5]

As a general account of rights and duties this is defective, since not all are so closely connected with benefit and harm. Nevertheless for our purposes it will do well. Let us speak of negative duties when thinking of the obligation to refrain from such things as killing or robbing, and of the positive duty, e.g., to look after children or aged parents. It will be useful, however, to extend the notion of positive duty beyond the range of things that are strictly called duties, bringing acts of charity under this heading. These are owed only in a rather loose sense, and some acts of charity could hardly be said to be *owed* at all, so I am not following ordinary usage at this point.

Let us now see whether the distinction of negative and positive duties explains why we see differently the action of the steering driver and that of the judge, of the doctors who withhold the scarce drug and those who obtain a body for medical purposes, of those who choose to rescue five men rather than one man from torture and those who are ready to torture the one man themselves in order to save five. In each case we have a conflict of duties, but what kind of duties are they? Are we, in each case, weighing positive duties against positive, negative against negative, or one against the other? Is the duty to refrain from injury, or rather to bring aid?

The steering driver faces a conflict of negative duties, since it is his duty to avoid injuring five men and also his duty to avoid injuring one. In the circumstances he is not able to avoid both, and it seems clear that he should do the least injury he can. The judge, however, is weighing the duty of not inflicting injury against the duty of bringing aid. He wants to rescue the innocent people threatened with death but can do so only by inflicting injury himself. Since one does not *in general* have the same duty to help people as to refrain from injuring them, it is not possible to argue to a conclusion about what he should do from the steering driver case. It is interesting that, even where the strictest duty of positive aid exists, this still does not weigh as if a negative duty were involved. It is not, for instance, permissible to commit a murder to bring one's starving children food. If the choice is between inflicting injury on one or many there seems only one rational course of action; if the choice is between aid to some at the cost of injury to others, and refusing to inflict the injury to bring the aid, the whole matter is open to dispute. So it is not inconsistent of us to think that the driver must steer for the road on which only one man stands while the judge (or his equivalent) may not kill the innocent person in order to stop the riots. Let us now consider the second pair of examples, which concern the scarce drug on the one hand and on the other the body needed to save lives. Once again we find a difference based on the distinction between the duty to avoid injury and the duty to provide aid. Where one man needs a massive dose of the drug and we withhold it from him in order to save five men, we are weighing aid against aid. But if we consider killing a man in order to use his body to save others, we are thinking of doing him an injury to bring others aid. In an interesting variant of the model, we may suppose that instead of killing someone we deliberately let him die. (Perhaps he is a beggar to whom we are thinking of giving food, but then we say 'No, they need bodies for medical research.') Here it does seem relevant that in allowing him to die we are aiming at his death, but presumably we are inclined to see this as a violation of negative rather than positive duty. If this is right, we see why we are unable in either case to argue to a conclusion from the case of the scarce drug.

In the examples involving the torturing of one man or five men, the principle seems to be the same as for the last pair. If we are bringing aid (rescuing people about to be tortured by the tyrant), we must obviously rescue the larger rather than the smaller group. It does not follow, however, that we would be justified in inflicting the injury, or getting a third person to do so, in order to save the five. We may therefore refuse to be forced into acting by the threats of bad men. To refrain from inflicting injury ourselves is a stricter duty than to prevent other people from inflicting injury, which is not to say that the other is not a very strict duty indeed.

So far the conclusions are the same as those at which we might arrive following the doctrine of the double effect, but in others they will be different, and the advantage seems to be all on the side of the alternative. Suppose, for instance, that there are five patients in a hospital whose lives could be saved by the manufacture of a certain gas, but that this inevitably releases lethal fumes into the room of another patient whom for some reason we are unable to move. His death, being of no use to us, is clearly a side effect, and not directly intended. Why then is the case different from that of the scarce drug, if the point about that is that we foresaw but did not strictly intend the death of the single patient? Yet it surely is different. The relatives of the gassed patient would presumably be successful if they sued the hospital and the whole story came out. We may find it particularly revolting that someone should be *used* as in the case where he is killed or allowed to die in the interest of medical research, and the fact of *using* may even determine what we would decide to do in some cases, but the principle seems unimportant compared with our reluctance to bring such injury for the sake of giving aid.

My conclusion is that the distinction between direct and oblique intention plays only a quite subsidiary role in determining what we say in these cases, while the distinction between avoiding injury and bringing aid is very important indeed. I have not, of course, argued that there are no other principles. For instance it clearly makes a difference whether our positive duty is a strict duty or rather an act of charity: feeding our own children or feeding those in faraway countries. It may also make a difference whether the person about to suffer is one thought of as uninvolved in the threatened disaster, and whether it is his presence that constitutes the threat to the others. In many cases we find it very hard to know what to say, and I have not been arguing for any general conclusion such as that we may never, whatever the balance of good and evil, bring injury to one for the sake of aid to others, even when this injury amounts to death. I have only tried to show that even if we reject the doctrine of the double effect we are not forced to the conclusion that the size of the evil must always be our guide.

Let us now return to the problem of abortion, carrying out our plan of finding parallels involving adults or children rather than the unborn. We must say something about the different cases in which abortion might be considered on medical grounds.

First of all there is the situation in which nothing that can be done will save the life of child and mother, but where the life of the mother can be saved by killing the child. This is parallel to the case of the fat man in the mouth of the cave who is bound to be drowned with the others if nothing is done. Given the certainty of the outcome, as it was postulated, there is no serious conflict of interests here, since the fat man will perish in either case, and it is reasonable that the action that will save someone should be done. It is a great objection to those who argue that the direct intention of the death of an innocent person is never justifiable that the edict will apply even in this case. The Catholic doctrine on abortion must here conflict with that of most reasonable men. Moreover we would be justified in performing the operation whatever the method used, and it is neither a necessary nor a good justification of the special case of hysterectomy that the child's death is not directly intended, being rather a foreseen consequence of what is done. What difference could it make as to how the death is brought about?

Secondly we have the case in which it is possible to perform an operation which will save the mother and kill the child or kill the mother and save the child. This is parallel to the famous case of shipwrecked mariners who believed that they must throw someone overboard if their boat was not to founder in a storm, and to the other famous case of the two sailors, Dudley and Stephens, who killed and ate the cabin boy when adrift on the sea without food. Here again there is no conflict of interests so far as the decision to act is concerned; only in deciding whom to save. Once again it would be reasonable to act, though one would respect someone who held back from the appalling action either because he preferred to perish rather than do such a thing or because he held on past the limits of reasonable hope. In real life the certainties postulated by philosophers hardly ever exist, and Dudley and Stephens were rescued not long after their ghastly meal. Nevertheless if the certainty were absolute, as it might be in the abortion case, it would seem better to save one than none. Probably we should decide in favour of the mother when weighing her life against that of the unborn child, but it is interesting that, a few years later, we might easily decide it the other way.

The worst dilemma comes in the third kind of example where to save the mother we must kill the child, say by crushing its skull, while if nothing is done the mother will perish but the child can be safely delivered after her death. Here the doctrine of the double effect has been invoked to show that we may not intervene, since the child's death would be directly intended while the mother's would not. On a strict parallel with cases not involving the unborn we might find the conclusion correct though the reason given was wrong. Suppose, for instance, that in later life the presence of a child was certain to bring death to the mother. We would surely not think ourselves justified in ridding her of it by a process that involved its death. For in general we do not think that we can kill one innocent person to rescue another, quite apart from the special care that we feel is due to children once they have prudently got themselves born. What we would be prepared to do when a great many people were involved is another matter, and this is probably the key to one quite common view of abortion on the part of those who take quite seriously the rights of the unborn child. They probably feel that if *enough* people were involved one must be sacrificed, and they think of the mother's life against the unborn child's life as if it were many against one. But of course many people do not view it like this at all, having no inclination to accord to the foetus or unborn child anything like ordinary human status in the matter of rights. I have not been arguing for or against these points of view but only trying to discern some of the currents that are pulling us back and forth. The levity of the examples is not meant to offend.

NOTES

* 'The Problem of Abortion and the Doctrine of the Double Effect' originally appeared in the *Oxford Review,* Number 5, 1967.

[1] H. L. A. Hart, 'Intention and Punishment', *Oxford Review*, Number 4, Hilary 1967. Reprinted in Hart, *Punishment and Responsibility* (Oxford, 1968). I owe much to this article and to a conversation with Professor Hart, though I do not know whether he will approve of what follows.

[2] For discussions of the Catholic doctrine on abortion see Glanville Williams, *The Sanctity of Life and the Criminal Law* (New York, 1957); also N. St. John Stevas, *The Right to Life* (London, 1963).

[3] It was Professor Hart who drew my attention to this distinction.

[4] See, e.g., J. Bennett, 'Whatever the Consequences', *Analysis*, January 1966, and G. E. M. Anscombe's reply in *Analysis*, June 1966. See also Miss Anscombe's 'Modern Moral Philosophy' in *Philosophy*, January 1958.

[5] J. Salmond, *Jurisprudence*, 11th edition, p. 283.

III

Euthanasia*

The widely used *Shorter Oxford English Dictionary* gives three meanings for the word 'euthanasia': the first, 'a quiet and easy death'; the second, 'the means of procuring this'; and the third, 'the action of inducing a quiet and easy death'. It is a curious fact that no one of the three gives an adequate definition of the word as it is usually understood. For 'euthanasia' means much more than a quiet and easy death, or the means of procuring it, or the action of inducing it. The definition specifies only the manner of death, and if this were all that was implied a murderer, careful to drug his victim, could claim that his act was an act of euthanasia. We find this ridiculous because we take it for granted that in euthanasia it is death itself, not just the manner of death, that must be kind to the one who dies.

To see how important it is that 'euthanasia' should not be used as the dictionary definition allows it to be used, merely to signify that a death was quiet and easy, one has only to remember that Hitler's 'euthanasia' programme traded on this ambiguity. Under this programme, planned before the War but brought into full operation by a decree of 1 September 1939, some 275,000 people were gassed in centres which were to be a model for those in which Jews were later exterminated. Anyone in a state institution could be sent to the gas chambers if it was considered that he could not be 'rehabilitated' for useful work. As Dr. Leo Alexander reports, relying on the testimony of a neuropathologist who received 500 brains from one of the killing centres,

In Germany the exterminations included the mentally defective, psychotics (particularly schizophrenics), epileptics and patients suffering from infirmities of old age and from various organic neurological disorders such as infantile paralysis, Parkinsonism, multiple sclerosis and brain tumors. . . . In truth, all those unable to work and considered nonrehabilitable were killed.[1]

These people were killed because they were 'useless' and 'a burden on society': only the manner of their deaths could be thought of as relatively easy and quiet.

Let us insist, then, that when we talk about euthanasia we are talking about a death understood as a good or happy event for the one who dies. This stipulation follows etymology, but is itself not exactly in line with current usage, which would be captured by the condition that the death should *not* be an evil rather than that it *should* be a good. That this is how people talk is shown by the fact that the case of Karen Ann Quinlan and others in a state of permanent coma is often discussed under the heading of 'euthanasia'. Perhaps it is not too late to object to the use of the word 'euthanasia' in this sense. Apart from the break with the Greek origins of the word there are other unfortunate aspects of this extension of the term. For if we say that the death must be supposed to be a good to the subject we can also specify that it shall be for his sake that an act of euthanasia is performed. If we say merely that death shall not be an evil to him, we cannot stipulate that benefiting him shall be the motive where euthanasia is in question. Given the importance of the question, For whose sake are we acting? it is good to have a definition of euthanasia which brings under this heading only cases of opting for death for the sake of the one who dies. Perhaps what is most important is to say either that euthanasia is to be for the good of the subject or at least that death is to be no evil to him, thus refusing to talk Hitler's language. However, in this paper it is the first condition that will be understood, with the additional proviso that by an act of euthanasia we mean one of inducing or otherwise opting for death for the sake of the one who is to die.

A few lesser points need to be cleared up. In the first place it must be said that the word 'act' is not to be taken to exclude omission: we shall speak of an act of euthanasia when someone is deliberately allowed to die, for his own good, and not only when positive measures are taken to see that he does. The very general idea we want is that of a choice of action or inaction directed at another man's death and causally effective in the sense that, in conjunction with actual circumstances, it is a sufficient condition of death. Of complications such as over-determination, it will not be necessary to speak.

A second, and definitely minor, point about the definition of an act of euthanasia concerns the question of fact versus belief. It has already been implied that one who performs an act of euthanasia thinks that death will be merciful for the subject since we have said that it is on account of this thought that the act is done. But is it enough that he acts with this thought, or must things actually be as he thinks them to be? If one man kills another, or allows him to die, thinking that he is in the last stages of a terrible disease, though in fact he could have been cured, is this an act of euthanasia or not? Nothing much seems to hang on our decision about this. The same condition has got to enter into the definition whether as an element in reality or only as an element in the agent's belief. And however we define an act of euthanasia culpability or justifiability will be the same: if a man acts through ignorance his ignorance may be culpable or it may not.[2]

These are relatively easy problems to solve, but one that is dauntingly difficult has been passed over in this discussion of the definition, and must now be faced. It is easy to say, as if this raised no problems, that an act of euthanasia is by definition one aiming at the *good* of the one whose death is in question, and that it is *for his sake* that his death is desired. But how is this to be explained? Presumably we are thinking of some evil already with him or to come on him if he continues to live, and death is thought of as a release from this evil. But this cannot be enough. Most people's lives contain evils such as grief or pain, but we do not therefore think that death would be a blessing to them. On the contrary, life is generally supposed to be a good even for someone who is unusually unhappy or frustrated. How is it that one can ever wish for death for the sake of the one who is to die? This difficult question is central to the discussion of euthanasia, and we shall literally not know what we are talking about if we ask whether acts of euthanasia defined as we have defined them are ever morally permissible without first understanding better the reason for saying that life is a good, and the possibility that it is not always so.

If a man should save my life he would be my benefactor. In

normal circumstances this is plainly true; but does one always benefit another in saving his life? It seems certain that he does not. Suppose, for instance, that a man were being tortured to death and was given a drug that lengthened his sufferings; this would not be a benefit but the reverse. Or suppose that in a ghetto in Nazi Germany a doctor saved the life of someone threatened by disease, but that the man once cured was transported to an extermination camp; the doctor might wish for the sake of the patient that he had died of the disease. Nor would a longer stretch of life always be a benefit to the person who was given it. Comparing Hitler's camps with those of Stalin, Dimitri Panin observes that in the latter the method of extermination was made worse by agonies that could stretch out over months.

Death from a bullet would have been bliss compared with what many millions had to endure while dying of hunger. The kind of death to which they were condemned has nothing to equal it in treachery and sadism.[3]

These examples show that to save or prolong a man's life is not always to do him a service: it may be better for him if he dies earlier rather than later. It must therefore be agreed that while life is normally a benefit to the one who has it, this is not always so.

The judgement is often fairly easy to make—that life is or is not a good to someone—but the basis for it is very hard to find. When life is said to be a benefit or a good, on what grounds is the assertion made?

The difficulty is underestimated if it is supposed that the problem arises from the fact that one who is dead has nothing, so that the good someone gets from being alive cannot be compared with the amount he would otherwise have had. For why should this particular comparison be necessary? Surely it would be enough if one could say whether or not someone whose life was prolonged had more good than evil in the extra stretch of time. Such estimates are not always possible, but frequently they are; we say, for example, 'He was very happy in those last years', or, 'He had little but unhappiness then'. If the balance of good and evil determined whether life was a good to someone we would expect to find a correlation in the judgements. In fact, of course, we find nothing of the kind. First, a man who has no doubt that existence is a good to him may have no idea about the balance of happiness and unhappiness in his life, or of any other positive and negative factors that may be suggested. So the supposed criteria are not always operating where the judgement is made. And secondly the application of the criteria gives an answer that is often wrong. Many people have more evil than good in their lives; we do not, however, conclude that we would do these people no service by rescuing them from death.

To get around this last difficulty Thomas Nagel has suggested that experience itself is a good which must be brought in to balance accounts.

. . . life is worth living even when the bad elements of experience are plentiful, and the good ones too meager to outweigh the bad ones on their own. The additional positive weight is supplied by experience itself, rather than by any of its contents.[4]

This seems implausible because if experience itself is a good it must be so even when what we experience is wholly bad, as in being tortured to death. How should one decide how much to count for this experiencing; and why count anything at all? Others have tried to solve the problem by arguing that it is a man's desire for life that makes us call life a good: if he wants to live then anyone who prolongs his life does him a benefit. Yet someone may cling to life where we would say confidently that it would be better for him if he died, and he may admit it too. Speaking of those same conditions in which, as he said, a bullet would have been merciful, Panin writes,

I should like to pass on my observations concerning the absence of suicides under the extremely severe conditions of our concentration camps. The more that life became desperate, the more a prisoner seemed determined to hold onto it.[5]

One might try to explain this by saying that hope was the ground of this wish to survive for further days and months in the camp. But there is nothing unintelligible in the idea that a man might cling to life though he knew those facts about his future which would make any charitable man wish that he might die.

The problem remains, and it is hard to know where to look for a solution. Is there a conceptual connexion between *life* and *good*? Because life is not always a good we are apt to reject this idea, and to think that it must be a contingent fact that life is usually a good, as it is a contingent matter that legacies are usually a benefit, if they are. Yet it seems not to be a contingent matter that to save someone's life is ordinarily to benefit him. The problem is to find where the conceptual connexion lies.

It may be good tactics to forget for a time that it is euthanasia we are discussing and to see how *life* and *good* are connected in the case of living beings other than men. Even plants have things done to them that are harmful or beneficial, and what does them good must be related in some way to their living and dying. Let us therefore consider plants and animals, and then come back to human beings. At least we shall get away from the temptation to think that the connexion between life and benefit must everywhere be a matter of happiness and unhappiness or of pleasure and pain; the idea being absurd in the case of animals and impossible even to formulate for plants.

In case anyone thinks that the concept of the beneficial applies only in a secondary or analogical way to plants, he should be reminded that we speak quite straightforwardly in saying, for instance, that a certain amount of sunlight is beneficial to most plants. What is in question here is the habitat in which plants of particular species flourish, but we can also talk, in a slightly different way, of what does them good, where there is some suggestion of improvement or remedy. What has the beneficial to do with sustaining life? It is tempting to answer, 'everything', thinking that a healthy condition just is the one apt to secure survival. In fact, however, what is beneficial to a plant may have to do with reproduction rather than survival of the individual member of the species. Nevertheless there is a plain connexion between the beneficial and the life-sustaining even for the individual plant; if something makes it better able to survive in conditions normal for that species it is ipso facto good for it. We need go no further, and could go no further, in explaining why a certain environment or treatment is good for a plant than to show how it helps this plant to survive.[6]

This connexion between the life-sustaining and the beneficial is reasonably unproblematic, and there is nothing fanciful
or zoomorphic in speaking of benefiting or doing good to
plants. A connexion with its survival can make something
beneficial to a plant. But this is not, of course, to say that we
count life as a good to a plant. We may save its life by giving it
what is beneficial; we do not benefit it by saving its life.

A more ramified concept of benefit is used in speaking of
animal life. New things can be said, such as that an animal is
better or worse off for something that happened, or that it was
a good or bad thing for it that it did happen. And new things
count as benefit. In the first place, there is comfort, which
often is, but need not be, related to health. When loosening a
collar which is too tight for a dog we can say, 'That will be
better for it.' So we see that the words 'better for it' have two
different meanings which we mark when necessary by a difference of emphasis, saying 'better *for* it' when health is
involved. And secondly an animal can be benefited by having
its life saved. 'Could you do anything for it?' can be answered
by, 'Yes, I managed to save its life.' Sometimes we may
understand this, just as we would for a plant, to mean that we
had checked some disease. But we can also do something for
an animal by scaring away its predator. If we do this, it is a
good thing for the animal that we did, unless of course it
immediately meets a more unpleasant end by some other
means. Similarly, on the bad side, an animal may be worse off
for our intervention, and this not because it pines or suffers but
simply because it gets killed.

The problem that vexes us when we think about euthanasia
comes on the scene at this point. For if we can do something
for an animal—can benefit it—by relieving its suffering but
also by saving its life, where does the greater benefit come
when only death will end pain? It seemed that life was a good
in its own right; yet pain seemed to be an evil with equal status
and could therefore make life not a good after all. Is it only life
without pain that is a good when animals are concerned? This
does not seem a crazy suggestion when we are thinking of
animals, since unlike human beings they do not have suffering
as part of their normal life. But it is perhaps the idea of
ordinary life that matters here. We would not say that we had

done anything for an animal if we had merely kept it alive, either in an unconscious state or in a condition where, though conscious, it was unable to operate in an ordinary way; and the fact is that animals in severe and continuous pain simply do not operate normally. So we do not, on the whole, have the option of doing the animal good by saving its life though the life would be a life of pain. No doubt there are borderline cases, but that is no problem. We are not trying to make new judgements possible, but rather to find the principle of the ones we do make.

When we reach human life the problems seem even more troublesome. For now we must take quite new things into account, such as the subject's own view of his life. It is arguable that this places extra constraints on the solution: might it not be counted as a necessary condition of life's being a good to a man that he should see it as such? Is there not some difficulty about the idea that a benefit might be done to him by the saving or prolonging of his life even though he himself wished for death? Of course he might have a quite mistaken view of his own prospects, but let us ignore this and think only of cases where it is life as he knows it that is in question. Can we think that the prolonging of this life would be a benefit to him even though he would rather have it end than continue? It seems that this cannot be ruled out. That there is no simple incompatibility between life as a good and the wish for death is shown by the possibility that a man should wish himself dead, not for his own sake, but for the sake of someone else. And if we try to amend the thesis to say that life cannot be a good to one who wishes *for his own sake* that he should die, we find the crucial concept slipping through our fingers. As Bishop Butler pointed out long ago not all ends are either benevolent or self-interested. Does a man wish for death for his own sake in the relevant sense if, for instance, he wishes to revenge himself on another by his death? Or what if he is proud and refuses to stomach dependence or incapacity even though there are many good things left in life for him? The truth seems to be that the wish for death is sometimes compatible with life's being a good and sometimes not, which is possible because the description 'wishing for death' is one covering diverse states of mind from that of the determined suicide, pathologically depressed, to that of one who is surprised to find that the thought of a fatal accident is viewed with relief. On the one hand, a man may see his life as a burden but go about his business in a more or less ordinary way; on the other hand, the wish for death may take the form of a rejection of everything that is in life, as it does in severe depression. It seems reasonable to say that life is not a good to one permanently in the latter state, and we must return to this topic later on.

When are we to say that life is a good or a benefit to a man? The dilemma that faces us is this. If we say that life as such is a good we find ourselves refuted by the examples given at the beginning of this discussion. We therefore incline to think that it is as bringing good things that life is a good, where it is a good. But if life is a good only because it is the condition of good things why is it not equally an evil when it brings bad things? And how can it be a good even when it brings more evil than good?

It should be noted that the problem has here been formulated in terms of the balance of good and evil, not that of happiness and unhappiness, and that it is not to be solved by the denial (which may be reasonable enough) that unhappiness is the only evil or happiness the only good. In this paper no view has been expressed about the nature of goods other than life itself. The point is that on any view of the goods and evils that life can contain, it seems that a life with more evil than good could still itself be a good.

It may be useful to review the judgements with which our theory must square. Do we think that life can be a good to one who suffers a lot of pain? Clearly we do. What about severely handicapped people; can life be a good to them? Clearly it can be, for even if someone is almost completely paralysed, perhaps living in an iron lung, perhaps able to move things only by means of a tube held between his lips, we do not rule him out of order if he says that some benefactor saved his life. Nor is it different with mental handicap. There are many fairly severely handicapped people—such as those with Down's Syndrome—for whom a simple affectionate life is possible. What about senility? Does this break the normal connexion between life and good? Here we must surely distinguish between forms of senility. Some forms leave a life which we count someone as better off having than not having, so that a doctor who prolonged it would benefit the person concerned. With some kinds of senility this is however no longer true. There are some in geriatric wards who are barely conscious, though they can move a little and swallow food put into their mouths. To prolong such a state, whether in the old or in the very severely mentally handicapped is not to do them a service or confer a benefit. But of course it need not be the reverse: only if there is suffering would one wish for the sake of the patient that he should die.

It seems, therefore, that merely being alive even without suffering is not a good, and that we must make a distinction similar to that which we made when animals were our topic. But how is the line to be drawn in the case of men? What is to count as ordinary human life in the relevant sense? If it were only the very senile or very ill who were said not to have this life it might seem right to describe it in terms of *operation*. But it will be hard to find the sense in which the men described by Panin were not operating, given that they dragged themselves out to the forest to work. What is it about the life that the prisoners were living that makes us put it on the other side of the dividing line from that of most of the physically or mentally handicapped and of some severely ill or suffering patients? It is not that they were in captivity, for life in captivity can certainly be a good. Nor is it merely the unusual nature of their life. In some ways the prisoners were living more as other men do than the patient in the iron lung.

The idea we need seems to be that of life which is ordinary human life in the following respect—that it contains a minimum of basic human goods. What is ordinary in human life—even in very hard lives—is that a man is not driven to work far beyond his capacity; that he has the support of a family or community; that he can more or less satisfy his hunger; that he has hopes for the future; that he can lie down to rest at night. Such things were denied to the men in the Vyatlag camps described by Panin; not even rest at night was allowed them when they were tormented by bed-bugs, by noise and stench, and by routines such as body-searches and bath-parades—arranged for the night time so that work norms would not be reduced. Disease too can so take over a man's life that the normal human goods disappear. When a patient is so overwhelmed by pain or nausea that he cannot eat with pleasure, if he can eat at all, and is out of the reach of even the most loving voice, he no longer has ordinary human life in the sense in which the words are used here. And we may now pick up a thread from an earlier part of the discussion by remarking that crippling depression can destroy the enjoyment of ordinary goods as effectively as external circumstances can remove them.

The suggested solution to the problem is, then, that there is a certain conceptual connexion between *life* and *good* in the case of human beings as in that of animals and even plants. Here, as there, however, it is not the mere state of being alive that can determine, or itself count as, a good, but rather life coming up to some standard of normality. It was argued that it is as part of ordinary life that the elements of good that a man may have are relevant to the question of whether saving his life counts as benefiting him. Ordinary human lives, even very hard lives, contain a minimum of basic goods, but when these are absent the idea of life is no longer linked to that of good. And since it is in this way that the elements of good contained in a man's life are relevant to the question of whether he is benefited if his life is preserved, there is no reason why it should be the balance of good and evil that counts.

It should be added that evils are relevant in one way when, as in the examples discussed above, they destroy the possibility of ordinary goods, but in a different way when they invade a life from which the goods are already absent for a different reason. So, for instance, the connexion between *life* and *good* may be broken because consciousness has sunk to a very low level, as in extreme senility or severe brain damage. In itself this kind of life seems to be neither good nor evil, but if suffering sets in one would hope for a speedy end.

This, admittedly inadequate, discussion of the sense in which life is normally a good, and of the reasons why it may not be so in some particular case, completes the account of what euthanasia is here taken to be. An act of euthanasia, whether literally act or rather omission, is attributed to an agent who opts for the death of another because in his case life seems to be an evil rather than a good. The question now to be asked is

whether acts of euthanasia are ever justifiable. But there are
two topics here rather than one. For it is one thing to say that
some acts of euthanasia considered only in themselves and
their results are morally unobjectionable, and another to say
that it would be all right to legalise them. Perhaps the practice
of euthanasia would allow too many abuses, and perhaps there
would be too many mistakes. Moreover the practice might
have very important and highly undesirable side effects,
because it is unlikely that we could change our principles about
the treatment of the old and the ill without changing fundamental emotional attitudes and social relations. The topics
must, therefore, be treated separately. In the next part of the
discussion, nothing will be said about the social consequences
and possible abuses of the practice of euthanasia, but only
about acts of euthanasia considered in themselves.

What we want to know is whether acts of euthanasia,
defined as we have defined them, are ever morally permissible.
To be more accurate, we want to know whether it is ever
sufficient justification of the choice of death for another that
death can be counted a benefit rather than harm, and that this is
why the choice is made.

It will be impossible to get a clear view of the area to which
this topic belongs without first marking the distinct grounds
on which objection may lie when one man opts for the death of
another. There are two different virtues whose requirements
are, in general, contrary to such actions. An unjustified act of
killing, or allowing to die, is contrary to justice or to charity,
or to both virtues, and the moral failings are distinct. Justice
has to do with what men *owe* each other in the way of noninterference and positive service. When used in this wide
sense, which has its history in the doctrine of the cardinal
virtues, justice is not especially connected with, for instance,
law courts but with the whole area of rights, and duties corresponding to rights. Thus murder is one form of injustice,
dishonesty another, and wrongful failure to keep contracts a
third; chicanery in a law court or defrauding someone of his
inheritance are simply other cases of injustice. Justice as such is
not directly linked to the good of another, and may require
that something be rendered to him even where it will do him
harm, as Hume pointed out when he remarked that a debt

must be paid even to a profligate debauchee who 'would rather receive harm than benefit from large possessions'.[7] Charity, on the other hand, is the virtue which attaches us to the good of others. An act of charity is in question only where something is not demanded by justice, but a lack of charity and of justice can be shown where a man is denied something which he both needs and has a right to: both charity and justice demand that widows and orphans are not defrauded, and the man who cheats them is neither charitable nor just.

It is easy to see that the two grounds of objection to inducing death are distinct. A murder is an act of injustice. A culpable failure to come to the aid of someone whose life is threatened is normally contrary, not to justice, but to charity. But where one man is under contract, explicit or implicit, to come to the aid of another injustice too will be shown. Thus injustice may be involved either in an act or an omission, and the same is true of a lack of charity; charity may demand that someone be aided, but also that an unkind word not be spoken.

The distinction between charity and justice will turn out to be of first importance when voluntary and nonvoluntary euthanasia are distinguished later on. This is because of the connexion between justice and rights, and something should now be said about this. I believe it is true to say that wherever a man acts unjustly he has infringed a right, since justice has to do with whatever a man is owed, and whatever he is owed is his as a matter of right. Something should therefore be said about the different kinds of rights. The distinction commonly made is between having a right in the sense of having a liberty, and having a 'claim-right' or 'right of recipience'.[8] The best way to understand such a distinction seems to be as follows. To say that a man has a right in the sense of liberty is to say that no one can demand that he do not do the thing which he has the right to do. The fact that he has a right to do it consists in the fact that a certain kind of objection does not lie against his doing it. Thus a man has a right in this sense to walk down a public street or park his car in a public parking space. It does not follow that no one else may prevent him from doing so. If for some reason I want a certain man not to park in a certain place I may lawfully park there myself or get my friends to do so, thus preventing him from doing what he has a right (in the sense of a liberty) to do. It is different, however, with a claim-right. This is the kind of right which I have in addition to a liberty when, for example, I have a private parking space; now others have duties in the way of noninterference, as in this case, or of service, as in the case where my claim-right is to goods or services promised to me. Sometimes one of these rights gives other people the duty of securing to me that to which I have a right, but at other times their duty is merely to refrain from interference. If a fall of snow blocks my private parking space there is normally no obligation for anyone else to clear it away. Claim rights generate duties; sometimes these duties are duties of noninterference; sometimes they are duties of service. If your right gives me the duty not to interfere with you I have 'no right' to do it; similarly, if your right gives me the duty to provide something for you I have 'no right' to refuse to do it. What *I* lack is the right which is a liberty: I am not 'at liberty' to interfere with you or to refuse the service.

Where in this picture does the right to life belong? No doubt people have the right to live in the sense of a liberty, but what is important is the cluster of claim-rights brought together under the title of the right to life. The chief of these is, of course, the right to be free from interferences that threaten life. If other people aim their guns at us or try to pour poison into our drink we can, to put it mildly, demand that they desist. And then there are the services we can claim from doctors, health officers, bodyguards, and firemen; the rights that depend on contract or public arrangement. Perhaps there is no particular point in saying that the duties these people owe us belong to the right to life; we might as well say that all the services owed to anyone by tailors, dressmakers, and couturiers belong to a right called the right to be elegant. But contracts such as those understood in the patient–doctor relationship come in in an important way when we are discussing the rights and wrongs of euthanasia, and are therefore mentioned here.

Do people have the right to what they need in order to survive, apart from the right conferred by special contracts into which other people have entered for the supplying of these necessities? Do people in the underdeveloped countries in which starvation is rife have the right to the food they so evidently lack? Joel Feinberg, discussing this question, suggests that they should be said to have 'a claim', distinguishing this from a 'valid claim', which gives a claim-right.

The manifesto writers on the other side who seem to identify needs, or at least basic needs, with what they call 'human rights', are more properly described, I think, as urging upon the world community the moral principle that *all* human needs ought to be recognized as *claims* (in the customary *prima facie* sense) worthy of sympathy and serious consideration right now, even though, in many cases, they cannot yet plausibly be treated as *valid* claims, that is, as grounds of any other people's duties. This way of talking avoids the anomaly of ascribing to all human beings now, even those in pre-industrial societies, such 'economic and social rights' as 'periodic holidays with pay'.[9]

This seems reasonable, though we notice that there are some actual rights to service which are not based on anything like a contract, as for instance the right that children have to support from their parents and parents to support from their children in old age, though both sets of rights are to some extent dependent on existing social arrangements.

Let us now ask how the right to life affects the morality of acts of euthanasia. Are such acts sometimes or always ruled out by the right to life? This is certainly a possibility; for although an act of euthanasia is, by our definition, a matter of opting for death for the good of the one who is to die, there is, as we noted earlier, no simple connexion between that to which a man has a right and that which is for his good. It is true that men have the right only to the kind of thing that is, in general, a good: we do not think that people have the right to garbage or polluted air. Nevertheless, a man may have the right to something which he himself would be better off without; where rights exist it is a man's will that counts not his or anyone else's estimate of benefit or harm. So the duties complementary to the right to life—the general duty of noninterference and the duty of service incurred by certain persons—are not affected by the quality of a man's life or by his prospects. Even if it is true that he would be, as we say, 'better off dead', so long as he wants to live this does not justify us in killing him and may not justify us in deliberately allowing him to die. All of us have the duty of noninterference, and some of us may have the duty to sustain his life. Suppose, for example, that a retreating army has to leave behind wounded or exhausted soldiers in the wastes of an arid or snowbound land where the only prospect is death by starvation or at the hands of an enemy notoriously cruel. It has often been the practice to accord a merciful bullet to men in such desperate straits. But suppose one of them demands that he should be left alive? It seems clear that his comrades have no right to kill him, though it is a quite different question as to whether they should give him a life-prolonging drug. The right to life can sometimes give a duty of positive service, but does not do so here. What it does give is the right to be left alone.

Interestingly enough we have arrived by way of a considera-tion of the right to life at the distinction normally labelled 'active' versus 'passive' euthanasia, and often thought to be irrelevant to the moral issue.[10] Once it is seen that the right to life is a distinct ground of objection to certain acts of euthanasia, and that this right creates a duty of noninterference more widespread than the duties of care there can be no doubt about the relevance of the distinction between passive and active euthanasia. Where everyone may have the duty to leave someone alone, it may be that no one has the duty to maintain his life, or that only some people do.

Where then do the boundaries of the 'active' and 'passive' lie? In some ways the words are themselves misleading, because they suggest the difference between act and omission which is not quite what we want. Certainly the act of shooting someone is the kind of thing we were talking about under the heading of 'interference', and omitting to give him a drug a case of refusing care. But the act of turning off a respirator should surely be thought of as no different from the decision not to start it; if doctors had decided that a patient should be allowed to die, either course of action might follow, and both should be counted as passive rather than active euthanasia if euthanasia were in question. The point seems to be that inter-ference in a course of treatment is not the same as other interference in a man's life, and particularly if the same body of people are responsible for the treatment and for its discon-tinuance. In such a case we could speak of the disconnecting of the apparatus as killing the man, or of the hospital as allowing him to die. By and large, it is the act of killing that is ruled out under the heading of noninterference, but not in every case.

Doctors commonly recognise this distinction, and the grounds on which some philosophers have denied it seem untenable. James Rachels, for instance, believes that if the difference between active and passive is relevant anywhere, it should be relevant everywhere, and he has pointed to an example in which it seems to make no difference which is done. If someone saw a child drowning in a bath it would seem just as bad to let it drown as to push its head under water.[11] If 'it makes no difference' means that one act would be as iniquitous as the other this is true. It is not that killing is *worse* than allowing to die, but that the two are contrary to distinct virtues, which gives the possibility that in some circumstances one is impermissible and the other permissible. In the circumstances invented by Rachels, both are wicked: it is contrary to justice to push the child's head under the water—something one has no right to do. To leave it to drown is not contrary to justice, but is a particularly glaring example of lack of charity. Here it makes no practical difference because the requirements of justice and charity coincide; but in the case of the retreating army they did not: charity would have required that the wounded soldier be killed had not justice required that he be left alive.[12] In such a case it makes all the difference whether a man opts for the death of another in a positive action, or whether he allows him to die. An analogy with the right to property will make the point clear. If a man owns something he has the right to it even when its possession does him harm, and normally we have no right to take it from him. But if one day it should blow away, maybe nothing requires us to get it back for him; we could not deprive him of it, but we may allow it to go. This is not to deny that it will often be an unfriendly act or one based on an arrogant judgement when we refuse to do what he wants. Nevertheless, we would be within our rights, and it might be that no moral objection of any kind would lie against our refusal.

It is important to emphasise that a man's rights may stand between us and the action we would dearly like to take for his sake. They may, of course, also prevent action which we would like to take for the sake of others, as when it might be tempting to kill one man to save several. But it is interesting that the limits of allowable interference, however uncertain, seem stricter in the first case than the second. Perhaps there are no cases in which it would be all right to kill a man against his will *for his own sake* unless they could equally well be described as cases of allowing him to die, as in the example of turning off the respirator. However, there are circumstances, even if these are very rare, in which one man's life would justifiably be sacrificed to save others, and 'killing' would be the only description of what was being done. For instance, a vehicle which had gone out of control might be steered from a path on which it would kill more than one man to a path on which it would kill one.[13] But it would not be permissible to steer a vehicle towards someone in order to kill him, against his will, for his own good. An analogy with property rights again illustrates the point. One may not destroy a man's property against his will on the grounds that he would be better off without it; there are however circumstances in which it could be destroyed for the sake of others. If his house is liable to fall and kill him that is his affair; it might, however, without injustice be destroyed to stop the spread of a fire.

We see then that the distinction between active and passive, important as it is elsewhere, has a special importance in the area of euthanasia. It should also be clear why James Rachels' other argument, that it is often 'more humane' to kill than to allow to die, does not show that the distinction between active and passive euthanasia is morally irrelevant. It might be 'more humane' in this sense to deprive a man of property that brings evil on him, or to refuse to pay what is owed to Hume's profligate debauchee; but if we say this we must admit that an act which is 'more humane' than its alternative may be morally objectionable because it infringes rights.

So far we have said very little about the right to service as opposed to the right to noninterference, though it was agreed that both might be brought under the heading of 'the right to life'. What about the duty to preserve life that may belong to special classes of persons such as bodyguards, firemen, or doctors? Unlike the general public they are not within their rights if they merely refrain from interfering and do not try to sustain life. The subject's claim-rights are two-fold as far as they are concerned and passive as well as active euthanasia may be ruled out here if it is against his will. This is not to say that he has the right to any and every service needed to save or prolong his life; the rights of other people set limits to what may be demanded, both because they have the right not to be interfered with and because they may have a competing right to services. Furthermore one must enquire just what the contract or implicit agreement amounts to in each case. Firemen and bodyguards presumably have a duty which is simply to preserve life, within the limits of justice to others and of reasonableness to themselves. With doctors it may however be different, since their duty relates not only to preserving life but also to the relief of suffering. It is not clear what a doctor's duties are to his patient if life can be prolonged only at the cost of suffering or suffering relieved only by measures that shorten life. George Fletcher has argued that what the doctor is under contract to do depends on what is generally done, because this is what a patient will reasonably expect.[14] This seems right. If procedures are part of normal medical practice then it seems that the patient can demand them however much it may be against his interest to do so. Once again it is not a matter of what is 'most humane'.

That the patient's right to life may set limits to permissible acts of euthanasia seems undeniable. If he does not want to die no one has the right to practise active euthanasia on him, and passive euthanasia may also be ruled out where he has a right to the services of doctors or others.

Perhaps few will deny what has so far been said about the impermissibility of acts of euthanasia, simply because we have so far spoken about the case of one who positively wants to live, and about his rights; whereas those who advocate euthanasia are usually thinking either about those who wish to die or about those whose wishes cannot be ascertained either because they cannot properly be said to have wishes or because, for one reason or another, we are unable to form a reliable estimate of what they are. The question that must now be asked is whether the latter type of case, where euthanasia though not *in*voluntary would again be *non*voluntary, is different from the one discussed so far. Would we have the right

to kill someone for his own good so long as we had no idea that
he positively wished to live? And what about the life-
prolonging duties of doctors in the same circumstances? This
is a very difficult problem. On the one hand, it seems ridiculous to suppose that a man's right to life is something which
generates duties only where he has signalled that he wants to
live; as a borrower does indeed have a duty to return something lent on indefinite loan only if the lender indicates that he
wants it back. On the other hand, it might be argued that there
is something illogical about the idea that a right has been
infringed if someone incapable of saying whether he wants it
or not is deprived of something that is doing him harm rather
than good. Yet on the analogy of property we would say that a
right has been infringed. Only if someone had earlier told us
that in such circumstances he would not want to keep the thing
could we think that his right had been waived. Perhaps if we
could make confident judgements about what anyone in such
circumstances would wish, or what he would have wished
beforehand had he considered the matter, we could agree to
consider the right to life as 'dormant', needing to be asserted if
the normal duties were to remain. But as things are we cannot
make any such assumption; we simply do not know what
most people would want, or would have wanted, us to do
unless they tell us. This is certainly the case so far as active
measures to end life are concerned. Possibly it is different, or
will become different, in the matter of being kept alive, so
general is the feeling against using sophisticated procedures on
moribund patients, and so much is this dreaded by people who
are old or terminally ill. Once again the distinction between
active and passive euthanasia has come on the scene, but this
time because most people's attitudes to the two are so different. It is just possible that we might presume, in the absence of
specific evidence, that someone would not wish, beyond a
certain point to be kept alive; it is certainly not possible to
assume that he would wish to be killed.

   In the last paragraph we have begun to broach the topic of
voluntary euthanasia, and this we must now discuss. What is
to be said about the case in which there is no doubt about
someone's wish to die? Either he has told us beforehand that he
would wish it in circumstances such as he is now in, and has

shown no sign of a change of mind, or else he tells us now, being in possession of his faculties and of a steady mind. We should surely say that the objections previously urged against acts of euthanasia, which it must be remembered were all on the ground of rights, had disappeared. It does not seem that one would infringe someone's right to life in killing him with his permission and in fact at his request. Why should someone not be able to waive his right to life, or rather, as would be more likely to happen, to cancel some of the duties of noninterference that this right entails? (He is more likely to say that he should be killed by this man at this time in this manner, than to say that anyone may kill him at any time and in any way.) Similarly someone may give permission for the destruction of his property, and request it. The important thing is that he gives a critical permission, and it seems that this is enough to cancel the duty normally associated with the right. If someone gives you permission to destroy his property it can no longer be said that you have no right to do so, and I do not see why it should not be the same with taking a man's life. An objection might be made on the ground that only God has the right to take life, but in this paper religious as opposed to moral arguments are being left aside. Religion apart, there seems to be no case to be made out for an infringement of rights if a man who wishes to die is allowed to die or even killed. But of course it does not follow that there is no moral objection to it. Even with property, which is after all a relatively small matter, one might be wrong to destroy what one had the right to destroy. For, apart from its value to other people, it might be valuable to the man who wanted it destroyed, and charity might require us to hold our hand where justice did not.

Let us review the conclusion of this part of the argument, which has been about nonvoluntary euthanasia and the right to life. It has been argued that from this side come stringent restrictions on the acts of euthanasia that could be morally permissible. Active nonvoluntary euthanasia is ruled out by that part of the right to life which creates the duty of noninterference, though passive nonvoluntary euthanasia is not necessarily ruled out, except where the right to life-preserving action has been created by some special condition such as a contract between a man and his doctor. Voluntary euthanasia is another matter: as the preceding paragraph suggested, no right is infringed if a man is allowed to die or even killed at his own request.

Turning now to the other objection that normally holds against inducing the death of another, that it is against charity, or benevolence, we must tell a very different story. Charity is the virtue that gives attachment to the good of others, and because life is normally a good, charity normally demands that it should be saved or prolonged. But as we so defined an act of euthanasia that it seeks a man's death for his own sake—for his good—charity will normally speak in favour of it. This is not, of course, to say that charity can require an act of euthanasia which justice forbids, but if an act of euthanasia is not contrary to justice—that is, it does not infringe rights—charity will rather be in its favour than against.

Once more the distinction between nonvoluntary and voluntary euthanasia must be considered. Could it ever be compatible with charity to seek a man's death although he wanted to live, or at least had not let us know that he wanted to die? I have argued that in such circumstances active euthanasia would infringe his right to life, but passive euthanasia would not do so, unless he had some special right to life-preserving service from the one who allowed him to die. What would charity dictate? Obviously when a man wants to live there is a presumption that he will be benefited if his life is prolonged, and if it is so the question of euthanasia does not arise. But it is, on the other hand, possible that he wants to live where it would be better for him to die: perhaps he does not realise the desperate situation he is in, or perhaps he is afraid of dying. So, in spite of a very proper resistance to refusing to go along with the man's own wishes in the matter of life and death, someone might justifiably refuse to prolong the life even of someone who asked him to prolong it, as in the case of refusing to give the wounded soldier a drug that would keep him alive to meet a terrible end. And it is even more obvious that charity does not always dictate that life should be prolonged where a man's own wishes, hypothetical or actual, are not known.

So much for the relation of charity to nonvoluntary passive euthanasia, which was not, like nonvoluntary active euthanasia, ruled out by the right to life. Let us now ask what charity has to say about voluntary euthanasia both active and passive. It was suggested in the discussion of justice that if of sound mind and steady desire a man might give others the *right* to allow him to die or even to kill him, where otherwise this would be ruled out. But it was pointed out that this would not settle the question of whether the act was morally permissible, and it is this that we must now consider. Could not charity speak against what justice allowed? Indeed it might do so. For while the fact that a man wants to die suggests that his life is wretched, and while his rejection of life may itself tend to take the good out of things he might have enjoyed, nevertheless his wish to die might here be opposed for his own sake just as it might be if suicide were in question. Perhaps there is hope that his mental condition will improve. Perhaps he is mistaken in thinking his disease is incurable. Perhaps he wants to die for the sake of someone else on whom he feels he is a burden, and we are not ready to accept this sacrifice whether for ourselves or others. In such cases, and there will surely be many of them, it could not be for his own sake that we kill him or allow him to die, and therefore euthanasia as defined in this paper would not be in question. But this is not to deny that there could be acts of voluntary euthanasia both passive and active against which neither justice nor charity would speak.

We have now considered the morality of euthanasia both voluntary and nonvoluntary, and active and passive. The conclusion has been that nonvoluntary active euthanasia (roughly, killing a man against his will or without his consent) is never justified; that is to say, that a man's being killed for his own good never justifies the act unless he himself has consented to it. A man's rights are infringed by such an action, and it is therefore contrary to justice. However, all the other combinations, nonvoluntary passive euthanasia, voluntary active euthanasia, and voluntary passive euthanasia are sometimes compatible with both justice and charity. But the strong condition carried in the definition of euthanasia adopted in this paper must not be forgotten; an act of euthanasia as here understood is one whose purpose is to benefit the one who dies.

In the light of this discussion let us look at our present practices. Are they good or are they bad? And what changes might be made, thinking now not only of the morality of particular acts of euthanasia but also of the indirect effects of instituting different practices, of the abuses to which they might be subject and of the changes that might come about if euthanasia became a recognised part of the social scene?

The first thing to notice is that it is wrong to ask whether we should introduce the practice of euthanasia as if it were not something we already had. In fact we do have it. For instance it is common, where the medical prognosis is very bad, for doctors to recommend against measures to prolong life, and particularly where a process of degeneration producing one medical emergency after another has already set in. If these doctors are not certainly within their legal rights this is something that is apt to come as a surprise to them as to the general public. It is also obvious that euthanasia is often practised where old people are concerned. If someone very old and soon to die is attacked by a disease that makes his life wretched, doctors do not always come in with life-prolonging drugs. Perhaps poor patients are more fortunate in this respect than rich patients, being more often left to die in peace; but it is in any case a well recognised piece of medical practice, and a form of euthanasia.

No doubt, the case of infants with mental or physical defects will be suggested as another example of the practice of euthanasia as we already have it, since such infants are sometimes deliberately allowed to die. That they are deliberately allowed to die is certain; children with severe spina bifida malformations are not always operated on even where it is thought that without the operation they will die; and even in the case of children with Down's Syndrome who have intestinal obstructions the relatively simple operation that would make it possible to feed them is sometimes not performed.[15] Whether this is euthanasia in our sense or only as the Nazis understood it is another matter. We must ask the crucial question, 'Is it for the sake of the child himself that the doctors and parents choose his death?' In some cases the answer may really be yes, and what is more important it may really be true that the kind of life which is a good is not possible or likely for this child, and that there is little but suffering and frustration in store for him.[16] But this must presuppose that the medical prognosis is wretchedly bad, as it may be for some spina bifida children. With children who are born with Down's Syndrome it is, however, quite different. Most of these are able to live on for quite a time in a reasonably contented way, remaining like children all their lives but capable of affectionate relationships and able to play games and perform simple tasks. The fact is, of course, that the doctors who recommend against life-saving procedures for handicapped infants are usually thinking not of them but rather of their parents and of other children in the family or of the 'burden on society' if the children survive. So it is not for their sake but to avoid trouble to others that they are allowed to die. When brought out into the open this seems unacceptable; at least we do not easily accept the principle that adults who need special care should be counted as too burdensome to be kept alive. It must in any case be insisted that if children with Down's Syndrome are deliberately allowed to die this is not a matter of euthanasia except in Hitler's sense. And for our children, since we scruple to gas them, not even the manner of their death is 'quiet and easy'; when not treated for an intestinal obstruction a baby simply starves to death. Perhaps some will take this as an argument for allowing active euthanasia, in which case they will be in the company of an S.S. man stationed in the Warthgenau who sent Eichmann a memorandum telling him that 'Jews in the coming winter could no longer be fed' and submitting for his consideration a proposal as to whether 'it would not be the most humane solution to kill those Jews who were incapable of work through some quicker means.'[17] If we say we are *unable* to look after children with handicaps we are no more telling the truth than was the S.S. man who said that the Jews could not be fed.

Nevertheless if it is ever right to allow deformed children to die because life will be a misery to them, or not to take measures to prolong for a little the life of a newborn baby whose life cannot extend beyond a few months of intense medical intervention, there is a genuine problem about active as opposed to passive euthanasia. There are well-known cases in which the medical staff has looked on wretchedly while an infant died slowly from starvation and dehydration because they did not feel able to give a lethal injection. According to the principles discussed in the earlier part of this paper they would indeed have had no right to give it, since an infant

cannot ask that it should be done. The only possible solution—supposing that voluntary active euthanasia were to be
legalised—would be to appoint guardians to act on the infant's
behalf. In a different climate of opinion this might not be
dangerous, but at present, when people so readily assume that
the life of a handicapped baby is of no value, one would be
loath to support it.

Finally, on the subject of handicapped children, another
word should be said about those with severe mental defects.
For them too it might sometimes be right to say that one
would wish for death for their sake. But not even severe
mental handicap automatically brings a child within the scope
even of a possible act of euthanasia. If the level of consciousness is low enough it could not be said that life is a good to
them, any more than in the case of those suffering from
extreme senility. Nevertheless if they do not suffer it will not
be an act of euthanasia by which someone opts for their death.
Perhaps charity does not demand that strenuous measures are
taken to keep people in this state alive, but euthanasia does not
come into the matter, any more than it does when someone is,
like Karen Ann Quinlan, in a state of permanent coma. Much
could be said about this last case. It might even be suggested
that in the case of unconsciousness this 'life' is not the life to
which 'the right to life' refers. But that is not our topic here.

What we must consider, even if only briefly, is the possibility that euthanasia, genuine euthanasia, and not contrary to
the requirements of justice or charity, should be legalised over
a wider area. Here we are up against the really serious problem
of abuse. Many people want, and want very badly, to be rid of
their elderly relatives and even of their ailing husbands or
wives. Would any safeguards ever be able to stop them
describing as euthanasia what was really for their own benefit?
And would it be possible to prevent the occurrence of acts
which were genuinely acts of euthanasia but morally impermissible because infringing the rights of a patient who wished
to live or whose wishes were unknown?

Perhaps the furthest we should go is to encourage patients to
make their own contracts with a doctor by making it known
whether they wish him to prolong their lives in case of painful terminal illness or of incapacity. A document such as the

Living Will seems eminently sensible, and should surely be allowed to give a doctor following the previously expressed wishes of the patient immunity from legal proceedings by relatives.[18] Legalising active euthanasia is, however, another matter. Apart from the special repugnance doctors feel towards the idea of a lethal injection, it may be of the very greatest importance to keep a psychological barrier up against killing. Moreover it is active euthanasia which is the most liable to abuse. Hitler would not have been able to kill 275,000 people in his 'euthanasia' programme if he had had to wait for them to need life-saving treatment. But there are other objections to active euthanasia, even voluntary active euthanasia. In the first place it would be hard to devise procedures that would protect people from being persuaded into giving their consent. And secondly the possibility of active voluntary euthanasia might change the social scene in ways that would be very bad. As things are, people do, by and large, expect to be looked after if they are old or ill. This is one of the good things that we have, but we might lose it, and be much worse off without it. It might come to be expected that someone likely to need a lot of looking after should call for the doctor and demand his own death. Something comparable could be good in an extremely poverty-stricken community where the children genuinely suffered from lack of food; but in rich societies such as ours it would surely be a spiritual disaster. Such possibilities should make us very wary of supporting large measures of euthanasia, even where moral principle applied to the individual act does not rule it out.

NOTES

* 'Euthanasia' originally appeared in *Philosophy and Public Affairs*, Volume 6, Number 2, Winter 1977.
I would like to thank Derek Parfit and the editors of *Philosophy & Public Affairs* for their very helpful comments.
[1] Leo Alexander, 'Medical Science under Dictatorship', *New England Journal of Medicine*, 14 July 1949, p. 40.
[2] For a discussion of culpable and nonculpable ignorance see Thomas Aquinas, *Summa Theologica*, First Part of the

Second Part, Question 6, article 8, and Question 19, articles 5 and 6.

[3] Dimitri Panin, *The Notebooks of Sologdin* (London, 1976), pp. 66–7.

[4] Thomas Nagel, 'Death', in James Rachels, ed., *Moral Problems* (New York, 1971), p. 362.

[5] Panin, *Sologdin*, p. 85.

[6] Yet some detail needs to be filled in to explain why we should not say that a scarecrow is beneficial to the plants it protects. Perhaps what is beneficial must either be a feature of the plant itself, such as protective prickles, or else must work on the plant directly, such as a line of trees which give it shade.

[7] David Hume, *Treatise*, book III, part II, section 1.

[8] See, for example, D. D. Raphael, 'Human Rights Old and New', in D. D. Raphael, ed., *Political Theory and the Rights of Man* (London, 1967), and Joel Feinberg, 'The Nature and Value of Rights', *The Journal of Value Inquiry* 4, no. 4 (Winter 1970): 243–57. Reprinted in Samuel Gorovitz, ed., *Moral Problems in Medicine* (Englewood Cliffs, New Jersey, 1976).

[9] Feinberg, 'Human rights', Gorovitz, *Moral Problems in Medicine*, p. 465.

[10] See, for example, James Rachels, 'Active and Passive Euthanasia', *New England Journal of Medicine* 292, no. 2 (9 Jan. 1975): 78–80.

[11] Ibid.

[12] It is not, however, that justice and charity conflict. A man does not lack charity because he refrains from an act of injustice which would have been for someone's good.

[13] For a discussion of such questions, see my article 'The Problem of Abortion and the Doctrine of the Double Effect', *Oxford Review*, no. 5 (1967); reprinted in Rachels, *Moral Problems*, and Gorovitz, *Moral Problems in Medicine*.

[14] George Fletcher, 'Legal Aspects of the Decision not to Prolong Life', *Journal of the American Medical Association* 203, no. 1 (1 Jan. 1968): 119–22. Reprinted in Gorovitz.

[15] I have been told this by a paediatrician in a well-known medical centre in the United States. It is confirmed by Anthony M. Shaw and Iris A. Shaw, 'Dilemma of Informed Consent in Children', *The New England Journal of Medicine* 289, no. 17 (25 Oct. 1973): 885–90. Reprinted in Gorovitz.

[16] It must be remembered, however, that many of the social miseries of spina bifida children could be avoided. Professor R. B. Zachary is surely right to insist on this. See, for example, 'Ethical and Social Aspects of Spina Bifida', *The Lancet*, 3 Aug. 1968, pp. 274–6. Reprinted in Gorovitz.

[17] Quoted by Hannah Arendt, *Eichmann in Jerusalem* (London, 1963), p. 90.

[18] Details of this document are to be found in J. A. Behnke and Sissela Bok, eds., *The Dilemmas of Euthanasia* (New York, 1975), and in A. B. Downing, ed., *Euthanasia and the Right to Life: The Case for Voluntary Euthanasia* (London, 1969).

IV

Free Will as Involving Determinism*

The idea that free will can be reconciled with the strictest determinism is now very widely accepted. To say that a man acted freely is, it is often suggested, to say that he was not constrained, or that he could have done otherwise if he had chosen, or something else of that kind; and since these things could be true even if his action was determined it seems that there could be room for free will even within a universe completely subject to causal laws. Hume put forward a view of this kind in contrasting the 'liberty of spontaneity . . . which is oppos'd to violence' with the nonexistent 'liberty of indifference . . . which means a negation of necessity and causes'.[1] A. J. Ayer, in his essay 'Freedom and Necessity'[2] was summing up such a position when he said, 'from the fact that my action is causally determined . . . it does not necessarily follow that I am not free'[3] and 'it is not when my action has any cause at all, but only when it has a special sort of cause, that it is reckoned not to be free'.[4]

I am not here concerned with the merits of this view but only with a theory which appears more or less incidentally in the writings of those who defend it. This is the argument that so far from being incompatible with determinism, free will actually requires it. It appears briefly in Hume's *Treatise* and was set out in full in an article by R. E. Hobart.[5] P. H. Nowell-Smith was expressing a similar view when he said of the idea that determinism is opposed to free will that 'the clearest proof that it is mistaken or at least muddled lies in showing that I could not be free to choose what I do *unless* determinism is correct. . . . Freedom, so far from being incompatible with causality implies it'.[6] Ayer has taken up a similar position, arguing that the absence of causal laws governing action 'does not give the moralist what he wants. For he is anxious to show that men are capable of acting freely in order to infer that they can be morally responsible for what they do. But if it is a matter of pure chance that a man should act in one way rather than another, he may be free but he can hardly be responsible.'[7]

This argument is not essential to the main thesis of those who use it; their own account of free will in such terms as the absence of *constraining* causes might be correct even though there were no inconsistencies in the suggestion put forward by their libertarian opponents. But if valid the argument would be a strong argument, disposing of the position of anyone who argued both that free will required the absence of determining causes and that free will was a possibility. That the argument is not valid, and indeed that it is singularly implausible, I shall now try to show. It is, I think, surprising that it should have survived so long; this is perhaps because it has not had to bear much weight. In any case the weapons which can be used against it are ones which are in general use elsewhere.

In discussing determinism and free will it is important to be clear about the sense which is given in this context to words such as 'determined' and 'caused'. Russell gave this account:

The law of universal causation . . . may be enunciated as follows: There are such invariable relations between different events at the same or different times that, given the state of the whole universe throughout any finite time, however short, every previous and subsequent event can theoretically be determined as a function of the given events during that time.[8]

This seems to be the kind of determinism which worries the defender of free will, for if human action is subject to a universal law of causation of this type, there will be for any action a set of sufficient conditions which can be traced back to factors outside the control of the agent.

We cannot of course take it for granted that whenever the word 'determined' or the word 'cause' is used this is what is implied, and what is intended may be in no way relevant to the question of free will. For instance, an action said to be determined by the desires of the man who does it is not necessarily an action for which there is supposed to be a sufficient condition. In saying that it is determined by his desires we may mean merely that he is doing something that he wants to do, or that he is doing it for the sake of something else he wants. There is nothing in this to suggest determinism in Russell's sense. On the whole it is wise to be suspicious of expressions such as 'determined by desire' unless these have been given a clear sense, and this is particularly true of the phrase 'determined by the agent's character'. Philosophers often talk about actions being determined by a man's character, but it is not certain that anyone else does, or that the words are given any definite sense. One might suppose that an action was so determined if it was *in* character, for instance the generous action of a generous man; but if this is so we will not have the kind of determinism traditionally supposed to raise difficulties for a doctrine of free will. For nothing has been said to suggest that where the character trait can be predicated the action will invariably follow; it has not been supposed that a man who can truly be said to be generous never acts ungenerously even under given conditions.

Keeping the relevant sense of 'determinism' in mind, we may now start to discuss the view that free will requires determinism. The first version which I shall consider is that put forward by R. B. Hobart, who suggests that an action which is not determined cannot properly be called an *action* at all, being something that happened to the agent rather than something he *did*. Hobart says, '*In proportion* as it [the action] is undetermined, it is just as if his legs should suddenly spring up and carry him off where he did not prefer to go.' To see how odd this suggestion is we have only to ask when we would say that a man's legs were carrying him where he did not prefer to go. One can imagine the scene: he is sitting quietly in his chair and has said that he is going to go on reading his book; suddenly he cries, 'Good heavens, I can't control my legs!' and as he moves across the room, he hangs on to the furniture or asks someone else to hold him. Here indeed his legs are carrying him where he does not want to go, but what has this to do with indeterminism, and what has the ordinary case, where he walks across the room, to do with determinism? Perhaps Hobart thinks that when a man does something meaning to do it, he does what he wants to do, and so his action is determined by his desire. But to do something meaning to do it is to do it in a certain way, not to do it as the result of the operation of a causal law. When one means to do something, one does not call out for help in preventing the movement of one's limbs; on the contrary, one is likely to stop other people from interfering, saying, 'I want to do this'. It is by such factors that walking across the room is distinguished from being carried off by one's legs. It is to be explained in terms of the things said and done by the agent, not in terms of some force, 'the desire', present before the action was done and still less in terms of some law telling us that whenever this 'desire' is found it will be followed by the action. The indeterminist has no difficulty in distinguishing an action from something that happens to the agent; he can say exactly the same as anyone else.

Nowell-Smith seems to be thinking along somewhat the same lines as Hobart when he attacks C. A. Campbell for saying that free will requires indeterminism:

The essence of Campbell's account is that the action should not be predictable from a knowledge of the agent's character. But, if this is so, can what he does be called *his* action at all? Is it not rather a *lusus naturae*, an Act of God or a miracle? If a hardened criminal, bent on robbing the poor-box, suddenly and *inexplicably* fails to do so, we should not say that he *chose* to resist or deserves *credit* for resisting the temptation; we should say, if we were religious, that he was the recipient of a sudden outpouring of Divine Grace or, if we were irreligious, that his 'action' was due to chance, which is another way of saying that it was inexplicable. In either case we should refuse to use the active voice.[9]

It is hard to see why a man who does something inexplicably does not really *do* it. Let us suppose that the hardened criminal's action really is inexplicable; we can only say, 'He just turned away', and not why he did so; this does not mean that he did it by accident, or unintentionally, or not of his own free will, and I see no reason for refusing to use the active voice. In any case, to explain an action is not necessarily to show that it could have been predicted from some fact about the agent's character—that he is weak, greedy, sentimental, and so forth. We may if we like say that an action is never *fully* explained unless it has been shown to be covered by a law

which connects it to such a character trait; but then it becomes
even more implausible to say that an action must be explicable
if we are to admit it as something genuinely *done*. In the
ordinary sense we explain the criminal's action if we say, for
instance, that a particular thought came into his mind; we do
not also have to find a law about the way such thoughts do
come into the minds of such men.

A rather different version of this argument runs as follows.
We hold responsible only a man who is a rational agent; if
someone were always to do things out of the blue, without
having any reason to do them, we should be inclined to count
him as a lunatic, one who could not be held responsible for his
actions, so that even if he *did* things he would do things for
which he could not be held responsible. And is it not through
being determined by motives that actions are those of a
rational agent whom we can praise or blame?

It certainly would be odd to suppose that free will required
the absence of motives for action. We do not of course expect
that everything that the rational man does should be done with
a motive; if he gets up and walks about the room he need not
be doing so in order to take exercise; it is quite usual for people
to do this kind of thing without any particular purpose in
view, and no one is counted irrational for doing so. And yet we
do expect a man to have a motive for a great number of things
that he does, and we would count anyone who constantly
performed troublesome actions without a motive as irrational.
So it looks as if a moral agent is a man whose actions are in
general determined, if determinism is involved in 'having a
motive' for what he does.

What does it mean to say that someone had a motive for
doing what he did? Often this particular expression means that
he did it with a particular intention, so we should first say
something about intentions and the sense in which they can be
said to determine action. We say that a man had a certain
intention in acting when he aimed at a certain thing, and 'his
motive for such and such' often means 'his aim in doing such
and such', for instance, 'His motive for going to the station
was to take a train to London'. But where motives are intentions it is clear that they cannot be determining causes; for
intending to do *x* and being ready to take the steps thought

necessary to do x are connected not empirically but analytically. A man cannot be said to have an intention unless he is reconciled to what he believes to be the intermediate steps. We cannot speak as if the intention were something which could be determined first, and 'being ready to take the necessary steps' were a second stage following on the first.

It might be objected that this does not cover the case of 'doing y because one wants x' where 'wanting x' does not imply trying to get x. In one sense of 'want' it is possible to say, 'He wants x' without knowing whether he is prepared to take steps to get it. (One might, for instance, want to go to London but not be prepared to spend the money to get there.) So that *wanting* seems here to be a separate condition, which might in certain cases be connected by an empirical law to the adoption of particular courses of action. Certainly wanting is not an event, but one gets rid of wanting as a determining factor too easily if one merely says that desires are not causes because they are not occurrences.

We say 'He wants' in this sense where he would adopt certain policies *if* there were no reasons for not doing so. We can say, 'He wants to get to London', even when he is not prepared to take the necessary steps to get to London, provided he can say, 'Trains are too expensive', or 'Hitchhiking is too uncomfortable'. If we offered him a spare railway ticket or otherwise disposed of his reasons against going, and he still did not go, we would have to say, 'He didn't really want to go after all'. So wanting in this sense is being prepared to act under certain conditions, though not being prepared to act under the given conditions. It is a description which could be applied to a man before we knew whether he was ready to act in a given situation, and it seems that there might then be a causal relation between the wanting and the acting where the latter took place. This is quite true; there could be a law to the effect that when the description 'He wants x' applied at t_1, the description 'He is taking the necessary steps to get x' applied at t_2. It would be possible to say this without making a mistake about what it is to *want* and inventing a hidden condition of body or mind. One could say, 'Wanting in this sense just is being prepared to act under some conditions', and still maintain that there could be an empirical law connecting wanting with acting under a particular set of conditions. The mistake lies not in the idea that such laws are *possible* but in the thought that there is a reference to them in the statement that a man did one thing because he wanted something else.

So far we have been dealing only with cases in which a question about a motive was answered by specifying something aimed at or wanted. Now we should turn to the cases in which the motive is said to be kindness, vanity, ambition, meanness, jealousy, and so on, to see whether determinism is involved.

It is easy to show that a motive is not a cause in Russell's sense, for it is clearly not an antecedent cause. Professor Gilbert Ryle has pointed out that a man who acts out of vanity is not a man who had a feeling of vanity immediately before he acted, and if it is objected that the vanity which preceded the action need not have manifested itself in a feeling, one may ask what else *would* count as the vanity which was causing him to act. A man's motives are not given by what was happening to him immediately before he started to act. Nor do we discover some independent condition contemporaneous with the action and a law linking the two, for again there is nothing which would count as vanity except the tendency to do this kind of thing.

So much is implied in what Ryle says about acting out of vanity, but his own account of what it is to do so still uses something which is objectionably like a causal model. The analogy which he thinks apt is that between saying a man acted out of vanity and saying a piece of glass broke because it was brittle: 'To explain an act as done from a certain motive is not analogous to saying that the glass broke because a stone hit it, but to the quite different type of statement that the glass broke, when the stone hit it, because the glass was brittle.'[10] The positive part of this statement seems to me mistaken. Acting out of vanity is not so closely connected with being vain as Ryle must suppose it to be. Let us suppose that his account of what it is to be vain is entirely correct; to say that a man is vain is to say that he tends to behave in certain ways, to feel aggrieved in particular situations, and so on.[11] It does not follow that ascribing vanity as a motive for an action is bringing this action under the 'lawlike' proposition that the agent is a man who tends to do these things. For it makes sense to say that a man acts out of vanity on a particular occasion although he is not in general vain, or even vain about this kind of thing. It cannot therefore be true that when we speak of an agent's motive for a particular action we are explaining it in terms of his character, as Ryle suggests; we are not saying 'he *would* do that'. It is of course possible to give a motive *and* to say that the agent has the character trait concerned, but the latter cannot be included in an account of what it is to assign a motive to a particular action.

The explanation of why Ryle says what he does seems to lie in the fact that he has taken a false example of explaining an action by giving a motive. He considers as his example the explanation, 'He boasted because he is vain', which is not in fact an explanation of the right type; considered as a statement assigning a motive to a particular action it would be uninformative, for except in very special cases *boasting* is acting out of vanity. It is not surprising that this particular sentence has a different function—that of relating this act of vanity to the character trait. What Ryle says about the example is correct, but it is not an example of the kind of thing he is trying to describe.

It might seem as if we could reformulate the theory to meet the objection about the man who acts out of vanity on one occasion by saying that a man's acting out of vanity is like glass breaking because of a brittleness which could be temporary. 'He acted out of vanity' would then be explained as meaning that at that particular time he tended to react in the ways described by Ryle. (If he finds a chance of securing admiration and envy of others, he does whatever he thinks will produce this admiration and envy.) This is wrong because, whereas glass which is even temporarily brittle has all the reactions which go by this name, a man who is temporarily acting out of vanity is not liable to do other things of this kind. To find concepts which this model would fit one must turn to such descriptions as 'a boastful mood', 'a savage frame of mind', or 'a fit of bad temper'. Assigning a motive to an action is not bringing it under any law; it is rather saying something about the kind of action it was, the direction in which it was tending, or what it was done *as*. A possible comparison would be with the explanation of a movement in a dance which consisted in saying what was being danced. Often in diagnosing motives we should look to purposes—to what the action was done for. This we should discover if we found out what the agent was prepared to go without and what he insisted on having; the fact that visitors are made to admire a garden even in the rain is strong evidence that they were invited out of vanity rather than kindness. In other cases finding the motive will be better described as finding what was being done—finding, for instance, that someone was *taking revenge*. We should take it that a man's motive was revenge if we discovered that he was intentionally harming someone and that his doing so was conditional on his believing that that person had injured him. In the same way we should take it that someone was acting out of gratitude if he (1) intended to confer a benefit and (2) saw this as called for by a past kindness. The fact that it is only the character of the particular action which is involved shows how far we are from anything which could involve motives as determining causes.

We have now considered two suggestions: (1) that an undetermined action would not be one which could properly be attributed to an agent as something that he *did* and (2) that an undetermined action would not be the action of a *rational* agent. A third version, the one put forward by Hume, suggests that an undetermined action would be one for which it would be impossible to praise or blame, punish or reward a man, because it would be connected with nothing permanent in his nature.

'Tis only [Hume says] upon the principles of necessity, that a person acquires any merit or demerit from his actions. . . . Actions are by their very nature temporary and perishing; and where they proceed not from some cause in the characters and disposition of the person, who perform'd them, they infix not themselves upon him, and can neither redound to his honour, if good, nor infamy, if evil. The action in itself may be blameable. . . . But the person is not responsible for it; and as it proceeded from nothing in him, that is durable and constant, and leaves nothing of that nature behind it, 'tis impossible he can, upon its account, become the object of punishment or vengeance.[12]

Hume is surely wrong in saying that we could not praise or blame, punish or reward, a person in whose character there was nothing 'permanent or durable'. As he was the first to point out, we do not need any *unchanging* element in order to say that a person is the same person throughout a period of time, and our concept of merit is framed to fit our concept of personal identity. We honour people as well as nations for what they have done in the past and do not consider what has been done merely as an indication of what may be expected in the future. Moreover, it is perfectly rational to punish people for what they have done, even if there is no reason to think that they would be likely to do it again. The argument that it will be a different *me* who will be beaten tomorrow carries no weight, for 'different' or not the back which will be beaten is the one about which I am concerned today. So we have no reason to invent something durable and constant underlying the actions which we punish or reward. And it is not in fact our practice to pick out for praise or blame only those actions for which something of the kind can be found. It would be possible, of course, that we should do this, punishing the cruel action of the cruel man but not that of one usually kind. But even in such a situation there would be no argument against the man who said that moral responsibility depended upon indeterminism; for a motive is not a determining cause, nor is an habitual motive. If we say that a man constantly acts out of cruelty, we no more say that his actions are determined than if we say that he acts out of cruelty on a particular occasion. There could of course be a law to the effect that no one who has been cruel for thirty years can turn to kindness after that, and this would throw responsibility back from the later to the earlier acts. But it is clear that this is a special assumption in no way involved in the statement that cruelty is a 'durable and constant' element in someone's character.

I have already mentioned Ayer's argument that moral responsibility cannot be defended on the basis of indeterminism and will now consider his version in detail. Ayer says that the absence of a cause will not give the moralist what he wants, because 'if it is a matter of pure chance that a man should act in one way rather than another, he may be free but he can hardly be responsible'.[13] To the suggestion that 'my actions are the result of my own free choice', Ayer will reply with a question about how I came to make my choice:

Either it is an accident that I choose to act as I do or it is not. If it is an accident, then it is merely a matter of chance that I did not choose otherwise; and if it is merely a matter of chance that I did not choose otherwise, it is surely irrational to hold me morally responsible for choosing as I did. But if it is not an accident that I chose to do one thing rather than another, then presumably there is some causal explanation in my choice: and in that case we are led back to determinism.[14]

The 'presumably' seems to be the weak link in the argument, which assumes a straightforward opposition between causality and chance that does not in general exist. It is not at all clear that when actions or choices are called 'chance' or 'accidental' this has anything to do with the absence of causes, and if it has not we will not be saying that they are in the ordinary sense a matter of chance if we say that they are undetermined.

When should we say that it was a matter of chance that a man did what he did? A typical example would be the case in which a man killed someone with a bullet which glanced off some object in a totally unforseeable way; here he could disclaim responsibility for the act. But in this instance, and that of something done 'by accident', we are dealing with what is done unintentionally, and this is not the case which Ayer has in mind. We may turn, as he does, to the actions which could be said to have been 'chosen' and ask how the words 'chance' and 'accident' apply to choices. Ayer says, 'Either it is an accident that I choose to act as I do, or it is not'. The notion of choosing by accident to do something is on the face of it puzzling; for usually choosing to do something is opposed to doing it by accident. What does it mean to say that the choice itself was accidental? The only application I can think of for the words 'I chose by accident' is in a case such as the following. I choose a firm with which to have dealings without meaning to pick on one run by an international crook. I can now rebut the charge of *choosing a firm run by an international crook* by saying that I chose it by accident. I cannot be held responsible for this but only for any carelessness which may have been involved. But this is because the relevant action—the one with which I am being charged—was unintentional; it is for this reason and not because my action was uncaused that I can rebut the charge. Nothing is said about my action being uncaused, and if it were, this could not be argued on my behalf; the absence of causes would not give me the same right to make the excuse.

Nor does it make any difference if we substitute 'chance' for accident'. If I say that it was a matter of chance that I chose to do something, I rebut the suggestion that I chose it for this reason or for that, and this can be a plea against an accusation which has to do with my reasons. But I do not imply that there was no reason for my doing what I did, and I say nothing whatsoever about my choice being undetermined. If we use 'chance' and 'accident' as Ayer wants to use them, to signify the absence of causes, we shall have moved over to a totally different sense of the words, and 'I chose it by chance' can no longer be used to disclaim responsibility.

NOTES

* 'Free Will as Involving Determinism' originally appeared in *The Philosophical Review*, Volume LXVI, Number 4, October 1957.

[1] *Treatise*, bk. II, pt. III, sec. 2.

[2] *Polemic*, no. 5 (1946); reprinted in his *Philosophical Essays* (London, 1954).

[3] *Philosophical Essays*, p. 278.

[4] Ibid., p. 281.

[5] 'Freewill as Involving Determinism', *Mind*, XLIII (1934), 1–27.

[6] 'Freewill and Moral Responsibility', *Mind*, LVII (1948), 46.

[7] *Philosophical Essays*, p. 275.

[8] 'On the Notion of Cause', in *Our Knowledge of the External World* (London, 1914), p. 221.

[9] *Ethics* (London, 1954), pp. 281–2.

[10] *Concept of Mind* (London, 1949), pp. 86–7.

[11] Ibid., p. 86.

[12] *Treatise*, bk. II, pt. III, sec 2.

[13] *Philosophical Essays*, p. 275.

[14] Ibid.

Additional note: The work by R. B. Hobart referred to on p. 64 is 'Freewill as Involving Determinism and Inconceivable Without It', *Mind*, LXIII (1934), pp. 1–27.

V

Hume on Moral Judgement*

Some philosophers talk about morality in an elevated tone;
and they seem to be entirely sincere, finding virtue a sublime
and noble subject, the pursuit of virtue an inspiring life's work.
So it is, for instance, with Kant, who writes in one place about
the moral law within and the starry heavens above filling the
mind with ever increasing awe and admiration, the oftener and
more steadily we reflect on them. It came quite naturally to
Kant, as it did to Rousseau, to talk about the sublimity of our
nature in its higher aspect, and of *reverence* for the moral law.
'Duty!' he says. 'Sublime and mighty name.' But Hume
speaks with a very different voice.

And as every quality which is useful or agreeable to ourselves or
others is, in common life, allowed to be a part of personal merit; so
no other will ever be received, where men judge of things by their
natural, unprejudiced reason, without the delusive glosses of superstition and false religion. Celibacy, fasting, penance, mortification,
self-denial, humility, silence, solitude, and the whole train of monk-
ish virtues; for what reason are they everywhere rejected by men of
sense, but because they serve to no manner of purpose; neither
advance a man's fortune in the world, nor render him a more
valuable member of society; neither qualify him for entertainment of
company, nor increase his power of self-enjoyment? We observe, on
the contrary, that they cross all these desirable ends; stupify the
understanding and harden the heart, obscure the fancy and sour the
temper. We justly, therefore, transfer them to the opposite column,
and place them in the catalogue of vices; nor has any superstition
force enough among men of the world, to pervert entirely these
natural sentiments. A gloomy, hair-brained enthusiast, after his
death, may have a place in the calendar; but will scarcely ever be
admitted, when alive, into intimacy and society, except by those
who are as delirious and dismal as himself.[1]

Where Kant, or Rousseau, close to Hume in time, but at a great distance in mental space, saw virtue as inspiring, Hume found it useful and agreeable, fitting a man for business and society. Indeed he actually identified a sense of virtue with a pleasing sentiment of approbation, which, he thought, men find within themselves on the contemplation of certain actions and qualities of mind. He defines virtue to be 'whatever mental action or quality gives to a spectator the pleasing sentiment of approbation; and vice the contrary'. Moreover, enquiring into the common characteristic of those actions or qualities which have this pleasant effect upon the spectator, he decides that they are all agreeable, or useful, to ourselves or other men. So a sense of virtue is itself a kind of pleasure, and this pleasure arises on the contemplation of what is useful or agreeable to mankind.

Hume's account of the common characteristics of the qualities called virtues is, it must be said, bad. It leads him to class with such things as honesty, justice, benevolence, and courage, not only cleanliness, which 'naturally renders us agreeable to others, and is a very considerable source of love and affection', but also such things as wit and eloquence. One does not find in Hume an account of the difference between skills or talents and virtues and he even says that there is no reason to consider virtue as something distinct. I suppose it is partly due to Hume's influence that this important topic, which was splendidly treated by Aristotle and Aquinas, is hardly discussed by modern moral philosophers.

But there is a much more serious charge to be laid at Hume's door. Even supposing that he had been right in saying that the things which we call virtues are the qualities useful and agreeable to ourselves and others—if these were their common characteristics—Hume's account of the *status* of the proposition 'virtues are qualities useful or agreeable, etc.' might still be attacked. For he seems to think that we find out *by observation* that these are the qualities which happen to arouse in a spectator the pleasing sentiment of approbation called the sense of virtue. We find that, as a matter of fact, people do feel the peculiar sentiment of approbation when they contemplate just these actions and qualities: but it might have been otherwise. He speaks as if we first identify the special sentiment of approbation, moral approval, and then look around to see what can be said about the things that arouse this feeling in us, thus implying that there is no difficulty in discovering that people *are* feeling approval before it is known what beliefs they hold about the things in question. Mr. Gardiner pointed out in his essay[2] that Hume held a similar theory about the identification of the internal sensation of pride, and objected that one could not really say that it was pride that someone was feeling unless he had the right thoughts about the thing of which he was supposed to feel proud. (He must, I suppose, see it as something like an achievement, and as in some way related to himself.) A feeling of pride is not identified like a tickle, but requires a special kind of thought about the thing of which one feels proud. Now I should say, though I do not know whether Mr. Gardiner would, that it is just as bad to try to identify a feeling as a feeling of approval, whether moral approval or any other, without its particular objects as it is to try to identify pride without talking about the only kinds of things about which one can *logically* feel proud. (I do not mean, of course, that one would be illogical in feeling pride towards something which one did not believe to be in some way splendid and in some way one's own, but that the concept of pride does not allow us to talk like that.) Similarly for the concept of approval, though the reader will kindly excuse me from giving an account of what exactly a man must believe of those things of which he can logically approve. Anyone who doubts this point about approval should ask what it would be to have *this* feeling when contemplating an object one did not see as useful, beautiful, efficient or anything like that. Does it make sense to suppose that one might wake up one morning feeling approval of something believed to be an ordinary, unnecessary, unbeautiful speck of dust? Hume was, I think, making a mistake when he tried to explain what it meant to say that an action or quality was virtuous in terms of a special feeling; for the explanation of the thought comes into the description of the feeling, not the other way round.

Now this theory of Hume's about moral sentiment commits him to a subjectivist theory of ethics. He could not consistently maintain both that a man calls qualities virtues when he happens to feel towards them this peculiar sentiment,

HUME ON MORAL JUDGEMENT

and that statements about virtue and vice are objective. For if they were objective, like ordinary statements of fact, there would have to be some method of deciding, in case of disagreement, whether one man's opinion or another's was correct—as the opinion that the earth is flat can be shown to be mistaken by a voyage round the globe. But since Hume has denied all logical connexions—all connexions of meaning—between moral approval and the objects of moral approval, and would have to allow anyone to assert any kinds of actions he chose to be virtuous on the strength of the supposed feeling of approbation, it follows that no one could get at an opponent who professed weird 'moral views'. And Hume himself, though he sometimes modifies his theory and talks about the sentiments of the majority, in most places accepts this subjectivism with ease, and even with relish.

Take any action allowed to be vicious: Wilful murder for instance. Examine it in all lights, and see if you can find that matter of fact, or real existence, which you call *vice*. In whichever way you take it, you find only certain passions, motives, volitions and thoughts. There is no other matter of fact in the case. The vice entirely escapes you, as long as you consider the object. You can never find it, till you turn your reflexion into your own breast, and find a sentiment of disapprobation, which arises in you, towards this action. Here is a matter of fact; but 'tis the object of feeling, not of reason. It lies in yourself, not in the object.[3]

Such a theory does not look at all plausible. We are not inclined to think that when a man says that an action is virtuous, or vicious, he is talking about his own feelings rather than a quality which he must show really to belong to what is done. It seems strange to suggest that he does not have to bring forward any special *fact about the action* in order to maintain what he says. So, of course, what one wants to know is why Hume adopted this strange theory: what drove him to say that the virtuousness of an action could not be a plain provable matter of fact. Sometimes, indeed, he suggests that one simply cannot find any such fact, but since he himself claims that all things called virtues are qualities agreeable or useful to mankind why should he not say that it is in this that their virtuousness *consists*? Why does he have to bring in his feeling of approbation, and by making this the essential part of moral judgement anchor statements about virtue to the sentiments of the observer and not to the facts?

Hume would reply that one must distinguish a judgement about morality from the whole class of what he calls 'conclusions of reason'—that is, ordinary provable propositions about what is the case. For, as he says, no such factual proposition could ever have a necessary connexion with the will of the man who accepted it, while it is an essential fact about a moral judgement that it does have this practical force.

'Morals excite passions, and produce or prevent actions. Reason of itself is utterly impotent in this particular. The rules of morality, therefore, are not conclusions of our reason.' Hume, who is not usually repetitious, says this kind of thing over and over again. 'As long as it is allowed, that reason has no influence on our passions and actions, 'tis in vain to pretend, that morality is discover'd only by a deduction of reason.' 'Reason is wholly inactive and can never be the source of so active a principle as conscience, or a sense of morals.'

What does Hume mean when he says that reason is wholly inactive? He argues that whenever a man is led by a judgement of reason to some action it is not reason *alone* which impels him, but reason with the co-operation of desire. Reason can tell us, for instance, that a certain action will have a particular effect, or, again, that a certain object exists within our reach; but if the effect is indifferent to us, the thing not wanted, the discovery of fact which Hume calls 'a conclusion of reason' will make no difference to what we do. And so, he says, reason alone is 'perfectly inert'; it may of course influence actions, but only when we happen to have certain desires. Thus conclusions of reason have a merely contingent connexion with action, whereas the propositions of morality are necessarily practical, going beyond the 'calm and indolent judgements of the understanding'. Between these calm and indolent judgements and the assertion that something should be done there is, Hume thinks, the famous gap between *is* and *ought*.

I cannot forbear adding to these reasonings an observation, which may, perhaps, be found of some importance. In every system of morality, which I have hitherto met with, I have always remarked, that the author proceeds for some time in the ordinary way of reasoning, and establishes the being of a God, or makes observations concerning human affairs; when of a sudden I am surpriz'd to find, that instead of the usual copulations of propositions, *is*, and *is not*, I meet with no proposition that is not connected with an *ought* or an *ought not*. This change is imperceptible; but is, however, of the last consequence. For as this *ought*, or *ought not* expresses some new relation or affirmation, 'tis necessary that it shou'd be observed and explain'd; and at the same time that a reason should be given, for what seems altogether inconceivable, how this new relation can be a deduction from others, which are entirely different from it.[4]

Hume thought that he himself had hit on the perfect solution to the problem. The new element in a proposition about virtue was the reference to a special sentiment of approbation: nothing new in the object, but something in ourselves. At a blow he seemed to have put an end to the hunt for mysterious extra properties, and also to have shown the necessary connexion between morality and the will. For the moral sentiment, the special feeling which we call approbation, was a pleasurable sentiment, by which we were inclined towards those actions whose contemplation gave rise to it. 'To know virtue is to love it.' This, Hume might have said, is a logical truth.

This extraordinarily interesting theory has been a great influence in contemporary ethics. Many modern moral philosophers have taken up Hume's argument and, starting from his premise about the necessarily practical nature of morality, assert his conclusion about the gap between *is* and *ought*. Indeed they often make the connexion between action and the propositions of morality even closer than he did, suggesting that an actual rule of conduct rather than a mere sentiment is required for moral judgement. 'To know virtue is to be prepared to follow it' is what they might say. And like Hume, having anchored moral judgement to the will of the judger, they have cut it loose from the world.

Such theories are, I believe, wrong, and the mistake can be traced back to the interpretation of the crucial premise: morality is necessarily practical. It is not that this is false, but that one may easily insist on too close a connexion between moral judgement and the will. I do not know quite what sense ought to be given to the proposition that morality is necessarily practical, but two things at least can be said. In the first place we take it as part of the meaning of what we call 'moral terms' that they are in general used for teaching particular kinds of conduct; though nothing follows about what any particular individual who uses the terms must feel or do. Secondly, since moral virtues are qualities necessary if men are to get on well in a world in which they are frightened, tempted by pleasure and liable to hurt rather than help each other, they need to make common plans. This general connexion between such things as courage, temperance, and justice and human good is quite enough to explain why people are often influenced by considerations of morality. They are not *necessarily* influenced, as Hume must have known; but they are concerned to teach and practise virtue in so far as they have taken this thought for their own and the common good. It is, therefore, unnecessary to posit a special sentiment to explain why observations about virtue have an influence on the will, and the *raison d'être* of Hume's subjectivist theory of ethics disappears.

NOTES

* 'Hume on Moral Judgement' originally appeared in David Pears, ed., *David Hume* (London, 1963).
[1] *An Enquiry Concerning The Principles of Morals*, sec. IX, pt. I.
[2] Patrick Gardiner, 'Hume's Theory of the Passions': David Pears (ed.), *David Hume.*
[3] *Treatise*, bk. III, pt. I, sec. 2.
[4] Ib. sec. 1.

VI

Nietzsche: The Revaluation of Values*

This problem of the *value* of pity and of the morality of pity . . . seems at first sight to be merely something detached, an isolated question mark; but whoever sticks with it and *learns* how to ask questions here will experience what I experienced—a tremendous new prospect opens up for him, a new possibility comes over him like a vertigo, every kind of mistrust, suspicion, fear leaps up, his belief in morality, in all morality, falters—finally a new demand becomes audible . . . we need a *critique* of moral values, *the value of these values themselves must just be called in question* . . . (GM Preface 6).[1]

What Nietzsche expresses here, his sense of the fearful strangeness of his thoughts, is something intensely felt and not unfitting given the facts of the case. For in his lonely, highly daring mental voyage he had come to a view of life which was quite unlike that of any of his contemporaries, and which brought him to challenge ways of thought and behaviour centuries old. He was ready, he said, to call in question Christian morality and even all morality, and when he had questioned he condemned. Yet Nietzsche saw as clearly as anyone that morality could fascinate and inspire. 'Thou shalt' he said is the name of a great dragon 'sparkling like gold' (Z I 'On the Three Metamorphoses' 10). He knew that what he was doing was almost unthinkable; he was branding as evil what seemed most certainly good.

Now one would expect that such a challenge from an undoubted genius must either be defeated or else shake the world. But neither of these things have happened. It is true that Nietzsche's theories (or a travesty of them) played a brief and inglorious part on the world's stage when he was proclaimed as a prophet by the Nazis, but by and large he has neither been accepted nor refuted, and this seems a remarkable fact. How is it, one may ask, that philosophers today do not even try to refute Nietzsche, and seem to feel morality as firm as ever under their feet? Why do we not argue with him as we argue with other philosophers of the past? Part of the answer seems to be that a confrontation with Nietzsche is a difficult thing to arrange. We find it hard to know where we could meet him because of the intrinsically puzzling nature of a project such as his. Nietzsche had demanded a critique of moral values and announced that he was calling in question 'the value of these values themselves'. But how can one value values? The idea of such a thing is enough to make one's head spin. It is, therefore, with a rueful sense of the difficulties that I shall try, in this essay, to confront Nietzsche, or at least to help to prepare the ground for a confrontation.

A problem arises at the outset. In the passage I quoted he spoke of the morality of pity but also of 'all morality'. Which shall we take his target to be? I shall consider first Nietzsche's special objection to Christian morality, with its teaching of the virtues of humility and compassion, and its rejection of 'the world'.

Nietzsche wanted to show Christian morality as a 'slave morality' rooted not in anything fine or admirable but rather in weakness, fear, and malice; these were its origins and to these origins its present nature conformed. In this morality the good man is the humble and compassionate man, the one who is not to be feared. But originally, he insists, it was quite otherwise. In the beginning it was the strong, noble, privileged aristocrat who called himself good, and called those who lacked his own qualities bad. These old concepts were turned on their heads when the perspective of the weak prevailed. For then the contrast of what was good and bad (*schlecht*) gave way to the contrast between what was good and evil (*böse*); the weak branded those they feared evil, and praised the 'propitiatory' qualities natural to men like themselves who were incapable of aggression. Where the old valuation had been positive the new was negative; the 'members of the herd' must first brand the enemies they feared as evil before they could see themselves as good. Moreover Nietzsche detects a large amount of malice under the professions of Christian humility and goodwill. When the weak call the strong evil the move is not merely defensive; it is also an expression of that peculiar malice which Nietzsche referred to as *ressentiment*. Those who cultivate humility and the other propitiatory virtues to cloak their weakness nourish an envious resentment against those stronger than themselves. They want revenge for their inferiority and have a deep desire to humiliate and harm. The wish to punish seems to Nietzsche one of the most evident signs of this hidden malice, and he sees the idea of free will, and accountability, as invented by those who desired to inflict punishment. Nor is punishment always directed outward; the man of self-sacrificing virtue is resentful and venomous also towards himself. 'But thus I counsel you, my friends: Mistrust all in whom the impulse to punish is powerful' (Z II 'On the Tarantulas').

The man professing Christian virtues is, Nietzsche insists, a sick individual, deeply malicious to himself and others. He has been taught to reject life as it is, to despise his own sensuality, and to torment himself and others in the name of his ideals. Even these ideals are inimical to health, since what is preached is compassion, and this Nietzsche sees as a kind of sickness in itself. Pity, he says, is a *temptation* to be resisted at all costs; he thinks of it as a kind of poison to the compassionate man, who becomes infected by the sufferings of others. 'The suffering of others infects us, pity is an infection' (WP 368).[2] Nor does he believe that pity relieves suffering. Now and then it may do so, but more often the object of our compassion suffers from our intervention in his affairs. He suffers first from the fact that we are helping him. 'Having seen the sufferer suffer, I was ashamed for the sake of his shame; and when I helped him I transgressed grievously against his pride' (Z II 'On the Pitying'). 'It seems to me that a human being with the very best intentions can do immeasurable harm, if he is immodest enough to wish to profit those whose spirit and will are concealed from him . . .' wrote Nietzsche in a letter to his sister in 1885 (quoted in Walter Kaufmann [ed.], *The Portable Nietzsche*, New York, Viking, 1956, p. 441). Nor did Nietzsche think that good motives lay behind most charitable acts. Charitable and helpful people 'dispose of the needy as of possessions. . . . One finds them jealous if one crosses or anticipates them when they want to help' (BGE 194). Concern for others often betrayed a man's dissatisfaction with himself; men who were dull tried to cheer themselves up with the sight of their neighbour's misfortunes, while those who had a low opinion of themselves would try to buy back a better opinion from those on whom they had conferred a benefit. Nietzsche saw the preoccupation with others as an evasion, and a sign of spiritual ill-health; what is important is to love oneself 'so that one can bear to be with oneself and need not roam' (Z III 'On the Spirit of Gravity' 2). The man who loves himself will be the one who most truly benefits others; in his own rejoicing he will forget how to contrive pain for them.

What shall we say of Nietzsche's attack on Christian moral-ity as it has so far been described? With what weapons is he attacking, and on what ground? Several different lines of attack can be discerned. In the first place he is suggesting that what is praised as Christian virtue is largely a sham, and that true goodwill would be produced not by teaching the morality of compassion but rather by encouraging 'a healthy egoism'. Secondly he is saying that judged by its own aims this morality is bad. Men suffer pity as a sickness, and by their pity they do more harm than good. Each of these charges would be damag-ing if it could be shown to be supported by the facts. But what of Nietzsche's account of the origins of Christian morality, and his insistence that it represents the ascendency of the weak over the strong? If proved would this be damaging or not? Could one reply that virtues such as compassion and justice are indeed of special interest to those liable to misfortune and vulnerable to oppression, and that they are none the worse for that? Such a reply would miss the point of Nietzsche's attack. He is trying to show the 'good and virtuous' as representatives of a mean and base section of mankind, as fawning, timid, incapable people who express in hidden form the malice they are afraid to express openly. He wants to suggest that they are both despicable and dislikable, and if he could really do this he would have struck a most telling blow. For how could a society which came to see things in Nietzsche's fashion have a morality of this kind? It is not, after all, enough for a moral system that particular actions should be rewarded and punished as in a system of laws. If a certain man is to be seen as a good man, and certain actions as good actions, then he and they must be generally esteemed. And no one is esteemed if he is the object of scorn and dislike. If Nietzsche could show that we have no reason either to admire the man of Christian virtue or to be grateful to him, he would have knocked away a psychological base without which this morality cannot stand.

In representing Christian morality as the weapon used by the weak to defend and exalt themselves Nietzsche was trying to show it and them in a disagreeable light. But it was much more important to him to show that in favouring the weak at the expense of the strong Christianity was the most powerful of the forces making for the degeneration of the human race. 'Nothing has preoccupied me more profoundly than the problem of decadence' he wrote (CW Preface). And he saw as decadent the type of man encouraged by Christian teaching, describing him as an accommodating, industrious, gregarious individual who was mediocre, and dull. Against this portrait he set that of a stronger 'higher' type of individual, bold, independent, and ready to say 'yes' to life. Such a man would not be much concerned about suffering, whether his own or that of others. Among his equals he would behave with restraint; to the weak he might be dangerous, but if he harmed them it would be rather from disregard than from malice. The weak man, however, is afraid of suffering for himself and preoccupied with the misfortunes of others. He tries to build himself a safe life which shall not require too much exertion. 'One has one's little pleasure for the day and one's little pleasure for the night: but one has a regard for health' (Z I 'Zarathustra's Prologue' 5). He preaches the morality of compassion, though filled with secret ill will towards others.

Much controversy has surrounded Nietzsche's writings on the 'higher' and 'lower' types of man. Is he to be taken as glorifying the cruel tyrant, the 'beast of prey', or did he have some less repulsive ideal? The answer seems to be neither an unqualified yes nor an unqualified no. There is no doubt that in the rank of men he preferred as the more healthy type 'even Caesare Borgia' to the mediocre submissive modern man. And there are some embarrassingly awful passages in which he speaks of the superior man's ruthlessness towards his inferiors as if it could be seen as something merely pranksome. But the cruel man is certainly not his ideal, and there are some to whom he refuses to preach egoism at all.

There are the terrible ones who carry around within themselves the beast of prey and have no choice but lust or self-laceration. And even their lust is still self-laceration. They have not even become human beings yet, these terrible ones: let them preach renunciation of life and pass away themselves! (Z I 'On the Preachers of Death').

In Nietzsche's eyes the important distinction was that of the 'ascending' and 'descending' types of men. One great question was to be asked about the history of any race: did it represent decline or ascent? And each individual should be scrutinised 'to see whether he represents the ascending or the descending line of life' (Twilight 'Skirmishes of an Untimely Man' 33). Nietzsche saw himself as the one, the only one, who saw clearly the contrast between ascending and declining mankind. 'I have a subtler sense of smell for the signs of ascent and decline than any other human being before me; I am the teacher *par excellence* for this . . .' (EH 'Why I Am So Wise' 1). It was in this context that he preached egoism to the strong:

Every individual consists of the whole course of evolution. . . . If he represents the ascending course of mankind, then his value is in fact extraordinary; and extreme care may be taken over the preservation and promotion of his development. (It is concern for the future promised him that gives the well-constituted individual such an extraordinary right to egoism.) If he represents the descending course, decay, chronic sickening, then he has little value: and the first demand of fairness is for him to take as little space, force, and sunshine as possible away from the well-constituted (WP 373).

And it was in this context that Nietzsche spoke least ambiguously about the fate he envisaged for the weak. 'The weak and the failures shall perish: first principle of *our* love of man' (A 2).

It was no wonder then that Nietzsche had a special hatred of Christianity. He saw it as the religion of the weak designed for their protection and glorification, and he saw it as the most powerful influence for decadence and decline. Above all he thought Christian morality harmful to the stronger and healthier type of man. By preserving the incapable and 'misbegotten', and by insisting that they be the object of compassionate attention, it would cause even the strong to be infected with gloom and nihilism. And even more importantly it would lead the 'higher' type of man to mistrust his own nature, and would create conditions in which it was impossible for him to find his health. To require a peaceable benevolence from such a man, to preach humility and pity to him, is necessarily to injure him.

To demand of strength that it should *not* express itself as strength, that it should *not* be a desire to overcome, a desire to throw down, a desire to become master, a thirst for enemies and resistances and triumphs, is just as absurd as to demand of weakness that it should express itself as strength (GM I 13).

The strong man condemned by society for doing what his nature demands will suffer from guilt and self-hatred, and may well be turned into a criminal.

The criminal type is the type of the strong human being under unfavourable circumstances: a strong human being made sick. . . . His *virtues* are ostracized by society; the most vivid drives with which he is endowed soon grow together with the depressing affects—with suspicion, fear and dishonour (Twilight 'Skirmishes of an Untimely Man' 45).

Nietzsche does not shrink from the conclusion that for some men ruthlessness may be the condition of health. It is the counterpart of his belief that 'everything evil, terrible, tyrannical in man, everything in him that is kin to beasts of prey and serpents, serves the enhancement of the species "man" as much as its opposite does' (BGE 44). If God is dead nothing guarantees that evil may not be the condition of good.

If . . . a person should regard even the affects of hatred, envy, covetousness, and the lust to rule as conditions of life, as factors which, fundamentally and essentially, must be present in the general economy of life (and must, therefore, be further enhanced if life is to be further enhanced)—he will suffer from such a view of things as from seasickness. And yet even this hypothesis is far from being the strangest and most painful in this immense and almost new domain of dangerous insights . . . (BGE 23).

It is, then, for the sake of the 'higher' man that the values of Christian morality must be abandoned, and it is from this perspective that the revaluation of values takes place. Is it Nietzsche's intention to present us with a clash of interests—the good of the strong against that of the weak? Obviously he has this intention, but just as obviously this is not all that he wants to suggest. A more puzzling aspect of his doctrines comes before us when we remind ourselves of what he says about the *value* of the 'higher' type of man.

The problem I pose is . . . what type of men shall be *bred*, shall be *willed*, for being higher in value, worthier of life, more certain of a future (A 3).

And again Nietzsche says:

We have a different faith; to us the democratic movement is . . . a form of decay, namely the diminution, of man, making him mediocre and *lowering his value* (BGE 203, italics added).

What does he mean when he speaks of the *value* of one type of man as greater than that of another? Nietzsche himself has remarked elsewhere that one can never too carefully consider the question 'value for what?' And in these terms one might try to explain what he says about the value of certain men. Perhaps he means that the contribution they make to life in general—by their optimism and fearlessness for instance—makes them *valuable* to us all. Or perhaps he is judging their value by the contribution they make to the future. Are they not a bridge to the superior man who may come in the future—to the *Übermensch*? Neither suggestion tells the whole story, and the second simply shifts the problem. If the 'Overman' or 'Superman' is the one who gives his forerunners value, this must be because he has value himself. In fact Nietzsche seems to want to say that anyone who is strong, independent, and so on—anyone who fits his description of the higher type of man—is one who *has value* in himself, and we are left with this puzzling idea. Is Nietzsche merely talking nonsense, or can we make sense of the word 'value' as it is used here? The answer seems to be that we can. For it does make sense to say that *we value* strong and exceptional individuals, whether or not Nietzsche's picture of these individuals rings true. We do find patterns of reaction to exceptional men that would allow us to see here a valuing rather similar to valuing on aesthetic grounds, even if it is one for which we have no special name. I am thinking of the interest and admiration which is the common attitude to remarkable men of exceptional independence of mind and strength of will. Such men hold our attention, and are often willingly served. When Nietzsche says that what is at stake is whether 'the *highest power and splendor* actually possible to the type man' is ever to be attained (GM Preface 6) it suggests that he is appealing to our tendency to *admire* certain individuals whom we see as powerful and splendid. He himself even says, in one passage, that 'This is at bottom a question of taste and of aesthetics: would it be desirable that the "most respectable", i.e., most tedious, species of man should survive?' (WP 353). But I think that the passage is untypical, and in any case does not quite describe the facts as they are; if there is an element of respect in the common reaction to strong and remarkable men then the analogy with an aesthetic valuation should not be pressed too far. Perhaps what we should do is simply to suggest a similarity between the way we attribute *value* (aesthetic value) to art objects and the *value* that Nietzsche attributes to a certain kind of man, both resting on a set of familiar reactions, and on reactions that have much in common.

If this were a correct account of the matter what would we conclude? Would Christian morality, or any other, be vulnerable to Nietzsche's attack? From the comparison with aesthetic values one would say that it might be vulnerable, not because something had been proved against it but because men might come to care more about producing and preserving interesting and 'splendid' individuals than about the ends of morality. For consider what the implications would be were it to be discovered that the human race would become physically uglier if morality flourished, or that justice and kindness destroyed beauty of some other kind. This could be considered irrelevant by those for whom moral values were more important than aesthetic values, and one might count as similarly irrelevant the discovery that 'the highest power and splendor' was inconsistent with moral ends; nevertheless morality might decline.

So far we have been considering Nietzsche's objections to one specific moral system—that of Christianity. But he had spoken of an attack on 'all morality' and was ready to call himself an immoralist. Does he really have arguments reaching so far? Some of his arguments against Christian morality will be brought also against other moral systems. But with others this will not be possible. Nietzsche could not, for instance, accuse Aristotle of preaching a morality of pity, nor of extolling humility. On the contrary Aristotle's description of the *megalopsychos* who possesses the virtue of greatness of soul and 'deserves and claims great things' (*Nicomachean Ethics* 1123 a 15) has much in common with Nietzsche's picture of the 'higher' type of man. Let us ask which part of Nietzsche's doctrines could justify us in thinking that morality—all morality—was indeed his target.

Is it relevant, for instance, that Nietzsche had no place in his ideology for the concept of *guilt*? About this he was quite explicit. He saw efforts to make men feel guilty as expressions of malice, and rejected guilt as a reaction to anything he himself would do. 'Not to perpetrate cowardice against one's own acts. Not to leave them in the lurch afterwards! The bite of conscience is indecent!' (Twilight 'Maxims and Arrows' 10). This seems to prove nothing about whether Nietzsche was, as he said, rejecting all morality; it does not seem impossible that a man should have a morality without accepting guilt as a response to moral failure. It would have been different had he been rejecting the aim of self-discipline, but this Nietzsche never did. Like Callicles in Plato's *Gorgias* Nietzsche objects to the 'taming' of the strong man by society, but where Callicles urges that the strong should throw away all restraint and allow their passions full rein Nietzsche was scornful of such a suggestion. He does indeed oppose those who would weaken or even destroy a man's passions, but insists that a strong will belongs only to one who has imposed discipline and unity on his desires. So instead of objecting to morality on the ground that it involves discipline of the passions he says that this is its one merit. 'What is essential and estimable in every morality is that it constitutes a long compulsion . . .' (BGE 188). Obviously drawing on his own experience he insists that what is most *natural* is a kind of self-discipline.

> Every artist knows how far from any feeling of letting himself go his 'most natural' state is—the free ordering, placing, disposing, giving form in the moment of 'inspiration'—and how strictly and subtly he obeys thousandfold laws precisely then . . . (BGE 188).

To this extent, then, Nietzsche is at one with the moralist: he is preaching self-discipline and control of the passions. Nevertheless it may be argued that he is rightly to be called an immoralist. It is relevant here to recall that the word 'morality' is derived from *mos* with its plural *mores*, and that in its present usage it has not lost this connexion with the *mores*—the rules of behaviour—of a society. For Nietzsche keeps some of his sharpest vituperation for those who try to impose social rules and a code of behaviour which shall be uniform throughout the community. He repeatedly rages against those who preach 'Good and evil, good and evil, the same for all'.

> Let us finally consider how naive it is altogether to say: 'Man *ought* to be such and such!' Reality shows us an enchanting wealth of types, the abundance of a lavish play and change of forms—and some wretched loafer of a moralist comments: 'No! Man ought to be different.' He even knows what man should be like, this wretched bigot and prig: he paints himself on the wall and comments, '*Ecce homo!*' (Twilight 'Morality as Anti-Nature 6').

What will create health in one will enfeeble another, and each man must discover the rule of his own health. To desire that men should be virtuous

> means that they should cease to be distinct
> means that they should begin to resemble one another in their needs and demands—more clearly that they should perish—
> The will to a single morality is thereby proved to be a tyranny over other types by that type whom this single morality fits: it is a destruction or a levelling for the sake of the ruling type (whether to render the others no longer fearsome or to render them useful) (WP 315).

It may be suggested that Nietzsche, even if he will not accept the rules of behaviour to be taught to all men, does at least set up ideals of character valid for all. Is it not the case that he refuses to praise anyone who is not, e.g., courageous and independent? This is of course true, and it does give some overlap, both in form and content, between a moral system and a set of teachings such as Nietzsche's. Nevertheless an injunction such as 'seek your own health' is so neutral as to actual behaviour as to fail to reestablish the link with social norms. And even injunctions such as this one were not preached to everyone, since Nietzsche thought that many men were simply incapable of health and strength. There were, as we have already seen, cruel monsters to whom Nietzsche would not preach egoism. And as for the members of 'the herd' he said that he had no wish to change them; the spirit of the herd should rule within the herd. He is not, he insists, trying to preach his kind of virtue generally: it belongs only to the rare and exceptional man.

These considerations should, I think, incline us to the view that Nietzsche is an immoralist rather than a special kind of moralist. And one is led in the same direction by the fact that he was prepared to throw out rules of justice in the interests of producing a stronger and more splendid type of man. I suggested that this implied a quasi-aesthetic rather than a moral set of values. Morality is necessarily connected with such things as justice and the common good, and it is a conceptual matter that this is so.

Why then should we still have a feeling, as I think we do, that Nietzsche has a great deal in common with the moralist and that he is not simply arguing from an incompatible and irreconcilable point of view? I think that this is due to the fact that in much of his work he can be seen as arguing about the way in which men must live in order to *live well*. It is the common ground between his system and that of traditional and particularly Greek morality that makes us inclined to think that he must be a moralist after all. For while Nietzsche loathed utilitarianism, with its concern for the greatest happiness of the greatest number, and its tendency to take pleasure and the absence of pain as the motive of all human action, he himself was interested, one might say, in the conditions in which men—at least strong men—would flourish. The issue is hard to get clear because Nietzsche, as well as introducing quasi-aesthetic criteria which are irrelevant in this context, also appeals to an idea of human good that is opposed to that of his opponents, and there is no concept that has proved more intractable than that of human happiness or human good. We are inclined to say at first sight that happiness is equivalent to contentment, and only see that this cannot be the case when we notice, for example, that we count someone as unfortunate, not fortunate, if he suffers brain damage and thereafter lives the life of a happy child. But this correction shows that however little we are able to give an account of the idea of human good we have reason to agree with Nietzsche that a man is harmed if he is taught to be content with small pleasures and made unfit for enterprises requiring daring and independence. So, insofar as Nietzsche is suggesting that morality in general, and Christian morality in particular, has this effect he is at least arguing on moral ground. And of course there were more obvious ways in which the 'good and virtuous' had been 'harmed'. For Nietzsche saw them as resentful, hating themselves and others, and without strong purpose or desire. No man can live happily if he lives like this.

The conclusion of this discussion must be that Nietzsche's 'revaluation of values' is a most complex matter, and there is no single answer to the question as to what he was attacking or as to what the basis might be for the attack. It is not, therefore, surprising that we should shy away from the attempt to say whether he was right. I shall, however, try to say one or two things about this. First of all I would like to point out that everything depends on his theories and observations of human nature. If his attack on Christian morality and on other moralities is going to be worth anything he has got to be *right* about the effect of teaching pity and justice—that it merely hides the *ressentiment* of the weak while it does injury to the strong. And he would have to be right in seeing compassion as necessarily harmful to the compassionate man and of little use to the unfortunate. Moreover he would have to be right about the possibilities of a 'healthy egoism' in the strong, even when this egoism could involve a ruthlessness to those who are less fortunately placed. Now on some points in his psychological observation Nietzsche undoubtedly was right; he was right for instance to teach us to be wary of one who finds other men most satisfactory when they are in need of his help, and to be wary also of the one who hates himself. At certain points his observation, and his anticipation of depth psychology, shows him as a brilliant psychologist. But one could not see Nietzsche as one who had a great knowledge of life and of the human heart. He describes convincingly what he knew thoroughly, as he knew the life of the lonely genius, the creative artist or thinker. It is, however, noticeable that his picture of the strong noble man fails to carry conviction when it deviates from this model; what he says about the conditions for this man's health seems to stem largely from his belief that the overriding and underlying principle of human behaviour is the will to power. Now it is notorious that general theories about the springs of action are traps for philosophers, and Nietzsche, who tried to work on a world historical scale, is an obvious victim of the delusion of having seen things whole. This charge would have to be proved against him, but *prima facie* one has no reason to trust Nietzsche's views of human nature beyond a very limited perspective, and one quite inadequate for his case. There is no reason to suppose that we really are in the dilemma that he insists on—that we either sacrifice the weak or else deform the strong. And in a way events have caught up with Nietzsche. How could one see the present dangers that the world is in as showing that there is too much pity and too little egoism around? One wonders what Nietzsche himself, in some ways a most humane man, would have said if he were living now, and could see inhumanity on its present scale, and in its present blatant forms.

NOTES

* 'Nietzsche: The Revaluation of Values' originally appeared in R. C. Solomon, ed., Nietzsche, *A Collection of Critical Essays*, New York, 1973.
[1] Translations, unless otherwise stated, by Walter Kaufmann. A list of abbreviations follows.
[2] Translation by Walter Kaufmann and R. J. Hollingdale.

List of abbreviations of titles of Nietzsche's works:
A: *The Antichrist*.

BGE: *Beyond Good and Evil.*
CW: *The Case of Wagner.*
EH: *Ecce Homo.*
GM: *The Genealogy of Morals.*
Twilight: *The Twilight of the Idols.*
WP: *The Will to Power.*
Z: *Thus Spake Zarathustra.*

VII

Moral Arguments*

Those who are influenced by the emotivist theory of ethics, and yet wish to defend what Hare has called 'the rationality of moral discourse', generally talk a lot about 'giving reasons' for saying that one thing is right, and another wrong. The fact that moral judgements need defence seems to distinguish the impact of one man's moral views upon others from mere persuasion or coercion, and the judgements themselves from mere expressions of likes and dislikes. Yet the version of argument in morals currently accepted seems to say that, while reasons must be given, no one need accept them unless he happens to hold particular moral views. It follows that disputes about what is right and wrong can be resolved only if certain contingent conditions are fulfilled; if they are not fulfilled, the argument breaks down, and the disputants are left face to face in opposition which is merely an expression of attitude and will. Much energy is expended in trying to show that no sceptical conclusion can be drawn. It is suggested, for instance, that anyone who has considered all the facts which could bear on his moral position has *ipso facto* produced a 'well founded' moral judgement; in spite of the fact that anyone else who has considered the same facts may well have come to the opposite conclusion. How 'x is good' can be a well founded moral judgement when 'x is bad' can be equally well founded it is not easy to see.

The statement that moral arguments 'may always break down' is often thought of as something that has to be accepted, and it is thought that those who deny it fail to take account of what was proved once for all by Hume, and elaborated by Stevenson, by Ayer, and by Hare. This article is an attempt to expose the assumptions which give the 'breakdown' theory so tenacious a hold, and to suggest an alternative view.

Looked at in one way, the assertion that moral arguments 'may always break down' appears to make a large claim. What is meant is that they may break down in a way in which other arguments may not. We are therefore working on a model on which such factors as shortage of time or temper are not shown; the suggestion is not that A's argument with B may break down because B refuses for one reason or another to go on with it, but that their positions are irreconcilable. Now the question is how can we assert that any disagreement about what is right and wrong may end like this? How do we know, without consulting the details of each argument, that there is always an impregnable position both for the man who says that X is right, or good, or what he ought to do, and for the man who denies it? How do we know that each is able to deal with every argument the other may bring?

Thus, when Hare describes someone who listens to all his adversary has to say and then at the end simply rejects his conclusion, we want to ask 'How can he?' Hare clearly supposes that he can, for he says that at this point the objector can only be asked to make up his mind for himself.[1] No one would ever paint such a picture of other kinds of argument—suggesting, for instance, that a man might listen to all that could be said about the shape of the earth, and then ask why he should believe that it was round. We should want, in such a case, to know how he met the case put to him; and it is remarkable that in ethics this question is thought not to be in place.

If a man making a moral judgement is to be invulnerable to criticism, he must be free from reproach on two scores: (a) he must have brought forward evidence, where evidence is needed; and (b) he must have disposed of any contrary evidence offered. It is worth showing why writers who insist that moral arguments may always break down assume, for both sides in a moral dispute, invulnerability on both counts. The critical assumption appears in different forms because different descriptions of moral arguments are given; and I shall consider briefly what has been said by Stevenson and by Hare.

I. Stevenson sees the process of giving reasons for ethical

conclusions as a special process of non-deductive inference, in which statements expressing beliefs (R) form the premises and emotive (evaluative) utterances (E) the conclusion. There are no rules validating particular inferences, but only causal connexions between the beliefs and attitudes concerned. 'Suppose', he writes,

that a theorist should *tabulate* the 'valid' inferences from R's to E's. It is difficult to see how he could be doing anything more than specify what R's he thereby resolves to *accept* as supporting the various E's. . . . Under the name of 'validity' he will be selecting those inferences to which he is psychologically disposed to give assent and perhaps inducing others to give a similar assent to them.[2]

It follows that disputes in which each man backs up his moral judgement with 'reasons' may always break down, and this is an implication on which Stevenson insists. So long as he does not contradict himself and gets his facts right, a man may argue as he chooses, or as he finds himself psychologically disposed. He alone says which facts are relevant to ethical conclusions, so that he is invulnerable on counts (a) and (b): he can simply assert that what he brings forward is evidence and can simply deny the relevance of any other. His argument may be ineffective, but it cannot be said to be wrong. Stevenson speaks of ethical 'inference' and of giving 'reasons', but the process he describes is rather that of trying to produce a result, an attitude, by means of a special kind of adjustment, an alteration in belief. All that is needed for a breakdown is for different attitudes in different people to be causally connected to the same beliefs. Then even complete agreement in belief will not settle a moral dispute.

II. Hare gives a picture of moral reasoning which escapes the difficulties of a special form of inference without rules of validity. He regards an argument to a moral conclusion as a syllogistic inference, with the ordinary rules. The facts, such as 'this is stealing', which are to back up a moral judgement are to be stated in a 'descriptive' minor premise, and their relevance is to be guaranteed by an 'evaluative' major premise in which that kind of thing is said to be good or bad. There is thus no difficulty about the validity of the argument; but one does arise about the status of the major premise. We are supposed to say that a particular action is bad because it is a case of stealing, and because stealing is wrong; but if we ask why stealing is wrong, we can only be presented with another argument of the same form, with another exposed moral principle as its major premise. In the end everyone is forced back to some moral principle which he simply asserts—and which someone else may simply deny. It can therefore be no reproach to anyone that he gives no reasons for a statement of moral principle, since any moral argument must contain some undefended premise of this kind. Nor can he be accused of failing to meet arguments put forward by opponents arguing from different principles; for by denying their ultimate major premises he can successfully deny the relevance of anything they say.

Both these accounts of moral argument are governed by the thought that there is no logical connexion between statements of fact and statements of value, so that each man makes his own decision as to the facts about an action which are relevant to its evaluation. To oppose this view we should need to show that, on the contrary, it is laid down that some things do, and some things do not, count in favour of a moral conclusion, and that a man can no more decide for himself what is evidence for rightness and wrongness than he can decide what is evidence for monetary inflation or a tumour on the brain. If such objective relations between facts and values existed, they could be of two kinds: descriptive, or factual, premises might *entail* evaluative conclusions, or they might count as *evidence* for them. It is the second possibility which chiefly concerns me, but I shall nevertheless consider the arguments which are supposed to show that the stronger relationship cannot exist. For I want to show that the arguments usually brought forward do not *even* prove this. I want to say that it has not even been proved that moral conclusions cannot be entailed by factual or descriptive premises.

It is often thought that Hume showed the impossibility of deducing 'ought' from 'is', but the form in which this view is now defended is, of course, that in which it was rediscovered by G. E. Moore at the beginning of the present century, and developed by such other critics of 'naturalistic' ethics as Stevenson, Ayer, and Hare. We need therefore to look into the case against naturalism to see exactly what was proved.

Moore tried to show that goodness was a non-natural property, and thus not to be defined in terms of natual properties;
the problem was to explain the concept of a 'natural property',
and to prove that no ethical definition in terms of natural
properties could be correct. As Frankena[3] and Prior[4] pointed
out, the argument against naturalism was always in danger of
degenerating into a truism. A natural property tended to
become one not identical with goodness, and the naturalistic
fallacy that of identifying goodness with 'some other thing'.

What was needed to give the attack on naturalism new life
was the identification of some deficiency common to the
whole range of definitions rejected by Moore, a reason why
they all failed. This was provided by the theory that value
terms in general, and moral terms in particular, were used for a
special function—variously identified as expressing feelings,
expressing and inducing attitudes, or commending. Now it
was said that words with emotive or commendatory force,
such as 'good', were not to be defined by the use of words
whose meaning was merely 'descriptive'. This discovery
tended to appear greater than it was, because it looked as if the
two categories of fact and value had been identified separately
and found never to coincide, whereas actually the factual or
descriptive was defined by exclusion from the realm of value.
In the ordinary sense of 'descriptive' the word 'good' is a
descriptive word and in the ordinary sense of 'fact' we say that
it is a fact about so and so that he is a good man, so that the
words must be used in a special sense in moral philosophy. But
a special philosopher's sense of these words has never, so far as
I know, been explained except by contrasting value and fact. A
word or sentence seems to be called 'descriptive' on account of
the fact that it is *not* emotive, does *not* commend, does *not* entail
an imperative, and so on according to the theory involved.
This might seem to reduce the case against naturalism once
more to an uninteresting tautology, but it does not do so. For if
the non-naturalist has discovered a special feature found in all
value judgements, he can no longer be accused of saying
merely that nothing is a definition of 'good' unless it is a
definition of 'good' and not 'some other thing'. His part is
now to insist that any definition which fails to allow for the
special feature of value judgements must be rejected, and to

label as 'naturalistic' all the definitions which fail to pass this test.

I shall suppose, for the sake of argument, that the non-naturalist really has identified some characteristic (let us call it f) essential to evaluative words; that he is right in saying that evaluations involve emotions, attitudes, the acceptance of imperatives, or something of the kind. He is therefore justified in insisting that no word or statement which does not have the property f can be taken as equivalent to any evaluation, and that no account of the use of an evaluative term can leave out f and yet be complete. What, if anything, follows about the relation between premises and conclusion in an argument designed to support an evaluation?

It is often said that what follows is that evaluative conclusion cannot be deduced from descriptive premises, but how is this to be shown? Of course, if a descriptive premise is redefined, as one which does not entail an evaluative conclusion, the non-naturalist will once more have bought security at the price of becoming a bore. He can once more improve his position by pointing to the characteristic f belonging to all evaluations, and asserting that no set of premises which do not entail an f proposition can entail an evaluation. If he takes this course he will be more like the man who says that a proposition which entails a proposition about a dog must be one which entails a proposition about an animal; he is telling us what to look out for in checking the entailment. What he is not so far telling us is that we can test for the entailment by looking to see whether the premise itself has the characteristic f. For all that has yet been shown it might be possible for a premise which is not f to entail a conclusion which is f, and it is obviously this proposition which the non-naturalist wants to deny.

Now it may seem obvious that a non-evaluative premise could not entail an evaluative conclusion, but it remains unclear how it is supposed to be proved.

In one form, the theory that an evaluative conclusion of a deductive argument needs evaluative premises is clearly unwarrantable; I mention it only to get it out of the way. We cannot possibly say that at least one of the premises must be evaluative if the conclusion is to be so; for there is nothing to tell us that whatever can truly be said of the conclusion of a deductive argument can truly be said of any of the premises. It is not necessary that the evaluative element should 'come in whole', so to speak. If f has to belong to the premises it can only be necessary that it should belong to the premises *together*, and it may be no easy matter to see whether a set of propositions has the property f.

How in any case is it to be proved that if the conclusion is to have the characteristic f the premises taken together must also have it? Can it be said that unless this is so it will always be possible to assert the premises and yet deny the conclusion? I shall try to show that this at least is false, and in order to do so I shall consider the case of arguments designed to show that a certain piece of behaviour is or is not rude.

I think it will be agreed that in the wide sense in which philosophers speak of evaluation, 'rude' is an evaluative word. At any rate it has the kind of characteristics upon which non-naturalists fasten: it expresses disapproval, is meant to be used when action is to be discouraged, implies that other things being equal the behaviour to which it is applied will be avoided by the speaker, and so on. For the purpose of this argument I shall ignore the cases in which it is admitted that there are reasons why something should be done in spite of, or even because of, the fact that it is rude. Clearly there are occasions when a little rudeness is in place, but this does not alter the fact that 'rude' is a condemnatory word.

It is obvious that there is something else to be said about the word 'rude' besides the fact that it expresses, fairly mild, condemnation: it can only be used where certain descriptions apply. The right account of the situation in which it is correct to say that a piece of behaviour is rude, is, I think, that this kind of behaviour causes offence by indicating lack of respect. Sometimes it is merely conventional that such behaviour does indicate lack of respect (e.g. when a man keeps his hat on in someone else's house); sometimes the behaviour is naturally disrespectful, as when when one man pushes another out of the way. (It should be mentioned that rudeness and the absence of rudeness do not exhaust the subject of etiquette; some things are not rude, and yet are 'not done'. It is rude to wear flannels at a formal dinner party, but merely not done to wear a dinner jacket for tennis.)

Given that this reference to offence is to be included in any account of the concept of rudeness, we may ask what the relation is between the assertion that these conditions of offence are fulfilled—let us call it O—and the statement that a piece of behaviour is rude—let us call it R. Can someone who accepts the proposition O (that this kind of offence is caused) deny the proposition R (that the behaviour is rude)? I should have thought that this was just what he could not do, for if he says that it is not rude, we shall stare, and ask him what sort of behaviour would be rude; and what is he to say? Suppose that he were to answer 'a man is rude when he behaves convention-ally', or 'a man is rude when he walks slowly up to a front door', and this not because he believes that such behaviour causes offence, but with the intention of leaving behind entirely the usual criteria of rudeness. It is evident that with the usual criteria of rudeness he leaves behind the concept itself; he may say the words 'I think this rude', but it will not on that account be right to describe him as 'thinking it rude'. If I *say* 'I am sitting on a pile of hay' and bring as evidence the fact that the object I am sitting on has four wooden legs and a hard wooden back, I shall hardly be described as thinking, even mistakenly, that I am sitting on a pile of hay; all I am doing is to use the *words* 'pile of hay'.

It might be thought that the two cases were not parallel, for while the meaning of 'pile of hay' is given by the characteris-tics which piles of hay must possess, the meaning of 'rude' is given by the attitude it expresses. The answer is that if 'think-ing a thing rude' is to be described as having a particular attitude to it, then having an attitude presupposes, in this case, believing that certain conditions are fulfilled. If 'attitudes' were solely a matter of reactions such as wrinkling the nose, and tendencies to such things as making resolutions and scold-ing, then thinking something rude would not be describable solely in terms of attitudes. Either thinking something rude is not to be described in terms of attitudes, or attitudes are not to be described in terms of such things. Even if we could suppose that a particular individual could react towards conventional behaviour, or to walking slowly up to an English front door, *exactly* as most people react to behaviour which gives offence, this would not mean that he was to be described as thinking these things rude. And in any case the supposition is nonsense. Although he could behave in some ways as if he thought them rude, e.g. by scolding conventional or slow-walking children, but not turning daughters with these proclivities out of doors, his behaviour could not be just as if he thought them rude. For as the social reaction to conventional behaviour is not the same as the social reaction to offensive behaviour, he could not act in just the same way. He could not for instance apologise for what he could call his 'rudeness', for he would have to admit that it had caused no offence.

I conclude that whether a man is speaking of behaviour as rude or not rude, he must use the same criteria as anyone else, and that since the criteria are satisfied if O is true, it is impossible for him to assert O while denying R. It follows that if it is a sufficient condition of P's entailing Q that the assertion of P is inconsistent with the denial of Q, we have here an example of a non-evaluative premise from which an evaluative conclusion can be deduced.

It is of course possible to admit O while refusing to assert R, and this will not be like the refusal to say about prunes what one has already admitted about dried plums. Calling an action 'rude' is using a concept which a man might want to reject, rejecting the whole practice of praising and blaming embodied in terms such as 'polite' and 'rude'. Such a man would refuse to discuss points of etiquette, and arguments with him about what is rude would not so much break down as never begin. But once he did accept the question 'Is this rude?' he would have to abide by the rules of this kind of argument; he could not bring forward any evidence he liked, and he could not deny the relevance of any piece of evidence brought forward by his opponent. Nor could he say that he was unable to move from O to R on this occasion because the belief in O had not induced in him feelings or attitudes warranting the assertion of R. If he had agreed to discuss rudeness he had commited himself to accepting O as evidence for R, and evidence is not a sort of medicine which is taken in the hope that it will work. To suggest that he could refuse to admit that certain behaviour was rude because the right psychological state had not been induced, is as odd as to suppose that one might refuse to speak of the world as round because in spite of the good evidence of roundness a feeling of confidence in the proposition had not been produced. When given good evidence it is one's business to act on it, not to hang around waiting for the right state of mind. It follows that if a man is prepared to discuss questions of rudeness, and hence to accept as evidence the fact that behaviour causes a certain kind of offence, he cannot refuse to admit R when O has been proved.

The point of considering this example was to show that there may be the strictest rules of evidence even where an evaluative conclusion is concerned. Applying this principle to the case of moral judgements, we see that—for all that the nonnaturalist has proved to the contrary—Bentham, for instance, may be right in saying that when used in conjunction with the principle of utility 'the words *ought* and *right* and *wrong*, and others of that stamp, have a meaning: when otherwise they have none'.[5] Anyone who uses moral terms at all, whether to assert or deny a moral proposition, must abide by the rules for their use, including the rules about what shall count as evidence for or against the moral judgement concerned. For anything that has yet been shown to the contrary these rules could be entailment rules, forbidding the assertion of factual propositions in conjunction with the denial of moral propositions. The only recourse of the man who refused to accept the things which counted in favour of a moral proposition as giving him a reason to do certain things or to take up a particular attitude, would be to leave the moral discussion and abjure altogether the use of moral terms.

To say what Bentham said is not, then, to commit any sort of 'naturalistic fallacy'. It is open to us to enquire whether moral terms do lose their meaning when divorced from the pleasure principle, or from some other set of criteria, as the word 'rude' loses its meaning when the criterion of offensiveness is dropped. To me it seems that this is clearly the case; I do not know what could be meant by saying that it was someone's duty to do something unless there was an attempt to show why it mattered if this sort of thing was not done. How can questions such as 'what does it matter?', 'what harm does it do?', 'what advantage is there in . . .?', 'why is it important?',

be set aside here? Is it even to be suggested that the harm done
by a certain trait of character could be taken, by some extreme
moral eccentric, to be just what made it a virtue? I suggest that
such a man would not even be a moral eccentric, any more
than the man who used the word 'rude' of conventional
behaviour was putting forward strange views about what was
rude. Both descriptions have their proper application, but it is
not here. How exactly the concepts of harm, advantage,
benefit, importance, etc. are related to the different moral
concepts, such as rightness, obligation, goodness, duty and
virtue is something that needs the most patient investigation,
but that they are so related seems undeniable, and it follows
that a man cannot make his own personal decision about the
considerations which are to count as evidence in morals.

Perhaps it will be argued that this kind of freedom of choice
is not ruled out after all, because a man has to decide for
himself what is to count as advantage, benefit, or harm. But is
this really plausible? Consider the man described by Hare as
thinking that torturing is morally permissible.[6] Apparently he
is not supposed to be arguing that in spite of everything
torture is justifiable as a means of extracting confessions from
enemies of the state, for the argument is supposed to be at an
end when he has said that torturing people is permissible, and
his opponent has said that it is not. How is he supposed to have
answered the objection that to inflict torture is to do harm? If
he is supposed to have said that pain is good for a man in the
long run, rather than bad, he will have to show the benefits
involved, and he can no more choose what shall count as a
benefit than he could have chosen what counted as harm. Is he
supposed perhaps to count as harm only harm to himself? In
this case he is guilty of *ignoratio elenchi*. By refusing to count as
harm anything except harm to himself, he puts himself outside
the pale of moral discussion, and should have explained that
this was his position. One might compare his case to that of a
man who in some discussion of common policy says 'this will
be the best thing to do', and announces afterwards that *he*
meant best for himself. This is not what the word 'best' does
mean in the context of such a discussion.

It may be objected that these considerations about the evidence which must be brought for saying that one thing is good

and another bad, could not in any case be of the least importance; such rules of evidence, even if they exist, only reflecting the connexion between our existing moral code and our existing moral terms; if there are no 'free' moral terms in our language it can always be supposed that some have been invented—as indeed they will have to be invented if we are to be able to argue with people who subscribe to a moral code entirely different from our own. This objection rests on a doubtful assumption about the concept of *morality*. It assumes that even if there are rules about the ground on which actions can be called good, right, or obligatory, there are no rules about the grounds on which a principle which is to be called a moral principle may be asserted. Those who believe this must think it possible to identify an element of feeling or attitude which carries the meaning of the word 'moral'. It must be supposed, for instance, that if we describe a man as being for or against certain actions, bringing them under universal rules, adopting these rules for himself, and thinking himself bound to urge them on others, we shall be able to identify him as holding moral principles, whatever the content of the principle at which he stops. But why should it be supposed that the concept of morality is to be caught in this particular kind of net? The consequences of such an assumption are very hard to stomach; for it follows that a rule which was admitted by those who obeyed it to be completely pointless could yet be recognised as a moral rule. If people happened to insist that no one should run round trees left handed, or look at hedgehogs in the light of the moon, this might count as a basic moral principle about which nothing more need be said.

I think that the main reason why this view is so often held in spite of these difficulties, is that we fear the charge of making a verbal decision in favour of our own moral code. But those who bring that charge are merely begging the question against arguments such as those given above. Of course if the rules we are refusing to call moral rules can really be given this name, then we are merely legislating against alien *moral codes*. But the suggestion which has been put forward is that this could not be the right description for rules of behaviour for which an entirely different defence is offered from that which we offer for our moral beliefs. If this suggestion is right, the difference

between ourselves and the people who have these rules is not
to be described as a difference of moral outlook, but rather as a
difference between a moral and a non-moral point of view.
The example of etiquette is again useful here. No one is
tempted to say that the ruling out, *a priori*, of rules of etiquette
which each man decides for himself when he feels so inclined,
represents a mere verbal decision in favour of our kind of
socially determined standards of etiquette. On what grounds
could one call a rule which someone was allowed to invent for
himself a rule of *etiquette*? It is not just a fact about the use of our
words 'rude', 'not done', etc., that they could not be applied in
such a case; it is also a fact about etiquette that if terms in
another language did appear in such situations they would not
be terms of etiquette. We can make a similar point about the
terms 'legal' and 'illegal' and the concept of law. If any individual was allowed to apply a certain pair of terms expressing
approval and disapproval off his own bat, without taking
notice of any recognised authority, such terms could not be
legal terms. Similarly it is a fact about etiquette and law that
they are both conventional as morality is not.

It may be that in attempting to state the rules which govern
the assertion of moral propositions we shall legislate against a
moral system radically opposed to our own. But this is only to
say that we may make a mistake. The remedy is to look more
carefully at the rules of evidence, not to assume that there
cannot be any at all. If a moral system such as Nietzsche's has
been refused recognition as a moral system, then we may have
got the criteria wrong. The fact that Nietzsche was arguably a
moralist cannot, however, be quoted in favour of the private
enterprise theory of moral criteria. Admittedly Nietzsche said
'You want to decrease suffering; I want precisely to increase it'
but he did not *just* say this. Nor did he offer as a justification the
fact that suffering causes a tendency to absent mindedness, or
lines on the human face. We are inclined to recognise Nietzsche
as a moralist because he tries to justify an increase in suffering
by connecting it with strength as opposed to weakness, and
individuality as opposed to conformity. That strength is a good
thing can only be denied by someone who can show that the
strong man overreaches himself, or in some other way brings
harm to himself or other people. That individuality is a good

thing is something that has to be shown, but in a vague way we connect it with originality, and with courage, and hence there is no difficulty in conceiving Nietzsche as a moralist when he appeals to such a thing.

In conclusion it is worth remarking that moral arguments break down more often than philosophers tend to think, but that the breakdown is of a different kind. When people argue about what is right, good, or obligatory, or whether a certain character trait is or is not a virtue, they do not confine their remarks to the adducing of facts which can be established by simple observation, or by some clear-cut technique. What is said may well be subtle or profound, and in this sort of discussion as in others, in the field of literary criticism for instance, or the discussion of character, much depends on experience and imagination. It is quite common for one man to be unable to see what the other is getting at, and this sort of misunderstanding will not always be resolvable by anything which could be called argument in the ordinary sense.

NOTES

* 'Moral Arguments' originally appeared in *Mind*, Volume 67, 1958.

¹ *The Language of Morals*, p. 69.

² *Ethics and Language*, pp. 170–1.

³ W. K. Frankena, 'The Naturalistic Fallacy', *Mind*, 1939.

⁴ A. N. Prior, *Logic and the Basis of Ethics*, chap. I.

⁵ *Principles of Morals and Legislation*, chap. I, x.

⁶ *Universalizability*, *Proceedings of the Aristotelian Society*, 1954–1955, p. 304.

VIII

Moral Beliefs*

I

To many people it seems that the most notable advance in moral philosophy during the past fifty years or so has been the refutation of naturalism; and they are a little shocked that at this late date such an issue should be reopened. It is easy to understand their attitude: given certain apparently unquestionable assumptions, it would be about as sensible to try to reintroduce naturalism as to try to square the circle. Those who see it like this have satisfied themselves that they know in advance that any naturalistic theory must have a catch in it somewhere, and are put out at having to waste more time exposing an old fallacy. This paper is an attempt to persuade them to look critically at the premises on which their arguments are based.

It would not be an exaggeration to say that the whole of moral philosophy, as it is now widely taught, rests on a contrast between statements of fact and evaluations, which runs something like this: 'The truth or falsity of statements of fact is shewn by means of evidence; and what counts as evidence is laid down in the meaning of the expressions occurring in the statement of fact. (For instance, the meaning of "round" and "flat" made Magellan's voyages evidence for the roundness rather than the flatness of the Earth; someone who went on questioning whether the evidence was evidence could eventually be shewn to have made some linguistic mistake.) It follows that no two people can make the same statement and count completely different things as evidence; in the end one at least of them could be convicted of linguistic ignorance. It also follows that if a man is given good evidence for a factual conclusion he cannot just refuse to accept the conclusion on the ground that in his scheme of things this evidence is not evidence at all. With evaluations, however, it is different. An evaluation is not connected logically with the factual statements on which it is based. One man may say that a thing is good because of some fact about it, and another may refuse to take that fact as any evidence at all, for nothing is laid down in the meaning of "good" which connects it with one piece of "evidence" rather than another. It follows that a moral eccentric could argue to moral conclusions from quite idiosyncratic premises; he could say, for instance, that a man was a good man because he clasped and unclasped his hands and never turned N.N.E. after turning S.S.W. He could also reject someone else's evaluation simply by denying that his evidence was evidence at all.

The fact about "good" which allows the eccentric still to use this term without falling into a morass of meaninglessness, is its "action-guiding" or "practical" function. This it retains; for like everyone else he considers himself bound to choose the things he calls "good" rather than those he calls "bad". Like the rest of the world he uses "good' in connexion only with a "pro-attitude"; it is only that he has pro-attitudes to quite different things, and therefore calls them good.'

There are here two assumptions about 'evaluations', which I will call assumption (1) and assumption (2).

Assumption (1) is that some individual may, without logical error, base his beliefs about matters of value entirely on premises which no one else would recognise as giving evidence at all. Assumption (2) is that, given the kind of statement which other people regard as evidence for an evaluative conclusion, he may refuse to draw the conclusion because *this* does not count as evidence for *him*.

Let us consider assumption (1). We might say that this depends on the possibility of keeping the meaning of 'good' steady through all changes in the facts about anything which are to count in favour of its goodness. (I do not mean, of course, that a man can make changes as fast as he chooses; only that, whatever he has chosen, it will not be possible to rule him out of order.) But there is a better formulation, which cuts out trivial disputes about the meaning which 'good' happens to have in some section of the community. Let us say that the assumption is that the evaluative function of 'good' can remain constant through changes in the evaluative principles; on this ground it could be said that even if no one can call a man *good* because he clasps and unclasps his hands, he can commend him or express his *pro-attitude* towards him, and if necessary can invent a new moral vocabulary to express his unusual moral code.

Those who hold such a theory will naturally add several qualifications. In the first place, most people now agree with Hare, against Stevenson, that such words as 'good' apply to individual cases only through the application of general principles, so that even the extreme moral eccentric must accept principles of commendation. In the second place 'commending', 'having a pro-attitude', and so on, are supposed to be connected with doing and choosing, so that it would be impossible to say, e.g., that a man was a good man only if he lived for a thousand years. The range of evaluation is supposed to be restricted to the range of possible action and choice. I am not here concerned to question these supposed restrictions on the use of evaluative terms, but only to argue that they are not enough.

The crucial question is this. Is it possible to extract from the meaning of words such as 'good' some element called 'evaluative meaning' which we can think of as externally related to its objects? Such an element would be represented, for instance, in the rule that when any action was 'commended' the speaker must hold himself bound to accept an imperative 'let me do these things'. This is externally related to its object because, within the limitation which we noticed earlier, to possible actions, it would make sense to think of anything as the subject of such 'commendation'. On this hypothesis a moral eccentric could be described as commending the clasping of hands as the action of a good man, and we should not have to look for some background to give the supposition sense. That is to say, on this hypothesis the clasping of hands could be commended without any explanation; it could be what those who hold such theories call 'an ultimate moral principle'.

I wish to say that this hypothesis is untenable, and that there is no describing the evaluative meaning of 'good', evaluation, commending, or anything of the sort, without fixing the object to which they are supposed to be attached. Without first laying hands on the proper object of such things as evaluation, we shall catch in our net either something quite different such as accepting an order or making a resolution, or else nothing at all.

Before I consider this question, I shall first discuss some other mental attitudes and beliefs which have this internal relation to their object. By this I hope to clarify the concept of internal relation to an object, and incidentally, if my examples arouse resistance, but are eventually accepted, to show how easy it is to overlook an internal relation where it exists.

Consider, for instance, pride.

People are often surprised at the suggestion that there are limits to the things a man can be proud of, about which indeed he can feel pride. I do not know quite what account they want to give of pride; perhaps something to do with smiling and walking with a jaunty air, and holding an object up where other people can see it; or perhaps they think that pride is a kind of internal sensation, so that one might naturally beat one's breast and say 'pride is something I feel *here*'. The difficulties of the second view are well known; the logically private object cannot be what a name in the public language is the name of.[1] The first view is the more plausible, and it may seem reasonable to say that given certain behaviour a man can be described as showing that he is proud of something, whatever that something may be. In one sense this is true, and in another sense not. Given any description of an object, action, personal characteristic, etc., it is not possible to rule it out as an object of pride. Before we can do so we need to know what would be said about it by a man who is to be proud of it, or feels proud of it; but if he does not hold the right beliefs about it then whatever his attitude is it is not pride. Consider, for instance, the suggestion that someone might be proud of the sky or the sea: he looks at them and what he feels is *pride*, or he puffs out his chest and gestures with *pride* in their direction. This makes sense only if a special assumption is made about his beliefs, for instance that he is under some crazy delusion and believes that he has saved the sky from falling, or the sea from drying up. The characteristic object of pride is something seen (*a*) as in some way a man's own, and (*b*) as some sort of achievement or advantage; without this object pride cannot be described. To see that the second condition is necessary, one should try supposing that a man happens to feel proud because he has laid one of his hands on the other, three times in an hour. Here again the supposition that it is pride that he feels will make perfectly good sense if a special background is filled in. Perhaps he is ill, and it is an achievement even to do this; perhaps this gesture has some religious or political significance, and he is a brave man who will so defy the gods or the rulers. But with no special background there can be no pride, not because no one could psychologically speaking feel pride in such a case, but because whatever he did feel could not logically be pride. Of course, people can see strange things as achievements, though not just anything, and they can identify themselves with remote ancestors, and relations, and neighbours, and even on occasions with Mankind. I do not wish to deny there are many far-fetched and comic examples of pride.

We could have chosen many other examples of mental attitudes which are internally related to their object in a similar way. For instance, fear is not just trembling, and running, and turning pale; without the thought of some menacing evil no amount of this will add up to fear. Nor could anyone be said to feel dismay about something he did not see as bad; if his thoughts about it were that it was altogether a good thing, he could not say that (oddly enough) what he felt about it was dismay. 'How odd, I feel dismayed when I ought to be pleased' is the prelude to a hunt for the adverse aspect of the thing, thought of as lurking behind the pleasant façade. But someone may object that pride and fear and dismay are feelings or emotions and therefore not a proper analogy for 'commendation', and there will be an advantage in considering a different kind of example. We could discuss for instance, the belief that a certain thing is dangerous, and ask whether this could logically be held about anything whatsoever. Like 'this is good', 'this is dangerous' is an assertion, which we should naturally accept or reject by speaking of its truth or falsity; we seem to support such statements with evidence, and moreover there may seem to be a 'warning function' connected with the word 'dangerous' as there is supposed to be a 'commending function' connected with the word 'good'. For suppose that philosophers, puzzled about the property of dangerousness, decided that the word did not stand for a property at all, but was essentially a practical or action-guiding term, used for *warning*. Unless used in an 'inverted comma sense' the word 'dangerous' was used to warn, and this meant that anyone using it in such a sense committed himself to avoiding the things he called dangerous, to preventing other people from going near them, and perhaps to running in the opposite direction. If the conclusion were not obviously ridiculous, it would be easy to infer that a man whose application of the term was different from ours throughout might say that the oddest things were dangerous without fear of disproof; the idea would be that he could still be described as 'thinking them dangerous', or at least as 'warning', because by his attitude and actions he would have fulfilled the conditions for these things. This is nonsense because without its proper object *warning*, like *believing dangerous*, will not be there. It is logically impossible to warn about anything not thought of as threatening evil, and for danger we need a particular kind of serious evil such as injury or death.

There are, however, some differences between thinking a thing dangerous and feeling proud, frightened or dismayed. When a man says that something is dangerous he must support his statement with a special kind of evidence; but when he says that he feels proud or frightened or dismayed the description of the object of his pride or fright or dismay does not have quite this relation to his original statement. If he is shown that the thing he was proud of was not his after all, or was not after all anything very grand, he may have to say that his pride was not justified, but he will not have to take back the statement that he was proud. On the other hand, someone who says that a thing is dangerous, and later sees that he made a mistake in thinking that an injury might result from it, has to go back on his original statement and admit that he was wrong. In neither case, however, is the speaker able to go on as before. A man who discovered that it was not his pumpkin but someone else's which had won the prize could only say that he still felt proud if he could produce some other ground for pride. It is in this way that even feelings are logically vulnerable to facts.

It will probably be objected against these examples that for part of the way at least they beg the question. It will be said that indeed a man can be proud only of something he thinks a good action, or an achievement, or a sign of noble birth; as he can feel dismay only about something which he sees as bad, or frightened of some threatened evil; similarly he can warn only if he is also prepared to speak, for instance, of injury. But this will limit the range of possible objects of those attitudes and beliefs only if the range of these terms is limited in its turn. To meet this objection I shall discuss the meaning of 'injury' because this is the simplest case. Anyone who feels inclined to say that anything could be counted as an achievement, or as the evil of which people were afraid, or about which they felt dismayed, should just try this out. I wish to consider the proposition that anything could be thought of as dangerous, because if it causes injury it is dangerous, and anything could be counted as an injury. I shall consider bodily injury because this is the injury connected with danger; it is not correct to put up a notice by the roadside reading 'Danger!' on account of bushes which might scratch a car. Nor can a substance be labelled 'dangerous' on the ground that it can injure delicate fabrics; although we can speak of the danger that it may do so, that is not the use of the word which I am considering here.

When a body is injured it is changed for the worse in a special way, and we want to know which changes count as injuries. First of all, it matters how an injury comes about; e.g., it cannot be caused by natural decay. Then it seems clear that not just any kind of thing will do, for instance, any unusual mark on the body, however much trouble a man might take to have it removed. By far the most important class of injuries are injuries to a part of the body, counting as injuries because there is an interference with the function of that part; injury to a leg, an eye, an ear, a hand, a muscle, the heart, the brain, the spinal cord. An injury to an eye is one that affects, or is likely to affect, its sight; an injury to a hand one which makes it less well able to reach out and grasp, and perform other operations of this kind. A leg can be injured because its movements and supporting power can be affected; a lung because it can become too weak to draw in the proper amount of air. We are most ready to speak of an injury where the function of a part of the body is to perform a characteristic operation, as in these examples. We might hesitate to say that a skull can be injured, and might prefer to speak of damage to it, since although there is indeed a function (a protective function) there is no operation. But thinking of the protective function of the skull we may want to speak of injury here. In so far as the concept of *injury* depends on that of *function* it is narrowly limited, since not even every use to which a part of the body is put will count as its function. Why is it that, even if it is the means by which they earn their living, we would never consider the removal of the dwarf's hump or the bearded lady's beard as a bodily injury? It will be tempting to say that these things are disfigurements, but this is not the point; if we suppose that a man who had some invisible extra muscle made his living as a court jester by waggling his ears, the ears would not have been injured if this were made to disappear. If it were natural to men to communicate by movements of the ear, then ears would have the function of signalling (we have no word for this kind of 'speaking') and an impairment of this function would be an injury; but things are not like this. This court jester would use his ears to make people laugh, but this is not the function of ears.

No doubt many people will feel impatient when such facts are mentioned, because they think that it is quite unimportant that this or that *happens* to be the case, and it seems to them arbitrary that the loss of the beard, the hump, or the ear muscle would not be called an injury. Isn't the loss of that by which one makes one's living a pretty catastrophic loss? Yet it seems quite natural that these are not counted as injuries if one thinks about the conditions of human life, and contrasts the loss of a special ability to make people gape or laugh with the ability to see, hear, walk, or pick things up. The first is only needed for one very special way of living; the other in any foreseeable future for any man. This restriction seems all the more natural when we observe what other threats besides that of injury can constitute danger: of death, for instance, or mental derangement. A shock which could cause mental instability or impairment of memory would be called dangerous, because a man needs such things as intelligence, memory, and concentration as he needs sight or hearing or the use of hands. Here we do not speak of injury unless it is possible to connect the impairment with some physical change, but we speak of danger because there is the same loss of a capacity which any man needs.

There can be injury outside the range we have been considering; for a man may sometimes be said to have received injuries where no part of his body has had its functions interfered with. In general, I think that any blow which disarranged the body in such a way that there was lasting pain would inflict an injury, even if no other ill resulted, but I do not know of any other important extension of the concept.

It seems therefore that since the range of things which can be called injuries is quite narrowly restricted, the word 'dangerous' is restricted in so far as it is connected with injury. We have the right to say that a man cannot decide to call just anything dangerous, however much he puts up fences and shakes his head.

So far I have been arguing that such things as pride, fear, dismay, and the thought that something is dangerous have an internal relation to their object, and hope that what I mean is becoming clear. Now we must consider whether those attitudes or beliefs which are the moral philosopher's study are similar, or whether such things as 'evaluation' and 'thinking something good' and 'commendation' could logically be found in combination with any object whatsoever. All I can do here is to give an example which may make this suggestion seem implausible, and to knock away a few of its supports. The example will come from the range of trivial and pointless actions such as we were considering in speaking of the man who clasped his hands three times an hour, and we can point to the oddity of the suggestion that this can be called a good action. We are bound by the terms of our question to refrain from adding any special background, and it should be stated once more that the question is about what can count in favour of the goodness or badness of a man or an action, and not what could be, or be thought, good or bad with a special background. I believe that the view I am attacking often seems plausible only because the special background is surreptitiously introduced.

Someone who said that clasping the hands three times in an hour was a good action would first have to answer the question 'How do you mean?' For the sentence 'this is a good action' is not one which has a clear meaning. Presumably, since our subject is moral philosophy, it does not here mean 'that was a good thing to do' as this might be said of a man who had done something sensible in the course of any enterprise whatever; we are to confine our attention to 'the moral use of "good"'. I am not clear that it makes sense to speak of 'a moral use of "good"', but we can pick out a number of cases which raise moral issues. It is because these are so diverse and because 'this is a good action' does not pick out any one of them, that we must ask 'How do you mean?' For instance, some things that are done fulfil a duty, such as the duty of parents to children or children to parents. I suppose that when philosophers speak of good actions they would include these. Some come under the heading of a virtue such as charity, and they will be included too. Others again are actions which require the virtues of courage or temperance, and here the moral aspect is due to the fact that they are done in spite of fear or the temptation of pleasure; they must indeed be done for the sake of some real or fancied good, but not necessarily what philosophers would want to call a moral good. Courage is not *particularly* concerned with saving other people's lives, or temperance with leaving them their share of the food and drink, and the goodness of *what is done* may here be all kinds of usefulness. It is because there are these very diverse cases included (I suppose) under the expression 'a good action' that we should refuse to consider applying it without asking what is meant, and we should now ask what is intended when someone is supposed to say that 'clasping the hands three times in an hour is a good action'. Is it supposed that this action fulfils a duty? Then in virtue of what does a man have this duty, and to whom does he owe it? We have promised not to slip in a special background, but he cannot possibly have a *duty* to clasp his hands unless such a background exists. Nor could it be an act of charity, for it is not thought to do anyone any good, nor again a gesture of humility unless a special assumption turns it into this. The action could be courageous, but only if it were done both in the face of fear and for the sake of a good; and we are not allowed to put in special circumstances which could make this the case.

I am sure that the following objection will now be raised.

'Of course clasping one's hands three times in an hour cannot be brought under one of the virtues which we recognise, but that is only to say that it is not a good action by our current moral code. It is logically possible that in a quite different moral code quite different virtues should be recognised, for which we have not even got a name.' I cannot answer this objection properly, for that would need a satisfactory account of the concept of a virtue. But anyone who thinks it would be easy to describe a new virtue connected with clasping the hands three times in an hour should just try. I think he will find that he has to cheat, and suppose that in the community concerned the clasping of hands has been given some special significance, or is thought to have some special effect. The difficulty is obviously connected with the fact that without a special background there is no possibility of answering the question 'What's the point?' It is no good saying that there would be a point in doing the action because the action was a morally good action: the question is how it can be given any such description if we cannot first speak about the point. And it is just as crazy to suppose that we can call *anything* the point of doing something without having to say what the point of *that* is. In clasping one's hands one may make a slight sucking noise, but what is the point of that? It is surely clear that moral virtues must be connected with human good and harm, and that it is quite impossible to call anything you like good or harm. Consider, for instance, the suggestion that a man might say he had been harmed because a bucket of water had been taken out of the sea. As usual it would be possible to think up circumstances in which this remark would make sense; for instance, when coupled with a belief in magical influences; but then the harm would consist in what was done by the evil spirits, not in the taking of the water from the sea. It would be just as odd if someone were supposed to say that harm had been done to him because the hairs of his head had been reduced to an even number.[2]

I conclude that assumption (1) is very dubious indeed, and that no one should be allowed to speak as if we can understand 'evaluation' 'commendation' or 'pro-attitude', whatever the actions concerned.

II

I propose now to consider what was called assumption (2), which said that a man might always refuse to accept the conclusion of an argument about values, because what counted as evidence for other people did not count for him. Assumption (2) could be true even if assumption (1) were false, for it might be that once a particular question of values—say a moral question—had been accepted, any disputant was bound to accept particular pieces of evidence as relevant, the same pieces as everyone else, but that he could always refuse to draw any moral conclusions whatsoever or to discuss any questions which introduced moral terms. Nor do we mean 'he might refuse to draw the conclusion' in the trivial sense in which anyone can perhaps refuse to draw *any* conclusion; the point is that any statement of value always seems to go beyond any statement of fact, so that he might have a reason for accepting the factual premises but refusing to accept the evaluative conclusion. That this is so seems to those who argue in this way to follow from the practical implication of evaluation. When a man uses a word such as 'good' in an 'evaluative' and not an 'inverted comma' sense, he is supposed to commit his will. From this it has seemed to follow inevitably that there is a logical gap between fact and value, for is it not one thing to say that a thing is so, and another to have a particular attitude towards its being so; one thing to see that certain effects will follow from a given action, and another to care? Whatever account was offered of the essential feature of evaluation—whether in terms of feelings, attitudes, the acceptance of imperatives or what not—the fact remained that with an evaluation there was a committal in a new dimension, and that this was not guaranteed by any acceptance of facts.

I shall argue that this view is mistaken; that the practical implication of the use of moral terms has been put in the wrong place, and that if it is described correctly the logical gap between factual premises and moral conclusion disappears.

In this argument it will be useful to have as a pattern the practical or 'action-guiding' force of the word 'injury', which is in some, though not all, ways similar to that of moral terms.

It is clear I think that an injury is necessarily something bad and therefore something which as such anyone always has a reason to avoid, and philosophers will therefore be tempted to say that anyone who uses 'injury' in its full 'action-guiding' sense commits himself to avoiding the things he calls injuries. They will then be in the usual difficulties about the man who says he knows he ought to do something but does not intend to do it; perhaps also about weakness of the will. Suppose that instead we look again at the kinds of things which count as injuries, to see if the connexion with the will does not start here. As has been shown, a man is injured whenever some part of his body, in being damaged, has become less well able to fulfil its ordinary function. It follows that he suffers a disability, or is liable to do so; with an injured hand he will be less well able to pick things up, hold on to them, tie them together or chop them up, and so on. With defective eyes there will be a thousand other things he is unable to do, and in both cases we should naturally say that he will often be unable to get what he wants to get or avoid what he wants to avoid.

Philosophers will no doubt seize on the word 'want', and say that if we suppose that a man happens to want the things which an injury to his body prevents him from getting, we have slipped in a supposition about a 'pro-attitude' already; and that anyone who does not happen to have these wants can still refuse to use 'injury' in its prescriptive, or 'action-guiding' sense. And so it may seem that the only way to make a *necessary* connexion between 'injury' and the things that are to be avoided, is to say that it is used in an 'action-guiding sense' only when applied to something the speaker intends to avoid. But we should look carefully at the crucial move in that argument, and query the suggestion that someone might happen not to want anything for which he would need the use of hands or eyes. Hands and eyes, like ears and legs, play a part in so many operations that a man could only be said not to need them if he had no wants at all. That such people exist, in asylums, is not to the present purpose at all; the proper use of his limbs is something a man has reason to want if he wants anything.

I do not know just what someone who denies this proposition could have in mind. Perhaps he is thinking of changing the facts of human existence, so that merely wishing, or the sound of the voice, will bring the world to heel? More likely he is proposing to rig the circumstances of some individual's existence within the framework of the ordinary world, by supposing for instance that he is a prince whose servants will sow and reap and fetch and carry for him, and so use their hands and eyes in his service that he will not need the use of his. Let us suppose that such a story could be told about a man's life; it is wildly implausible, but let us pretend that it is not. It is clear that in spite of this we could say that any man had a reason to shun injury; for even if at the end of his life it could be said that by a strange set of circumstances he had never needed the use of his eyes, or his hands, this could not possibly be foreseen. Only by once more changing the facts of human existence, and supposing every vicissitude foreseeable, could such a supposition be made.

This is not to say that an injury might not bring more incidental gain than necessary harm; one has only to think of times when the order has gone out that able-bodied men are to be put to the sword. Such a gain might even, in some peculiar circumstances, be reliably foreseen, so that a man would have even better reason for seeking than for avoiding injury. In this respect the word 'injury' differs from terms such as 'injustice'; the practical force of 'injury' means only that anyone has *a* reason to avoid injuries, not that he has an overriding reason to do so.

It will be noticed that this account of the 'action-guiding' force of 'injury' links it with reasons for acting rather than with actually doing something. I do not think, however, that this makes it a less good pattern for the 'action-guiding' force of moral terms. Philosophers who have supposed that actual action was required if 'good' were to be used in a sincere evaluation have got into difficulties over weakness of will, and they should surely agree that enough has been done if we can show that any man has reason to aim at virtue and avoid vice. But is this impossibly difficult if we consider the kinds of things that count as virtue and vice? Consider, for instance, the cardinal virtues, prudence, temperance, courage and justice. Obviously any man needs prudence, but does he not also need to resist the temptation of pleasure when there is harm involved? And how could it be argued that he would never need to face what was fearful for the sake of some good? It is not obvious what someone would mean if he said that temperance or courage were not good qualities, and this not because of the 'praising' sense of these *words*, but because of the things that courage and temperance are.

I should like to use these examples to show the artificiality of the notions of 'commendation' and of 'pro-attitudes' as these are commonly employed. Philosophers who talk about these things will say that after the facts have been accepted—say that X is the kind of man who will climb a dangerous mountain, beard an irascible employer for a rise in pay, and in general face the fearful for the sake of something he thinks worth while—there remains the question of 'commendation' or 'evaluation'. If the word 'courage' is used they will ask whether or not the man who speaks of another as having courage is supposed to have commended him. If we say 'yes' they will insist that the judgement about courage *goes beyond the facts*, and might therefore be rejected by someone who refused to do so; if we say 'no' they will argue that 'courage' is being used in a purely descriptive or 'inverted comma sense', and that we have not got an example of the evaluative use of language which is the moral philosopher's special study. What sense can be made, however, of the question 'does he commend?' What is this extra element which is supposed to be present or absent after the facts have been settled? It is not a matter of liking the man who has courage, or of thinking him altogether good, but of 'commending him for his courage'. How are we supposed to do that? The answer that will be given is that we only commend someone else in speaking of him as courageous if we accept the imperative 'let me be courageous' for ourselves. But this is quite unnecessary. I can speak of someone else as having the virtue of courage, and of course recognise it as a virtue in the proper sense, while knowing that I am a complete coward, and making no resolution to reform. I know that I should be better off if I were courageous and so have a reason to cultivate courage, but I may also know that I will do nothing of the kind.

If someone were to say that courage was not a virtue he would have to say that it was not a quality by which a man came to act well. Perhaps he would be thinking that someone might be worse off for his courage, which is true, but only because an incidental harm might arise. For instance, the courageous man might have underestimated a risk, and run into some disaster which a cowardly man would have avoided because he was not prepared to take any risk at all. And his courage, like any other virtue, could be the cause of harm to him because possessing it he fell into some disastrous state of pride.[3] Similarly, those who question the virtue of temperance are probably thinking not of the virtue itself but of men whose temperance has consisted in resisting pleasure for the sake of some illusory good, or those who have made this virtue their pride.

But what, it will be asked, of justice? For while prudence, courage and temperance are qualities which benefit the man who has them, justice seems rather to benefit others, and to work to the disadvantage of the just man himself. Justice as it is treated here, as one of the cardinal virtues, covers all those things owed to other people: it is under injustice that murder, theft and lying come, as well as the withholding of what is owed for instance by parents to children and by children to parents, as well as the dealings which would be called unjust in everyday speech. So the man who avoids injustice will find himself in need of things he has returned to their owner, unable to obtain an advantage by cheating and lying; involved in all those difficulties painted by Thrasymachus in the first book of the Republic in order to show that injustice is more profitable than justice to a man of strength and wit. We will be asked how, on our theory, justice can be a virtue and injustice a vice, since it will surely be difficult to show that any man whatsoever must need to be just as he needs the use of his hands and eyes, or needs prudence, courage and temperance?

Before answering this question I shall argue that if it cannot be answered, then justice can no longer be recommended as a virtue. The point of this is not to show that it must be answerable, since justice is a virtue, but rather to suggest that we should at least consider the possibility that justice is not a virtue. This suggestion was taken seriously by Socrates in the Republic, where it was assumed by everyone that if Thrasymachus could establish his premise—that injustice was more profitable than justice—his conclusion would follow:

that a man who had strength to get away with injustice had reason to follow this as the best way of life. It is a striking fact about modern moral philosophy that no one sees any difficulty in accepting Thrasymachus' premise and rejecting his conclusion, and it is because Nietzsche's position is at this point much closer to that of Plato that he is remote from academic moralists of the present day.

In the Republic it is assumed that if justice is not a good to the just man, moralists who recommend it as a virtue are perpetrating a fraud. Agreeing with this, I shall be asked where exactly the fraud comes in; where the untruth that justice is profitable to the individual is supposed to be told. As a preliminary answer we might ask how many people are prepared to say frankly that injustice is more profitable than justice? Leaving aside, as elsewhere in this paper, religious beliefs which might complicate the matter, we will suppose that some tough atheistical character has asked 'Why should I be just?' (Those who believe that this question has something wrong with it can employ their favourite device for sieving out 'evaluative meaning', and suppose that the question is 'Why should I be "just"?') Are we prepared to reply 'As far as you are concerned you will be better off if you are unjust, but it matters to the rest of us that you should be just, so we are trying to get you to be just'? He would be likely to enquire into our methods, and then take care not to be found out, and I do not think that many of those who think that it is not necessary to show that justice is profitable to the just man would easily accept that there was nothing more they could say.

The crucial question is: 'Can we give anyone, strong or weak, a reason why he should be just?'—and it is no help at all to say that since 'just' and 'unjust' are 'action-guiding words' no one can even ask 'Why should I be just?' Confronted with that argument the man who wants to do things has only to be careful to avoid the *word*, and he has not been given a reason why he should not do the things which other people call 'unjust'. Probably it will be argued that he has been given a reason so far as anyone can ever be given a reason for doing or not doing anything, for the chain of reasons must always come to an end somewhere, and it may seem that one may always reject the reason which another man accepts. But this is a mistake; some answers to the question 'why should I?' bring the series to a close and some do not. Hume showed how *one* answer closed the series in the following passage:

> Ask a man *why he uses exercise*; he will answer, *because he desires to keep his health*. If you then enquire, *why he desires health*, he will readily reply, *because sickness is painful*. If you push your enquiries farther, and desire a reason *why he hates pain*, it is impossible he can ever give any. This is an ultimate end, and is never referred to any other object. (*Enquiries*, Appendix I, V.)

Hume might just as well have ended this series with boredom: sickness often brings boredom, and no one is required to give a reason why he does not want to be bored, any more than he has to give a reason why he does want to pursue what interests him. In general, anyone is given a reason for acting when he is shown the way to something he wants; but for some wants the question 'Why do you want that?' will make sense, and for others it will not.[4] It seems clear that in this division justice falls on the opposite side from pleasure and interest and such things. 'Why shouldn't I do that?' is not answered by the words 'because it is unjust' as it is answered by showing that the action will bring boredom, loneliness, pain, discomfort or certain kinds of incapacity, and this is why it is not true to say that 'it's unjust' gives a reason in so far as any reasons can ever be given. 'It's unjust' gives a reason only if the nature of justice can be shown to be such that it is necessarily connected with what a man wants.

This shows why a great deal hangs on the question of whether justice is or is not a good to the just man, and why those who accept Thrasymachus' premise and reject his conclusion are in a dubious position. They recommend justice to each man, as something he has a reason to follow, but when challenged to show why he should do so they will not always be able to reply. This last assertion does not depend on any 'selfish theory of human nature' in the philosophical sense. It is often possible to give a man a reason for acting by showing him that someone else will suffer if he does not; someone else's good may really be more to him than his own. But the affection which mothers feel for children, and lovers for each other, and friends for friends, will not take us far when we are asked for reasons why a man should be just; partly because it will not extend far enough, and partly because the actions dictated by benevolence and justice are not always the same. Suppose that I owe someone money:

'. . . what if he be my enemy, and has given me just cause to hate him? What if he be a vicious man, and deserves the hatred of all mankind? What if he be a miser, and can make no use of what I would deprive him of? What if he be a profligate debauchee, and would rather receive harm than benefit from large possessions?'[5]

Even if the general practice of justice could be brought under the motive of universal benevolence—the desire for the greatest happiness of the greatest number—many people certainly do not have any such desire. So that if justice is only to be recommended on these grounds a thousand tough characters will be able to say that they have been given no reason for practising justice, and many more would say the same if they were not too timid or too stupid to ask questions about the code of behaviour which they have been taught. Thus, given Thrasymachus' premise Thrasymachus' point of view is reasonable; we have no particular reason to admire those who practise justice through timidity or stupidity.

It seems to me, therefore, that if Thrasymachus' thesis is accepted things cannot go on as before; we shall have to admit that the belief on which the status of justice as a virtue was founded is mistaken, and if we still want to get people to be just we must recommend justice to them in a new way.[6] We shall have to admit that injustice is more profitable than justice, at least for the strong, and then do our best to see that hardly anyone can get away with being unjust. We have, of course, the alternative of keeping quiet, hoping that for the most part people will follow convention into a kind of justice, and not ask awkward questions, but this policy might be overtaken by a vague scepticism even on the part of those who do not know just what is lacking; we should also be at the mercy of anyone who was able and willing to expose our fraud.

Is it true, however, to say that justice is not something a man needs in his dealings with his fellows, supposing only that he be strong? Those who think that he can get on perfectly well without being just should be asked to say exactly how such a man is supposed to live. We know that he is to practise injustice whenever the unjust act would bring him advantage; but what is he to say? Does he admit that he does not recognise the rights of other people, or does he pretend? In the first case even those who combine with him will know that on a change of fortune, or a shift of affection, he may turn to plunder them, and he must be as wary of their treachery as they are of his. Presumably the happy unjust man is supposed, as in Book II of the Republic, to be a very cunning liar and actor, combining complete injustice with the appearance of justice: he is prepared to treat others ruthlessly, but pretends that nothing is further from his mind. Philosophers often speak as if a man could thus hide himself even from those around him, but the supposition is doubtful, and in any case the price in vigilance would be colossal. If he lets even a few people see his true attitude he must guard himself against them; if he lets no one into the secret he must always be careful in case the least spontaneity betray him. Such facts are important because the need a man has for justice in dealings with other men depends on the fact that they are men and not inanimate objects or animals. If a man only needed other men as he needs household objects, and if men could be manipulated like household objects, or beaten into a reliable submission like donkeys, the case would be different. As things are, the supposition that injustice is more profitable than justice is very dubious, although like cowardice and intemperance it might turn out incidentally to be profitable.

The reason why it seems to some people so impossibly difficult to show that justice is more profitable than injustice is that they consider in isolation particular just acts. It is perfectly true that if a man is just it follows that he will be prepared, in the event of very evil circumstances, even to face death rather than to act unjustly—for instance, in getting an innocent man convicted of a crime of which he has been accused. For him it turns out that his justice brings disaster on him, and yet like anyone else he had good reason to be a just and not an unjust man. He could not have it both ways and while possessing the virtue of justice hold himself ready to be unjust should any great advantage accrue. The man who has the virtue of justice is not ready to do certain things, and if he is too easily tempted we shall say that he was ready after all.

NOTES

* 'Moral Beliefs' originally appeared in the *Proceedings of the Aristotelian Society*, Volume 59, 1958–1959.

[1] See Wittgenstein, *Philosophical Investigations*, especially §§ 243–315.

[2] In face of this sort of example many philosophers take refuge in the thicket of aesthetics. It would be interesting to know if they are willing to let their whole case rest on the possibility that there might be aesthetic objections to what was done.

[3] Cp. Aquinas, *Summa Theologica*, I–II, q. 55, Art. 4.

[4] For an excellent discussion of reasons for action, see G. E. M. Anscombe, *Intention* §34–40.

[5] Hume, *Treatise* book III, part II, sect. 1.

[6] I was in this difficulty because I had supposed—with my opponents—that the thought of a good action must be related to the choices of each individual in a very special way. It had not occurred to me to question the often repeated dictum that moral judgements give reasons for acting to each and every man. This now seems to me to be a mistake. Quite generally the reason why someone choosing an A may 'be expected' to choose good A's rather than bad A's is that our criteria of goodness for any class of things are related to certain interests that someone or other has or takes in those things. When someone shares these interests he will have reasons to choose the good A's; otherwise not. Since, in the case of actions, we may distinguish good and bad on account of the interest we take in the common good, someone who does not care a damn about it may ask why *he* should be just, and we must take this question seriously, as Plato did. Nor need we be frightened by the thought that there does not *have* to be an answer to be given, and that the rational cooperation of others in moral practices is not to be taken for granted. Things might get better, not worse, if we recognized that the reasons men have for acting justly and charitably depend on contingent human

attitudes, and the identification of one man with another in society. For then we would see that it is up to us to cherish these things, and (above all) that it is no good treating people despitefully and divisively and then demanding morality of them with an alien 'ought'.

On these topics see 'Morality as a System of Hypothetical Imperatives', reprinted in this volume, and also the Introduction, pp. xiii–xvi.

IX

Goodness and Choice*

It is often said nowadays that the meaning of the word 'good' is to be explained by talking about some necessary connexion between calling things good and choosing them. This theory is thought to have the following merits. (1) It seems to distinguish 'good' from such terms as 'yellow' and 'square' without talking about peculiar non-natural properties. (2) It seems to show how a value judgement in general, and a moral judgement in particular, is, as Hume insisted, essentially practical, being supposed 'to influence our passions and actions, and to go beyond the calm and indolent judgments of the understanding'. (*Treatise*, Bk. III, Part 1, Section 1.) (3) It seems to solve the problem of how 'good' can have the same meaning when applied to many diverse things; the relation to choice being offered as the thread on which these different uses are all strung. Nevertheless, the subject is full of obscurities and uncertainties, as we can see if we try to answer questions such as these. (1) Is a connexion with the choices of the speaker ever a *sufficient* condition for the use of the word 'good', as it would be if a man could ever call certain things (let us call them *A*'s) good *A*'s merely because these were the *A*'s which he was thereafter ready to choose? Is there any case in which he could defend his use of the word 'good' by saying, for instance, 'I committed myself to a choice'? Or, if 'committing himself to choosing' is not thought quite the right condition, will it do if he fills in more detail, e.g., about the way he feels if he fails to choose these *A*'s, and how he encourages others to make the same choice? (2) Is it even true to say that a connexion with the choices of the speaker is a *necessary* condition of the use of 'good', or of the use of this word 'in its proper evaluative sense'? Might there not be cases in which calling an *A* a good *A* does not commit one to anything at all in the way of choices, perhaps not even to the admission of any reason for preferring the A's which are good? And where calling an A a good A and choosing it are connected, will they be connected in just the same way for all the different things that A is supposed to be?

I shall first deal with the question of choice as a sufficient condition. Are facts about the speaker's choices ever a sufficient defence for his calling a certain kind of A a good A, no matter what that kind of A may be? No one, I think, would try to maintain such a view quite generally; it is certain that the expression 'a good A' cannot always be used in this way. Such a theory could not be right, for instance, for the use of 'good' in the expression 'a good knife'; the man who uses these words correctly must use them in conjunction with particular criteria of goodness: those which really are the criteria for the goodness of knives. No matter what he may do in the way of choosing knives which are M he cannot say 'M knives are good knives' unless M is a relevant characteristic, or unless he is prepared to show that M knives are also N knives, and N is a characteristic of the right kind. He could not, for example, say that a good knife was the one which rusted quickly, defending his use of the word 'good' by showing that he picked out such knives for his own use. I imagine that almost everyone would agree about this, saying that there are some cases in which the correct use of the expression 'a good A' requires that one set of criteria rather than another should be used for judging the goodness of the things. But many people who would admit this think that in other cases *any* criteria of goodness would be logically possible, so that for some A's the individual calling an A a good A has to decide for himself which characteristics he will take as counting in favour of the goodness of an A. The example which they most often have in mind is that in which 'A' is 'man' or 'action'; for it has seemed to them that moral judgements must be construed in this way. Nevertheless it is supposed that the account given of the use of 'good' in these expressions is one that goes for many other cases as well; indeed the suggestion often seems to be that this is a typical use of 'good', and sometimes other examples are given, as for instance by Hare when he talks about good cacti in *The Language of Morals*.[1] A man is described as having imported a cactus, the first cactus, into his own country, and it is implied that he can decide which of the plants he shall count as good cacti, laying down criteria in respect of such things as size and shape. There is no suggestion of any limits to the criteria which can be criteria of goodness in cacti, and Hare obviously thinks that this is quite an ordinary case of the use of the word 'good'. I shall argue that, on the contrary, it is hard to find any genuine example of this kind, so that if Hare's account of the 'good' in 'good man' were correct then this use of the word would seem to be different from all other cases in which we speak of a good such-and-such. My thesis is not, of course, that criteria for the goodness of each and every kind of thing are determined in the same way as they are determined for such things as knives, but rather that they are always determined, and not a matter for decision. (The only qualification to this statement comes from consideration of the range of cases which I shall call 'competition examples'; these are discussed on pp. 140–2 infra.)

What is peculiar about a word such as 'knife' is that it names an object in respect of its function. This is not to say (simply) that it names an object which has a function, but also that the function is involved in the meaning of the word, and I shall call such words functional in the strong sense. That 'knife' is a functional word in the strong sense is shown by describing another community supposed to have objects exactly like our knives but never used for cutting. To save complications let us suppose that never in the history of this community were knife-shaped objects used as we use knives. These people have objects which look just like knives, are made of the same material and so on, but they only use them for some quite different purpose, such as marking plots of land. If asked whether they had knives we should not say, 'Yes, but they use them for quite different purposes from us', but rather 'No', explaining that they did as a matter of fact have things just like our knives, but that these were actually markers. The equivalent of our word 'knife' would not exist in their language just because they had a word to name these objects indistinguishable by such things as shape and colour from our knives. This is not, of course, to deny that given the use of knives in a particular community one can have things which are, so to speak, degenerate knives, used only as ornaments, hung upon the wall, and perhaps manufactured for this purpose; it is another matter to suppose that in a community which used knife-like objects only for the purpose of ornaments the word which names them would be properly translated as 'knife'.

Where a thing has a function the primary (but by no means necessarily the only) criterion for the goodness of that thing will be that it fulfils its function well. Thus the primary criterion of goodness in a knife is its ability to cut well. If a man goes into a shop and asks for a knife, saying that he wants a good knife, he can be understood as wanting one that cuts well, and since 'knife' is a functional word in the strong sense 'good knives cut well' must be held to be some kind of analytic proposition. Moreover, since 'cutting' is the name of an operation with a particular point, different, for example, from the activity of producing noises by running steel over wood, no one is at liberty to pick on just any kind of cutting to count as cutting well. We may compare the activity of writing, and its connexion with the goodness of pens. The word 'pen' means something used in writing, and writing is making a set of marks designed to be read; so the minimum condition for a good pen is that it writes legibly. One would not know the meaning of the word 'pen' if one did not know that a good pen had to write well, or the meaning of 'writing' without understanding that good writing had to be writing which it was possible to read.[2]

Knives and pens have functions not only because we use them for a central purpose but also because they are manufactured for a specific use. But it is obvious that there are examples of words which, without naming manufactured things, are functional in the strong sense: 'eye', for instance, and 'lung' are words like this. Moreover words can be functional in the 'strong' sense without naming anything that we ourselves use or need. Any part of a plant or animal may have a function, and often we would refuse to call by the same name something that played no part, or a quite different part, in the life of the living thing. Such things as roots and claws are named in this way.

Are there, in fact, any examples of words naming things which have a function without being functional words in the strong sense? I suppose that this would be the case where the function of some organ was discovered, but it was not renamed. We ask, for instance, 'Has the appendix a function?', and an affirmative answer would surely give us a contingent proposition, at least for a time. A good appendix would thereafter be judged by its ability to perform this function well, but we could not be expected to know what, if anything, had to be done well in knowing the meaning of the word.

It has been common for philosophers to call all words which allow one to derive criteria of goodness from their meaning 'functional words'. This is confusing, for it suggests either a quite improper use of the word 'function' or the denial of clear examples for which the condition stated in the last sentence is fulfilled. This may be seen by considering expressions such as 'good farmer', 'good rider' and 'good liar'. Neither 'farmer', 'rider' nor 'liar' picks a man out by reference to a *function*, though of course they name him in respect of something that he does. It would be comic to speak of the function of a rider or a liar, and we can only think of a farmer as having a function if we think of him in some special way, as serving the community. In any ordinary context we should be puzzled if asked for the function of a farmer, thinking the questioner must mean something very odd. But although words such as 'farmer', 'rider' and 'liar' are not functional words, in either the weak or the strong sense, when joined with 'good' they yield criteria of goodness as functional words were seen to do. We say that a man is a good farmer only because of his farming, while what counts as good farming must be e.g., maintaining crops and herds in healthy condition, and obtaining the maximum from the soil. What is good farming will naturally vary somewhat from place to place: a nomadic race could exhaust a piece of land in farming it, though a settled race could not. But within such limits the standards by which farming is judged depend on the meaning of the word, since what counts as farming is only something which has a particular point. If in another community there was an activity (let us call it 'snodding'), and people said that a man snodded well, and was a good snodder, when plants and animals died in his charge, we should not consider translating 'snodding' as 'farming'; perhaps a snodder would be a black magician or something like that. Similarly, a good liar must tell convincing or artistic untruths, and the minimum condition of good riding is an ability to control a horse.

These examples show that the range of words whose meaning determines criteria of goodness is much wider than that of functional words. And perhaps the range is even greater than these examples suggest. We might consider whether, for instance, 'daughter', 'father' and 'friend' might not be added to the list. It might seem that since 'daughter' simply means 'female offspring' nothing is laid down in the language about the criteria of goodness in daughters, as nothing is laid down about the meaning of 'good female offspring'—if this has a meaning at all. Is it, however, true that a word in another language would be translated by our word 'daughter' whatever the criteria of goodness for those named by this name? Does it make sense to say that they speak of good daughters, but judge daughters on quite different grounds? Of course it will depend on the structure of a particular society—its economic arrangements for instance, and its marriage rules—as to just what is expected of daughters, and to this extent at least what counts as being a good daughter can vary from place to place. But surely it is wrong to suppose that even anything expected of a female offspring could be part of what counted when the goodness of a daughter was being weighed. If it were expected, as in Nazi Germany, that a daughter (like a son) should denounce disloyal parents to the police, this still could not be part of being a good *daughter*; a word which combined with 'good' to give this result would be closer to our word 'citizen' or 'patriot'. Only in the context of a belief that denunciation would lead to regeneration could this be seen as one of the things by which the goodness of a daughter could be judged.

'Father' seems to be another word of roughly the same kind; for a man can only be said to be a good father if he looks after his children as best he can. Being a good *father* must have something to do with bringing up children, and more specifically caring for them. While opinions may differ as to what is best for children, and while more or less of the children's care may be assigned to parents in different communities, it is only within such limits that the criteria of a good father will differ from place to place. If, in a certain community, a man were said to be a good *A* in so far as he offered his children up for sacrifice, '*A*' could not be translated by our word 'father', but would be like 'citizen' again, or 'provider of children for the state'. Similarly, a good *friend* must be one who is well disposed towards the man whose friend he is; it makes no sense to say that he would be a good friend in so far as he cheated the other, or left him in the lurch. One interesting point about being a good father, daughter, or friend is that it seems to depend on one's intentions, rather than on such things as cleverness and strength. No one could be counted a bad father because he failed to make a living, though he tried as hard as he could. Similarly, the best of daughters might lack the capacity to provide for aged parents, while good friends are those who want to help us rather than those who actually have the capacity to succeed. This is not to deny that in such a context much may be held against people besides the things they *intended* to do, and that it is hard to know where to draw the line, but if for instance someone were said to be a bad friend on grounds of tactless or obtuse behaviour, it would be a fault of character and not mere lack of cleverness which was involved. On investigation we might decide that 'father', 'daughter' and 'friend' should be called moral terms, especially if we thought that a wholly good man could not be bad in any of these respects.

We have now described two classes of words whose meaning determines criteria of goodness for the things they name: functional words such as 'knife', 'pen', 'eye' and 'root', and non-functional words such as 'farmer', 'liar' and 'father'. This is not, however, the only way in which criteria of goodness are fixed; they can be just as determinate, leaving the individual as little scope for decision, in cases where it would be impossible to get them from the meaning of a word. We have mentioned one example of this kind in speaking of things that have a function, but are not named in respect of their function, and there will be many more. Take, for instance, the word 'coal'. The question is 'What could be counted as good coal?' and the answer seems to be that that depends on what coal happens to be used for. 'Happens to be used for' is the right expression here, though it would not have been had we still been talking about knives or pens. For it makes sense to suppose that in some

other community coal—the same stuff—was mined as we
mine it but used quite differently, for some magical or orna-
mental purpose perhaps. Because of these different purposes,
what counts as good coal here might count as bad coal there,
though within either community prospectors and coal merchants must take these purposes into account in promising
their customers good coal. Within each society the goodness
of coal is settled by the purposes for which coal is used, while
outside such a context it is not clear how anyone could talk
about coal as good or bad at all.

There will obviously be many cases of this sort, where the
criteria of goodness are fixed by the use to which the thing is
usually put; but there is another range of examples rather like
this where it would be better to speak of the interest we have in
something, and what we expect from it, than the use to which
it is put. We do not, for instance, *use* works of literature, or not
normally, and could not say that it is by their use that the
criteria for their goodness are determined. On the other hand,
the interest which we have in books and pictures determines
the grounds on which their excellence is judged. Just as we
cannot consider the question 'Is this a good piece of coal?'
without taking into account the use which we have for coal, so
we cannot consider the criteria of goodness in books and
pictures without noticing the part which literature and art play
in a civilisation such as ours. First of all, we treat works of art
very seriously, and while we may expect to enjoy reading a
good novel or looking at a good picture, we are prepared to
take trouble about them. We study pictures, and may learn
new languages to read works of literature, all of which
depends on the fact that we expect a lot from such things. We
expect them to interest us profoundly, and this must have
something to do with the fact that we are not allowed to give
as support for a judgement of aesthetic merit the mere fact that
a book passes the time easily, or makes us cry, or cheers us up.
That when we speak about a good book or picture we do very
often mean to judge it as a work of art depends on the rôle
which these things have, though perhaps only in the lives of a
minority whose word has become law. Obviously it would be
possible to imagine a society in which things would be quite
different, where, for instance pictures though hung on the

walls were never looked at with concentration except by chance. Pictures might in fact be treated rather as we usually treat wall-paper, as a cheerful background decoration which should not demand full attention for itself. There are thus some similarities between 'a good picture' and a 'good piece of coal', and in neither case can someone seize on anything he likes as the criteria of goodness and badness, justifying his use of the word 'good' by pointing to his own choices. He might resolve to read only novels which would send him to sleep, and might choose them only for this reason, but he could not say that for him this was the characteristic which made a novel a good novel.

This is not, however, to deny that sometimes a particular man's interests determine what is good and bad. For it is always possible to speak of an A as being 'a good A for X's purposes', when the criteria of goodness may be quite different from those by which the goodness of A's is judged. But since it is one thing to speak of 'a good A' and another to speak of 'a good A for so-and-so's purposes' this cannot be used to show anything about the use of the former expression. Nor does it give us a case in which criteria of goodness have to be *decided upon* by the man who uses the word 'good'. He can choose what he will try to do, which games he will play, and so on; but given his purposes, and in general his interests, it is a plain matter of fact that particular A's will be good *for his purposes*, or *from his point of view*. In such a context he will be able to attach the word 'good' even to such things as pebbles or twigs, implying 'for my purposes' or 'for someone playing this game'. But even here it is not by his readiness to pick up the pebbles that he legitimises his words.

Where then are the cases to be found in which someone can simply decide to take anything he likes as criteria of goodness for a certain kind of thing? A perfect example might seem to be that of the show dog pronounced by the judge to be 'better' than others of his breed because of some fancy quality such as length of ears. Here the standard may be simply conventional; it is decided, in some more or less deliberate way, that a twist in the tail or an extra inch on the ears shall be the criterion of goodness in a particular breed. There is usually no point in picking on these characteristics; it is not a matter of beauty or strength in the animal, but simply what we have decided to call 'good'. This case belongs with a number of others which we might call 'competition examples', belonging to the game of 'Let's see who can do this'. Suppose, for instance, that people decide, for a joke, to see who can produce something—say the longest sentence containing only Anglo-Saxon words, or the musical instrument which will produce the lowest note. Then, although there may be no point in having such instruments or such sentences, there is a point in producing one once the competition has been set, and it is by its ability to serve as a good entry in the competition that the sentence or instrument is then judged good. That long ears can be one of the criteria of goodness in a spaniel depends entirely on the competition element in the breeding of show dogs. If we take away this background, and suppose that someone says 'Good spaniels have long ears', it will not be clear what he means. It is true that in such cases a man who is in a special position can lay down standards quite arbitrarily, but he must be in the position of setting the competition, so that when he says 'This is to be the mark of a good X' he means 'This is the target you are to try to hit'. In one sense the man who is allowed to choose the target decides 'what shall be the criterion of a good shot', but in another sense he does not; the criterion of a good shot is that it should hit the target, and he merely chooses what the target shall be.

What has just been said may be applied to the discussion of statements about good cacti in *The Language of Morals*.[3] Hare supposes that someone has just imported the first cactus into the country, and that since no one has ever seen them before no one has yet called one cactus good and another bad. But other people bring them in too, and eventually someone claims that his is a good cactus; he sets up standards for cacti, and people may set up rival standards of their own. This is all quite possible, but what Hare does not give us is the necessary background, and as he describes it, it is not clear how the criteria could be criteria of *goodness* at all. There is no reference to the fact that a cactus is a living organism, which can therefore be called healthy or unhealthy, and a good or bad specimen of its kind. But in that case we must be told what the rôle of the cacti is to be. If they are to be used as ornaments, then good cacti must possess the kind of shape and colour that we find pleasing or curious, and the criteria of goodness are determined by the interest which we have in the things, and not by any standard set up by the importer. If, on the other hand, cacti are to be collected and grown for cactus shows, standards may be *set*, but only by those who are in some special position of authority. In this case we have a 'competition example', and this will hardly seem suitable as a model for the use of 'good' in moral contexts.

The reason why it seems as if choice alone, or some condition connected with choice, might be a sufficient condition for the use of the word 'good' probably lies in certain facts about the concept of choice. Of course choosing is not just pointing at something; for while even pointing is not simply extending one's hand in the direction of a certain object, given our institution of pointing I can say, 'Point to one of the windows in this room' without giving any idea of what if anything is to happen next. Whereas if I said 'Choose one of the windows in this room' the question would be 'For what?' It would hardly count as choosing if people made pointing gestures, or touched particular objects, and nothing followed, or was meant to follow. Nevertheless it may look as if choosing could be just distinguishing, or marking, or separating out, because we are used to games in which people are told for instance to choose a card, and they do not necessarily know what they are choosing it for. But there are two points to notice about this example:

(1) The context of a card trick does tell us roughly the rôle which the chosen card will play, and children who were used to choosing sweets and toys, not knowing about card tricks, might be puzzled when asked to choose a card.

(2) Choosing for a rôle which is kept secret is itself a kind of game. But then the whole point is that X knows the rôle but is keeping it from Y: it is not a case of choosing but not for anything, but rather of choosing 'for whatever X has in mind'.

So when one chooses one chooses for a rôle. One chooses something to have, or to throw away, to sit on, or to put on the mantelpiece; a road to drive down or to have closed. But now the question arises—will anything that happens as the intended consequence of the distinguishing gesture do as the

rôle for which one is choosing the thing? Suppose, for
instance, that someone said 'Choose a window pane for me to
put my finger on' or 'Choose a pebble to have a handkerchief
waved at.' Could these things be the object of choice? One is
inclined to say that choosing is rather the kind of picking out for
a rôle, which has a ground; we choose one thing rather than
another because it has some advantage in the context, as a flat
pebble is best for playing ducks and drakes, and a heavy stone
to stop a car from running downhill. There are, indeed, what
we might call peripheral cases of choosing, when we 'just pick'
a card from the pack for instance, or take any one of a number
of objects which would serve equally well. But a word which
applies *only* to such activities would not properly be translated
by our word 'choice', and we are inclined to say in such cases
that 'there was nothing to choose' between the alternatives. In
any case these are certainly not the examples which we have in
mind when we think that there is a very close connexion
between choosing something and calling it good. For in so far
as the choosing was supposed to be choosing of this kind it is
not guaranteed that the word 'good' will be given an application by the connexion with choice. However strictly a man
might set himself to choose a card in a certain position in the
pack when told to 'choose a card' by someone showing a card
trick, we should not be able to describe him as thinking cards
in this position the best cards or the best cards to take unless he
were prepared to *justify* his choice. And he could do that only
by asserting, for instance, that this was the best card to take in
order to beat the trick. He could never say, 'Those just are, to
my mind, the best ones to take.'

In the beginning we raised two questions about the relation
between choosing something and calling it good, asking
whether some connexion with choice (1) could give a sufficient condition, and (2) was a necessary condition for the
application of the word. The rest of this paper will be about
question (2).

It is very often said that the use of 'good' in its 'proper
evaluative sense' commits a man to choosing the things he
calls good in preference to others, or at least that 'other things
being equal' this what he must do. Such statements are quite
misleading in so far as they suggest that a man is only at liberty

to call an A a good A if he thinks that such A's are A's he has reason to choose. Consider, for example, someone who is choosing a pen. Since a good pen is one which will write well, he will have reason to choose a good pen if he wants to write with it and to write well. But what if his purposes are different? Suppose that he wishes to cover a piece of paper with blots? Perhaps we might say that he is not choosing a pen to write with, and so not as a pen, hoping to keep the connexion between good pens and the pens which a man should choose (other things being equal) if he is choosing a pen as a pen. But there is also the case of the man who wants a pen to write with, but has some reason for wanting to write untidily or illegibly, or to whom it does not matter either way. We could hardly say that he was not choosing a pen as a pen, and he would have no reason to choose a good pen, perhaps rather the reverse. That most men must have a reason to choose good pens depends on the purposes which we take for granted in talking about good and bad pens at all: we cannot suppose that the standard case is that of wanting pens for the creation of blots, or undecipherable marks without dissociating pens from writing, and changing the concept *pen*. The necessary connexion lies here, and not in some convention about what the individual speaker must be ready to choose if he uses the word 'good'.

There seems to be an exact parallel in the case where 'good' is used with a word such as 'rider', naming a man in respect of some activity with a characteristic point. (It is only where the activity has a point that we can speak of a good —er or a bad; there are no good foot-wagglers, or tree-touchers, because nothing counts as doing these things well.) Since the point of riding is pleasure, exercise, or locomotion, riders are judged good or bad by their ability to do such things as staying in the saddle and controlling the horse, with additional requirements of elegance and style. Anyone who shares the typical purposes of the rider has a reason to ride well rather than badly, and will want to be a good rider rather than a bad. But it is quite possible for someone to be riding with different purposes in view; perhaps he wants to play the fool and make people laugh. It is tempting to say that anyone must be called a good rider if he is achieving what he wants, but on reflection one sees that this is not 'the language of mankind'. Good riding is the kind of riding likely to achieve the characteristic purposes of the rider, not those which a particular individual may happen to have.

In such cases the point of the activity lies in something commonly wanted by the man who engages in it, but there are other things normally done for hire. Then the one who hires is the one who has a direct interest in what is done, and will normally want it done well. For instance, someone going to a tailor, or engaging a teacher, will usually have reason to choose a good one, though here again we cannot say that there is a necessary connexion between calling an A a good A and having reasons for choice. For someone may choose a teacher, and even choose him as a teacher—that is with an interest in his teaching—without wanting the teaching to be done well. A wicked uncle choosing a tutor for his nephew would be a case in point.

If this is a correct account of the connexion that there is between calling an A a good A and choosing it where an A is something that we use, or where 'A' is the name of a man who does something that he or others want done, it is not surprising that the word 'good' can sometimes be used without any implications for choice. For where there is no connexion with anything that we use, or need, or want doing, the A that is called good may be one that *no one* has reason to choose. We say, in a straightforward way, that a tree has good roots, meaning by this that they are well suited to the performance of their function, serving the plant by anchoring it and drawing moisture out of the soil. Our interests are not involved, and only someone in the grip of a theory would insist that when we speak of a good root we commit ourselves in some way to choosing a root like that. Nor do we need to look for such a connexion in order to find 'what is common' to the different cases where we apply the word 'good'. Because the root plays a part in the life of the organism we can say 'it has a function', relating what it does to the welfare of the plant. And good roots are like good eyes, good pens, and many other things that are good, in being of the kind to perform their function well.

If someone should say that in the expression 'a good root' 'good' is not used 'evaluatively' this would only increase the artificiality of the notion of 'evaluation' as used in moral philosophy, and it would raise a number of awkward problems as well. For if the 'good' in 'good roots' is said to lack 'evaluative meaning' because good roots are not things that we should have any reason to choose, then presumably 'good claws' and 'good fangs' are expressions which must be treated in the same way. But then we shall be in difficulties over examples such as 'good eyes', 'good muscles' and 'good stomachs'. We could hardly say that the meaning of 'good' changes when the word is applied to those parts of organisms which can belong to our bodies; it would seem therefore that if 'good roots' and 'good claws' are non-evaluative expressions, 'good eyes' must be the same.

Nor is it easy to see how a distinction between 'evaluative' and 'non-evaluative' uses of 'good' would be applied in cases such as that of the good pen. I suppose it would be said that one who, wanting to write illegibly, rejected the pen he called a good pen, must use the word in its 'non-evaluative sense'. This case might seem easy to decide, but what of a man discussing the merits of something like a pen or a motor car in the abstract, as people often do? What criteria would we introduce for deciding whether he was using 'good' evaluatively or not? Should we take into account his last choice, or his next choice, or the choices he made in the majority of cases, or what he thought he would choose if he were to choose just now? If he himself had no use for the kind of thing under discussion the last clause would lack a definite sense. And in any case it seems entirely arbitrary, and unimportant, that any particular decision should be made. The man who calls roots good roots uses 'good' in a straightforward sense, which has nothing to do with the irony or reported speech marked by the use of inverted commas. So too does the man who calls a pen a good pen, and says that being a good one it is not one that he has any reason to choose.

The conclusion seems to be that a connexion with the choices of the speaker is not a necessary condition of the use of the word 'good' in its ordinary sense. If a man who calls an A a good A has reason, other things being equal, to prefer it to other A's, this is because of the kind of thing that an A is, and its connexion with his wants and needs. It is clear that most people will have reason to choose good pens and good knives if they are choosing pens and knives, and that they will have reason to try to ride well if they are riding, and to tell good lies if they are going in for lying. But this is because the word 'good' is here joined to the name of objects or activities which are characteristically chosen with given ends in view. It is not nearly so easy to see just when someone will have reason for choosing to be, or to have, a good A where 'A' is e.g., 'parent' or 'daughter' or 'friend'. Since the most basic needs and desires are involved here it is not at all surprising that the word 'good' should have an application in cases like these; but while there will often be obvious reason to be given for choosing to be, or to have, a good A, when 'A' is a word in this range, it is impossible to say offhand how far these reasons will extend. Anyone may properly ask why he should choose to have, or to be, the kind of A he has called a good A, and we may or may not be able to give him a reply.

NOTES

* 'Goodness and Choice' originally appeared in *The Aristotelian Society Supplementary Volume*, 1961.

[1] Pp. 96–7.

[2] Things are not, of course, really as simple as this paragraph might suggest. Some people (hunters, for instance) use their knives as much for stabbing as cutting, and cutting will not be the primary function of their knives. There are also derivative concepts such as 'palette-knife' to be explained. But I do not think that complications of this kind will affect my main point.

[3] Pp. 96–7.

X
Reasons for Action and Desires*

Mr. Woods wants to disprove a certain theory of what it is for an agent to have a reason for acting.[1] This theory is the one that makes reasons dependent on desires, saying that every statement of a reason, when fully spelled out, must contain a reference to something wanted or desired by the person whose reason it is to be. As an account of sufficient conditions this is quite implausible, as Mr. Woods shows. Nevertheless it might truly state a necessary condition, and it is to this suggestion that Mr. Woods addresses himself. He wants to show, by producing examples, that there are reasons for acting not dependent on the agent's desires.

Two questions arise, first whether Mr. Woods is right in rejecting the theory he rejects, and secondly whether his arguments are sound. It will be argued here that the answer to the first question is 'yes' and the answer to the second 'no'. I shall first give my own counter-example and then go on to say why I reject those put forward by Mr. Woods.

Prudential reasons seem to me to provide the most obvious counter-examples to the thesis that all reasons for action depend on the agent's desires. By 'prudential reasons' I mean those having to do with the agent's interests. There are, of course, problems about the limits of this class, but these need not concern us here. It will be enough to take some uncontroversial example of a prudential reason.

Let us, then, consider the case of a man who knows he will go hungry tomorrow unless he goes shopping today. We will suppose that circumstances are normal; he has no reason for wanting to be hungry tomorrow, and his house is not on fire. He has a prudential reason for visiting the shops. Now according to the theory we are discussing, the statement of his reason, if fully spelled out, must contain a reference to one of his desires. What desire will this be? The desire *not to be hungry tomorrow* seems the most obvious candidate. For we may tell ourselves that this is the desire that will be present in every case. We should pause, however, and ask why we say that the man who has reason to go shopping today has a *desire* not to be hungry tomorrow. Do we find ourselves, in such circumstances, with thoughts and feelings that allow us to speak of 'desire'? Sometimes this is exactly how it is; the prospect of tomorrow fills us with anxiety and apprehension, together with a lively hope that the evil may be averted. But in most ordinary cases we would have nothing of the kind to report; it is not on such grounds that we can speak of a desire, and if reasons depended on such things there would be few reasons indeed. Yet surely we cannot deny that when a man goes shopping today because otherwise he will be hungry tomorrow he wants, or has a desire to, avoid being hungry? This is true, but an analysis of the use of expressions such as 'want' and 'has a desire to' in such contexts shows that these 'desires' cannot be the basis of the reason for acting. Thomas Nagel, in an excellent discussion of prudence, has explained the matter in the following way:

That I have the appropriate desire simply *follows* from the fact that these considerations motivate me; if the likelihood that an act will promote my future happiness motivates me to perform it now, then it is appropriate to ascribe to me a desire for my own future happiness (*The Possibility of Altruism* (O.U.P., 1970) pp. 29–30).

What we have here is a use of 'desire' which indicates a motivational direction and nothing more. One may compare it with the use of 'want' in 'I want to φ' where only intentionality is implied. Can *wanting* in this sense create the reason for acting? It seems that it cannot. For in the first place the desires of which we are now speaking are to be attributed to the agent only in case he is moved to action, or would be so moved in the absence of counteracting reasons or causes, and it is a mistake to set corresponding limits to the scope of reasons for acting. Moreover a false account is given even of the cases in which action occurs. For what happens there is that a man is moved to action by the recognition that he has reason to act. This would be impossible if there were not reason to be recognised until the agent has been moved.[2]

It seems, then, that the agent's present desire to avert the future evil cannot be the basis of his prudential reason for acting. Would it be more plausible to suggest that it is on future desires that prudential reasons depend? It might be said, for instance, that suffering is something we necessarily want away *at the time we are suffering*, so the thought of future suffering contains the thought of future desire. Whether or not it is right to see a connexion as close as this between every prudential consideration and future desire, the theory seems to put the emphasis in the wrong place. For it is not as implying a desire, but rather *as suffering*, that future pain is something we have reason to avoid. If we postulate the future desire alone it is not at all certain that a reason for action in the present remains, as we can see by considering the case of future *whims*. Suppose we believe today that tomorrow we shall want to do something, which will, however, be a mere whim. Suppose, moreover, that we do not expect to get pleasure from the satisfaction of our whim, and do not think we will feel frustrated or annoyed if the whim is not gratified. Have we any reason to make provision now for the satisfaction of this future desire? We are inclined to say that we have not; at the very least our intuitions become uncertain, and even this suggests that in stripping down to future desire we have not reached the essential factor in prudential reasoning.

Mr. Woods himself did not discuss prudential reasons except as refuting the suggestion that reasons must necessarily move to action. I hope he may agree with most of what I have said up to this point. But whether or not he thinks that prudential reasons could be used as a counter-example to the thesis that statements of reason, when fully spelled out, must contain a reference to the desires of the person for whom they are to be reasons, he himself relied on examples of another kind. He believes that the theory can be refuted by showing that moral beliefs, aesthetic opinions and 'evaluative beliefs in general' give reasons that are not dependent on the agent's desires. I want to show that Mr. Woods is mistaken in thinking that evaluative beliefs give reasons in this special way. They have a special connexion with reasons for action, but this depends on their special connexions with interests and desires.

How then, do evaluative judgements give reasons for acting? Let us put aside moral and aesthetic examples for the moment, and look at familiar everyday instances of evaluation outside these fields. We may think, for instance, about good doctors and good philosophers, good arguments and good parties, good houses and good land. If a patient has a reason to choose a good doctor, and a tenant a good house, why is this so? Obviously it is because the qualities by which a doctor is judged a good doctor, and a house a good house, are those which make them useful to patients and tenants respectively. Good qualities are exactly those which are of some interest or use, and it is not surprising that *someone* has a reason to choose good F's and good G's where F's and G's are the kind of things one can choose. In general very many people will have reason to choose to have good ones, or, in some cases, to choose to be good ones, since the good will be judged from some standard point of view. But not everyone will have these reasons, since he may not have standard desires and interests, and may not be the one whose desires and interests are taken into account. There is no magical reason-giving force in evaluative judgements, and it would be ludicrous carefully to choose a good F or a good G, rather than a bad F or a bad G, if one's own desires and interests were not such as to provide a reason in one's own case.

The reason-giving force of aesthetic judgement has a similar dependence on interests and desires. A man has reason to read an interesting book just so far as he thinks it will interest him, or if he expects the reading to be pleasing or profitable in some other way. The idea that one should have good works of art around just because they are good works of art, and even if one can get nothing from them, must depend on hopes of improvement in one's taste. This is probably bad policy, and in any case does nothing to support the thesis that aesthetic beliefs provide reasons for action that are independent of what the agent wants.

Are moral evaluations linked with reasons for acting only when connected with the agent's interests and desires? There are many who will refuse to admit that it is so, agreeing with

Mr. Woods at least so far as this class of evaluations is concerned. It seems to them essential that moral considerations give reason for acting to each and every man, and they rightly say that such universal reasons cannot be provided for moral action if the basis is interest and desire. Why, however, do they insist that each and every man whatever his situation and whatever his nature, must have reason to do what morality requires? Is there perhaps some confusion between the moral judgement, which undoubtedly stands for any man, and the judgement about reasons which may not? Or is it that they want to be able to call a wicked, amoral man irrational, as if by that they can hit him where it will hurt? Some would admit that the cool, calculating, amoral man is not to be called *irrational*, but nevertheless say that he has reason to act morally whatever his interests and desires. This seems to be an inconsistent position, as we may show in the following way.

Suppose a man to assert these propositions:

A. 1. I have a reason to do action *a*.
    2. I have no reason not to do *a*.
    3. I am not going to do *a*.

From these premises he must conclude

    4. I am going to act irrationally.

On the other hand the following are admitted consistent:

B. 1. I shall act immorally unless I do *a*.
    2. I have no reason not to do *a*.
    3. I am not going to do *a*.
    4. I am not going to act irrationally.

We can show by a simple argument that when B. 1–4 are true, A. 1 is false; from which it follows that B. 1 cannot entail A. 1.

What proof can be given of the special reason-giving force of moral considerations? What is its source supposed to be? Mr. Woods is impressed by the fact that moral judgement, and evaluation generally, is connected with 'intelligible human pursuits and practices'. But as we saw in discussing non-moral evaluations this will not guarantee that every man has a reason to choose what is properly called good. Perhaps good men are those who have qualities useful to society not to themselves; perhaps it is others who have reason to want them to be good? Or perhaps it is sometimes one and sometimes another, with no guarantee that on each occasion each man will have reason to do what morality requires.

Why is it, one may ask, that these particular evaluations—moral evaluations—are supposed by so many people to be different from the rest? The reason why they should be *thought* to be different is not hard to find. For moral judgements are not only evaluative but also normative. Moral language is used not simply to pick out actions and qualities which are of interest or use, but also to teach that these actions should be performed, and these qualities acquired. Moral behaviour is the subject of social teaching and social demand. There is thus no doubt that people are taught to *take* moral considerations as reasons for acting, without any reference to what they want, or what their interests are. They are to say 'It's immoral, so I won't do it' or 'Justice requires that I act in this way, so that is what I shall do'. This kind of teaching explains why it should be thought that moral judgements give reasons for acting which are independent of interests and desires, but it does nothing to prove that it is so. For we certainly do not think that independent reasons could be created by social pressures, and elsewhere we are quite ready to throw over the rules of behaviour that we were taught when we were young. We were taught, for instance, that we should follow rules of etiquette. Later we ask whether there is any reason to do what we were taught.

It may be suggested that we are looking for the special connexion between reason for acting and morality in the wrong place. Perhaps it is to be found not in the form of moral judgements but rather in their content. Morality, or a large part of morality, has to do with a man's actions so far as these affect other men for good or ill. If it can be shown that we have reason to aim at the good of others, as much as we have reason to aim at our own, then we shall have reason to follow a great many of morality's laws. Theories have, of course, been constructed along these lines. A version of the argument was put forward by G. E. Moore in the following well known passage:

. . . The only reason I can have for aiming at 'my own good' is that it is *good absolutely* that what I so call should belong to me . . . But if it is *good absolutely* that I should have it, then everyone else has as much reason for aiming at *my* having it, as I have myself (*Principia Ethica* (Cambridge, 1903) p. 99).

What Moore is saying is that if I have reason to promote state *S* then *it is good* that state *S* comes about, and if *it is good* that *S* comes about then anyone has reason to promote *S*. The argument is faulty because there is no such thing as an objectively good *state of affairs*. Such constructions as 'a good state of affairs', 'a good thing that *p*', are used subjectively, to mark what fits in with the aims and interests of a particular indi-vidual or group. Divorced from such a background these expressions lose their sense, and an argument of the type that Moore suggested will not, for this reason, go through.

Thomas Nagel, who has recently argued the case against rational egoism with much subtlety, employs what is basically the same argument as Moore's. When anyone has a reason for bringing anything about there has to be a reason for that thing 'to happen', and Nagel says that in acting for a reason one must be able to regard oneself as 'promoting an objectively valuable end' (*The Possibility of Altruism* (O.U.P. 1970) pp. 96–7). But if it means nothing to speak of an 'objectively valuable end' then there are no reasons such as Nagel describes and I may say that another has reason to aim at his own good without implying that I too have reason to promote this end.

It seems, then, that we lack a convincing argument for the special, automatic reason–giving force of moral judgement, and should be prepared to think that moral considerations give reasons for action only in ordinary ways. Can we explain how men do have reasons for acting morally if we confine ourselves to reasons based on interests and desires? It seems that we can do so, and that without placing too much emphasis on self-interested reasons for doing what ought to be done. One does not want to deny a general connexion between virtue and happiness, but no one who acts justly or charitably only where it pays him to do so will qualify as a just or benevolent man. A moral man must be ready to go against his interests in the particular case, and if he has reason to act morally the reason will lie rather in what he wants than in what is to his advan-tage. On this basis reasons will exist for many kind and upright men. We readily accept private affection as giving reasons for actions without the least hint of self-interest; why should a more extended fellow-feeling not do the same? If a man has that basic sense of identification with others that makes him care whether or not they live wretched lives, has he not the best possible reason for charitable action? And would it not be misrepresentation to speak of this as a charity dependent on the feelings and inclinations of the moment, since both public and private affections endure through periods of coldness, and lack of inclination never destroys the reason to act?

The case of justice may be thought to present greater difficulties for such an account of moral reasons for acting, since justice is notoriously not to be reduced to benevolence, and a man's affections, however extended, would not necessarily lead him to be just. Two different types of example have to be considered. There is first the case where the life or liberty of an individual is set against the good of the majority. This seems to pose no special problems. There are some who have a special concern for those who are vulnerable to oppression, and one who is a lover of justice will be a man such as this. The second case is more puzzling: it is that of Hume's profligate creditor to whom a debt should be paid though no good is foreseen. Why does anyone think that he has reason to be honest in such a case? It could be mere superstition. Perhaps we have been bewitched by the idea that we *just do* have reason to obey this part of our moral code. But such a suggestion may well be wrong. It seems that we cannot get on well without the kind of justice that is 'without reason' in the particular case. We need *just men* who are prepared to follow rules of justice even where these are not coincident with any benevolence, and men act justly because they believe that this is so. We should also take into account, here and elsewhere, the desires that people have to live a certain kind of life. Of course these desires vary greatly from person to person. One man likes to be useful; another demands a part in some great or noble cause. Perhaps it will be said that such people choose the life they choose because they think they *ought* to do so—because this is how a man ought to live. But perhaps no such thought, with its problematic reason-giving force, enters into the matter at all. Without any moral imperatives a man may have such desires.

POSTSCRIPT

I am sure that I do not understand the idea of a reason for acting, and I wonder whether anyone else does either. I myself incline to the view that all such reasons depend either on the agent's interest (meaning here what is in his interest) or else on his desires. I take these to be independent sources of reasons for action, so that the fact that a man is indifferent to his future welfare does not destroy the reason he has for paying attention to it, but this particular thesis is not one on which I place any importance. Perhaps all reasons for action are desire-dependent, even if some Humean arguments for it are faulty.

Is it not, however, possible that if we come to understand reasons for action better we shall find that some are dependent neither upon the agent's interests nor upon his desires? Indeed it is possible, and then it is possible that moral considerations will be found to be reasons of this kind. I do not claim to have shown that it is not so, but rather that no one has offered any valid argument for the proposition that moral considerations have an automatic reason-giving force, and that until such arguments are given it merely expresses a pious hope.

I should add here, that I have never at any time held an egoistic theory of human action, or thought that all reasons for action were in some sense self-interested. Nor have I thought that a means–ends model was suitable for all cases of acting for a reason.

NOTES

* 'Reasons for Action and Desires' originally appeared in *The Aristotelian Society Supplementary Volume*, 1972.

1 Michael Woods, 'Reasons for Actions and Desires', *Aristotelian Society Supp. Vol.*, 1972.

2 This paragraph did not make my point as clearly as it should have done. The fact that if I go to the shops in order not to be hungry tomorrow I can *ipso facto* be said to have a desire not to be hungry tomorrow cannot show that reasons are necessarily based on desires. For it seems reasonable to say that I have the reason even in the absence of this, or any other, ground for attributing the desire.

XI

Morality as a System of Hypothetical Imperatives*

There are many difficulties and obscurities in Kant's moral philosophy, and few contemporary moralists will try to defend it all. Many, for instance, agree in rejecting Kant's derivation of duties from the mere form of the law expressed in terms of a universally legislative will. Nevertheless, it is generally supposed, even by those who would not dream of calling themselves his followers, that Kant established one thing beyond doubt—namely, the necessity of distinguishing moral judgements from hypothetical imperatives. That moral judgements cannot be hypothetical imperatives has come to seem an unquestionable truth. It will be argued here that it is not.

In discussing so thoroughly Kantian a notion as that of the hypothetical imperative, one naturally begins by asking what Kant himself meant by a hypothetical imperative, and it may be useful to say a little about the idea of an imperative as this appears in Kant's works. In writing about imperatives Kant seems to be thinking at least as much of statements about what ought to be or should be done, as of injunctions expressed in the imperative mood. He even describes as an imperative the assertion that it would be 'good to do or refrain from doing something'[1] and explains that for a will that 'does not always do something simply because it is presented to it as a good thing to do' this has the force of a command of reason. We may therefore think of Kant's imperatives as statements to the effect that something ought to be done or that it would be good to do it.

The distinction between hypothetical imperatives and

categorical imperatives, which plays so important a part in Kant's ethics, appears in characteristic form in the following passages from the *Foundations of the Metaphysics of Morals*:

All imperatives command either hypothetically or categorically. The former present the practical necessity of a possible action as a means to achieving something else which one desires (or which one may possibly desire). The categorical imperative would be one which presented an action as of itself objectively necessary, without regard to any other end.[2]

If the action is good only as a means to something else, the imperative is hypothetical; but if it is thought of as good in itself, and hence as necessary in a will which of itself conforms to reason as the principle of this will, the imperative is categorical.[3]

The hypothetical imperative, as Kant defines it, 'says only that the action is good to some purpose' and the purpose, he explains, may be possible or actual. Among imperatives related to actual purposes Kant mentions rules of prudence, since he believes that all men necessarily desire their own happiness. Without committing ourselves to this view it will be useful to follow Kant in classing together as 'hypothetical imperatives' those telling a man what he ought to do because (or if) he wants something and those telling him what he ought to do on grounds of self-interest. Common opinion agrees with Kant in insisting that a moral man must accept a rule of duty whatever his interests or desires.[4]

Having given a rough description of the class of Kantian hypothetical imperatives it may be useful to point to the heterogeneity within it. Sometimes what a man should do depends on his passing inclination, as when he wants his coffee hot and should warm the jug. Sometimes it depends on some long-term project, when the feelings and inclinations of the moment are irrelevant. If one wants to be a respectable philosopher one should get up in the mornings and do some work, though just at that moment when one should do it the thought of being a respectable philosopher leaves one cold. It is true nevertheless to say of one, at that moment, that one wants to be a respectable philosopher,[5] and this can be the foundation of a desire-dependent hypothetical imperative.

The term 'desire' as used in the original account of the hypothetical imperative was meant as a grammatically convenient substitute for 'want', and was not meant to carry any implication of inclination rather than long-term aim or project. Even the word 'project', taken strictly, introduces undesirable restrictions. If someone is devoted to his family or his country or to any cause, there are certain things he wants, which may then be the basis of hypothetical imperatives, without either inclinations or projects being quite what is in question. Hypothetical imperatives should already be appearing as extremely diverse; a further important distinction is between those that concern an individual and those that concern a group. The desires on which a hypothetical imperative is dependent may be those of one man, or may be taken for granted as belonging to a number of people engaged in some common project or sharing common aims.

Is Kant right to say that moral judgements are categorical, not hypothetical, imperatives? It may seem that he is, for we find in our language two different uses of words such as 'should' and 'ought', apparently corresponding to Kant's hypothetical and categorical imperatives, and we find moral judgements on the 'categorical' side. Suppose, for instance, we have advised a traveller that he should take a certain train, believing him to be journeying to his home. If we find that he has decided to go elsewhere, we will most likely have to take back what we said: the 'should' will now be unsupported and in need of support. Similarly, we must be prepared to withdraw our statement about what he should do if we find that the right relation does not hold between the action and the end—that it is either no way of getting what he wants (or doing what he wants to do) or not the most eligible among possible means. The use of 'should' and 'ought' in moral contexts is, however, quite different. When we say that a man should do something and intend a moral judgement we do not have to back up what we say by considerations about his interests or his desires; if no such connexion can be found the 'should' need not be withdrawn. It follows that the agent cannot rebut an assertion about what, morally speaking, he should do by showing that the action is not ancillary to his interests or desires. Without such a connexion the 'should' does not stand unsupported and in need of support;[6] the support that *it* requires is of another kind.[7]

There is, then, one clear difference between moral judgements and the class of 'hypothetical imperatives' so far discussed. In the latter 'should' is 'used hypothetically', in the sense defined, and if Kant were merely drawing attention to this piece of linguistic usage his point would easily be proved. But obviously Kant meant more than this; in describing moral judgements as non-hypothetical—that is, categorical imperatives—he is ascribing to them a special dignity and necessity which this usage cannot give. Modern philosophers follow Kant in talking, for example, about the 'unconditional requirement' expressed in moral judgements. These, they say, tell us what we have to do whatever our interests or desires, and by their inescapability they are distinguished from hypothetical imperatives.

The problem is to find proof for this further feature of moral judgements. If anyone fails to see the gap that has to be filled it will be useful to point out to him that we find 'should' used non-hypothetically in some non-moral statements to which no one attributes the special dignity and necessity conveyed by the description 'categorical imperative'. For instance, we find this non-hypothetical use of 'should' in sentences enunciating rules of etiquette, as, for example, that an invitation in the third person should be answered in the third person, where the rule does not *fail to apply* to someone who has his own good reasons for ignoring this piece of nonsense, or who simply does not care about what, from the point of view of etiquette, he should do. Similarly, there is a non-hypothetical use of 'should' in contexts where something like a club rule is in question. The club secretary who has told a member that he should not bring ladies into the smoking-room does not say, 'Sorry, I was mistaken' when informed that this member is resigning tomorrow and cares nothing about his reputation in the club. Lacking a connexion with the agent's desires or interests, this 'should' does not stand 'unsupported and in need of support'; it requires only the backing of the rule. The use of 'should' is therefore 'non-hypothetical' in the sense defined.

It follows that if a hypothetical use of 'should' gave a hypothetical imperative, and a non-hypothetical use of 'should' a categorical imperative, then 'should' statements based on rules of etiquette, or rules of a club would be categorical imperatives. Since this would not be accepted by defenders of the categorical imperative in ethics, who would insist that these other 'should' statements give hypothetical imperatives, they must be using this expression in some other sense. We must therefore ask what they mean when they say that 'You should answer . . . in the third person' is a hypothetical imperative. Very roughly the idea seems to be that one may reasonably ask why anyone should bother about what should (from the point of view of etiquette) be done, and that such considerations deserve no notice unless reason is shown. So although people give as their reason for doing something the fact that it is required by etiquette, we do not take this consideration as *in itself giving us reason to act*. Considerations of etiquette do not have any automatic reason-giving force, and a man might be right if he denied that he had reason to do 'what's done'.

This seems to take us to the heart of the matter, for, by contrast, it is supposed that moral considerations necessarily give reasons for acting to any man. The difficulty is, of course, to defend this proposition which is more often repeated than explained. Unless it is said, implausibly, that all 'should' or 'ought' statements give reasons for acting, which leaves the old problem of assigning a special categorical status to moral judgement, we must be told what it is that makes the moral 'should' relevantly different from the 'shoulds' appearing in normative statements of other kinds.[8] Attempts have sometimes been made to show that some kind of irrationality is involved in ignoring the 'should' of morality: in saying 'Immoral—so what?' as one says 'Not *comme il faut*—so what?' But as far as I can see these have all rested on some illegitimate assumption, as, for instance, of thinking that the amoral man, who agrees that some piece of conduct is immoral but takes no notice of that, is inconsistently disregarding a rule of conduct that he has accepted; or again of thinking it inconsistent to desire that others will not do to one what one proposes to do to them. The fact is that the man who rejects morality because he sees no reason to obey its rules can be convicted of villainy but not of inconsistency. Nor will his action necessarily be irrational. Irrational actions are those in which a man in some way defeats his own purposes, doing what is calculated to be disadvantageous or to frustrate his ends. Immorality does not *necessarily* involve any such thing.

It is obvious that the normative character of moral judgement does not guarantee its reason-giving force. Moral judgements are normative, but so are judgements of manners, statements of club rules, and many others. Why should the first provide reasons for acting as the others do not? In every case it is because there is a background of teaching that the non-hypothetical 'should' can be used. The behaviour is required, not simply recommended, but the question remains as to why we should do what we are required to do. It is true that moral rules are often enforced much more strictly than the rules of etiquette, and our reluctance to press the non-hypothetical 'should' of etiquette may be one reason why we think of the rules of etiquette as hypothetical imperatives. But are we then to say that there is nothing behind the idea that moral judgements are categorical imperatives but the relative stringency of our moral teaching? I believe that this may have more to do with the matter than the defenders of the categorical imperative would like to admit. For if we look at the kind of thing that is said in its defence we may find ourselves puzzled about what the words can even mean unless we connect them with the feelings that this stringent teaching implants. People talk, for instance, about the 'binding force' of morality, but it is not clear what this means if not that we *feel* ourselves unable to escape. Indeed the 'inescapability' of moral requirements is often cited when they are being contrasted with hypothetical imperatives. No one, it is said, escapes the requirements of ethics by having or not having particular interests or desires. Taken in one way this only reiterates the contrast between the 'should' of morality and the hypothetical 'should', and once more places morality alongside of etiquette. Both are inescapable in that behaviour does not cease to offend against either morality or etiquette because the agent is indifferent to their purposes and to the disapproval he will incur by flouting them. But morality is supposed to be inescapable in some special way and this may turn out to be merely the reflection of the way morality is taught. Of course, we must try other ways of expressing the fugitive thought. It may be said, for instance, that moral judgements have a kind of necessity since they tell us what we 'must do' or 'have to do' whatever our interests and desires. The sense of this is, again, obscure. Sometimes when we use such expressions we are referring to physical or mental compulsion. (A man has to go along if he is pulled by strong men and he has to give in if tortured beyond endurance.) But it is only in the absence of such conditions that moral judgements apply. Another and more common sense of the words is found in sentences such as 'I caught a bad cold and had to stay in bed' where a penalty for acting otherwise is in the offing. The necessity of acting morally is not, however, supposed to depend on such penalties. Another range of examples, not necessarily having to do with penalties, is found where there is an unquestioned acceptance of some project or rôle, as when a nurse tells us that she has to make her rounds at a certain time, or we say that we have to run for a certain train.[9] But these too are irrelevant in the present context, since the acceptance condition can always be revoked.

No doubt it will be suggested that it is in some other sense of the words 'have to' or 'must' that one has to or must do what morality demands. But why should one insist that there must be such a sense when it proves so difficult to say what it is? Suppose that what we take for a puzzling thought were really no thought at all but only the reflection of our *feelings* about morality? Perhaps it makes no sense to say that we 'have to' submit to the moral law, or that morality is 'inescapable' in some special way. For just as one may feel as if one is falling without believing that one is moving downward, so one may feel as if one has to do what is morally required without believing oneself to be under physical or psychological compulsion, or about to incur a penalty if one does not comply. No one thinks that if the word 'falling' is used in a statement reporting one's sensations it must be used in a special sense. But this kind of mistake may be involved in looking for the special sense in which one 'has to' do what morality demands. There is no difficulty about the idea that we feel we *have to* behave morally, and given the psychological conditions of the learning of moral behaviour it is natural that we should have such feelings. What we cannot do is quote them in support of the doctrine of the categorical imperative. It seems, then, that in so far as it is backed up by statements to the effect that the moral law *is* inescapable, or that we *do* have to do what is morally required of us, it is uncertain whether the doctrine of the categorical imperative even makes sense.

The conclusion we should draw is that moral judgements have no better claim to be categorical imperatives than do statements about matters of etiquette. People may indeed follow either morality or etiquette without asking why they should do so, but equally well they may not. They may ask for reasons and may reasonably refuse to follow either if reasons are not to be found.

It will be said that this way of viewing moral considerations must be totally destructive of morality, because no one could ever act morally unless he accepted such considerations as in themselves sufficient reason for action. Actions that are truly moral must be done 'for their own sake', 'because they are right', and not for some ulterior purpose. This argument we must examine with care, for the doctrine of the categorical imperative has owed much to its persuasion.

Is there anything to be said for the thesis that a truly moral man acts 'out of respect for the moral law' or that he does what is morally right because it is morally right? That such propositions are not prima facie absurd depends on the fact that moral judgement concerns itself with a man's reasons for acting as well as with what he does. Law and etiquette require only that certain things are done or left undone, but no one is counted as charitable if he gives alms 'for the praise of men', and one who is honest only because it pays him to be honest does not have the virtue of honesty. This kind of consideration was crucial in shaping Kant's moral philosophy. He many times contrasts acting out of respect for the moral law with acting from an ulterior motive, and what is more from one that is self-interested. In the early *Lectures on Ethics* he gave the principle of truth-telling under a system of hypothetical imperatives as that of not lying *if it harms one* to lie. In the *Metaphysics of Morals* he says that ethics cannot start from the ends which a man may propose to himself, since these are all 'selfish'.[10] In the *Critique of Practical Reason* he argues explicitly that when acting not out of respect for moral law but 'on a material maxim' men do what they do for the sake of pleasure or happiness.

All material practical principles are, as such, of one and the same kind and belong under the general principle of self love or one's own happiness.[11]

Kant, in fact, was a psychological hedonist in respect of all actions except those done for the sake of the moral law, and this faulty theory of human nature was one of the things preventing him from seeing that moral virtue might be compatible with the rejection of the categorical imperative.

If we put this theory of human action aside, and allow as ends the things that seem to be ends, the picture changes. It will surely be allowed that quite apart from thoughts of duty a man may care about the suffering of others, having a sense of identification with them, and wanting to help if he can. Of course he must want not the reputation of charity, nor even a gratifying rôle helping others, but, quite simply, their good. If this is what he does care about, then he will be attached to the end proper to the virtue of charity and a comparison with someone acting from an ulterior motive (even a respectable ulterior motive) is out of place. Nor will the conformity of his action to the rule of charity be merely contingent. Honest action may happen to further a man's career; charitable actions do not *happen* to further the good of others.[12]

Can a man accepting only hypothetical imperatives possess other virtues besides that of charity? Could he be just or honest? This problem is more complex because there is no end related to such virtues as the good of others is related to charity. But what reason could there be for refusing to call a man a just man if he acted justly because he loved truth and liberty, and wanted every man to be treated with a certain respect? And why should the truly honest man not follow honesty for the sake of the good that honest dealing brings to men? Of course, the usual difficulties can be raised about the rare case in which no good is foreseen from an individual act of honesty. But it is not evident that a man's desires could not give him reason to act honestly even here. He wants to live openly and in good faith with his neighbours; it is not all the same to him to lie and conceal.

If one wants to know whether there could be a truly moral man who accepted moral principles as hypothetical rules of conduct, as many people accept rules of etiquette as hypothetical rules of conduct, one must consider the right kind of example. A man who demanded that morality should be brought under the heading of self-interest would not be a good candidate, nor would anyone who was ready to be charitable or honest only so long as he felt inclined. A cause such as justice makes strenuous demands, but this is not peculiar to morality, and men are prepared to toil to achieve many ends not endorsed by morality. That they are prepared to fight so hard for moral ends—for example, for liberty and justice—depends on the fact that these are the kinds of ends that arouse devotion. To sacrifice a great deal for the sake of etiquette one would need to be under the spell of the emphatic 'ought'. One could hardly be devoted to behaving *comme il faut*.

In spite of all that has been urged in favour of the hypothetical imperative in ethics, I am sure that many people will be unconvinced and will argue that one element essential to moral virtue is still missing. This missing feature is the recognition of a *duty* to adopt those ends which we have attributed to the moral man. We have said that he *does* care about others, and about causes such as liberty and justice; that it is on this account that he will accept a system of morality. But what if he never cared about such things, or what if he ceased to care? Is it not the case that he *ought* to care? This is exactly what Kant would say, for though at times he sounds as if he thought that morality is not concerned with ends, at others he insists that the adoption of ends such as the happiness of others is itself dictated by morality.[13] How is this proposition to be regarded by one who rejects all talk about the binding force of the moral law? He will agree that a moral man has moral ends and cannot be indifferent to matters such as suffering and injustice. Further, he will recognise in the statement that one *ought* to care about these things a correct application of the non-hypothetical moral 'ought' by which society is apt to voice its demands. He will not, however, take the fact that he ought to have certain ends as in itself reason to adopt them. If he himself is a moral man then he cares about such things, but not 'because he ought'. If he is an amoral man he may deny that he has any reason to trouble his head over this or any other moral demand. Of course he may be mistaken, and his life as well as others' lives may be most sadly spoiled by his selfishness. But this is not what is urged by those who think they can close the matter by an emphatic use of 'ought'. My argument is that they are relying on an illusion, as if trying to give the moral 'ought' a magic force.[14]

This conclusion may, as I said, appear dangerous and subversive of morality. We are apt to panic at the thought that we ourselves, or other people, might stop caring about the things we do care about, and we feel that the categorical imperative gives us some control over the situation. But it is interesting that the people of Leningrad were not struck by the thought that only the *contingent* fact that other citizens shared their loyalty and devotion to the city stood between them and the Germans during the terrible years of the siege. Perhaps we should be less troubled than we are by fear of defection from the moral cause; perhaps we should even have less reason to fear it if people thought of themselves as volunteers banded together to fight for liberty and justice and against inhumanity and oppression. It is often felt, even if obscurely, that there is an element of deception in the official line about morality. And while some have been persuaded by talk about the authority of the moral law, others have turned away with a sense of distrust.[15]

NOTES

* 'Morality as a System of Hypothetical Imperatives' originally appeared in *The Philosophical Review*, Volume 81, Number 3, July 1972.

[1] *Foundations of the Metaphysics of Morals*, Sec. II, trans. by L. W. Beck.

[2] Ibid.

[3] Ibid.

[4] According to the position sketched here we have three

forms of hypothetical imperative: 'If you want x you should do y', 'Because you want x you should do y', and 'Because x is in your interest you should do y'. For Kant the third would automatically be covered by the second.

[5] To say that at that moment one wants to be a respectable philosopher would be another matter. Such a statement requires a special connexion between the desire and the moment.

[6] I am here going back on something I said in an earlier article ('Moral Beliefs', reprinted in this volume) where I thought it necessary to show that virtue must benefit the agent. I believe the rest of the article can stand.

[7] Op. cit., p. 119. See also Foot, 'Moral Arguments', p. 105.

[8] To say that moral considerations are *called* reasons is blatantly to ignore the problem.

In the case of etiquette or club rules it is obvious that the non-hypothetical use of 'should' has resulted in the loss of the usual connexion between what one should do and what one has reason to do. Someone who objects that in the moral case a man cannot be justified in restricting his practical reasoning in this way, since every moral 'should' gives reasons for acting, must face the following dilemma. Either it is possible to create reasons for acting simply by putting together any silly rules and introducing a non-hypothetical 'should', or else the non-hypothetical 'should' does not necessarily imply reasons for acting. If it does not necessarily imply reasons for acting we may ask why it is supposed to do so in the case of morality. Why cannot the indifferent amoral man say that for him 'should$_m$' gives no reason for acting, treating 'should$_m$' as most of us treat 'should$_e$'? Those who insist that 'should$_m$' is categorical in this second 'reason-giving' sense do not seem to realise that they never prove this to be so. They sometimes say that moral considerations 'just do' give reasons for acting, without explaining why some devotee of etiquette could not say the same about the rules of etiquette.

[9] I am grateful to Rogers Albritton for drawing my attention to this interesting use of expressions such as 'have to' or 'must'.

[10] Pt. II, Introduction, sec. II.

[11] Immanuel Kant, *Critique of Practical Reason*, trans. L. W. Beck, p. 133.

[12] It is not, of course, necessary that charitable actions should *succeed* in helping others; but when they do so they do not *happen* to do so, since that is necessarily their aim. (Footnote added, 1977.)

[13] See, e.g., *The Metaphysics of Morals*, pt. II, sec. 30.

[14] See G. E. M. Anscombe, 'Modern Moral Philosophy', *Philosophy* (1958). My view is different from Miss Anscombe's, but I have learned from her.

[15] So many people have made useful comments on drafts of this article that I despair of thanking them all. Derek Parfit's help has been sustained and invaluable, and special thanks are also due to Barry Stroud.

An earlier version of this paper was read at the Center for Philosophical Exchange, Brockport, N.Y., and published in *Philosophical Exchange* (Summer 1971). Footnote 8 is mostly from this paper, and I add here some other paragraphs that may throw light on the present paper.

My own view is that while there are ends within ethics which one should adopt (as e.g. that one's children get a good education) there are difficulties about saying that one 'ought' to take account of the general good. For either the 'ought' means 'morally ought' or 'ought from a moral point of view' or else it does not. If it does we have a tautological principle. If it does not the problem is to know what is being said. By hypothesis a prudential 'ought' is not intended here, or one related to others of the agent's contingent ends. Nor do we have the 'ought' and 'ought not' operating within the system of etiquette, or some system of institutional rules. This 'ought'—the one in the sentence 'One ought to be moral'—is supposed to be free floating and unsubscripted, and I have never found anyone who could explain the use of the word in such a context. (They are apt to talk about the expressing of resolves, or of decisions, but it is then not clear why we need the 'ought' terminology when 'I resolve' and 'I've decided' are already in use.) My own conclusion is that 'One ought to be moral' makes no sense at all unless the 'ought' has the moral subscript, giving a tautology, or else relates morality to some other system such as prudence or etiquette. I am, therefore putting forward quite seriously a theory that disallows the possibility of saying that a man ought (free unsubscripted 'ought') to have ends other than those he does have: e.g. that the uncaring, amoral man ought to care about the relief of suffering or the protection of the weak. In my view we must start from the fact that some people do care about such things, and even devote their lives to them; they may therefore talk about what should be done presupposing such common aims. These things are necessary, but only subjectively and conditionally necessary, as Kant would put it.

Kant would of course object that I am treating men as if, in the army of duty, they were volunteers, and this is exactly my thought. Why does Kant so object to the idea that those who are concerned about morality are joining together with like-minded people to fight against injustice and oppression, or to try to relieve suffering, and that they do so because, caring about such things, they are ready to volunteer in the cause? Kant says that there is a kind of conceit involved in such a conception. Why does he think this? He supposes that in so viewing the matter (in seeing ourselves as volunteers) we are forgetting our nature as human beings, members of the phenomenal as well as the noumenal world, whose will may be determined by the moral law but also by desire, so that we do not automatically act as a being with a holy will would act, and are beings for whom the dictates of reason take the form of a command. Let us agree that a human being doesn't necessarily have moral ends, and that even when he does his inclination may be stronger than his moral resolves. Both of these things being true a man could be mistaken either in supposing that his concern for others could not fail, or in supposing that by merely following his inclinations he could serve moral causes with no need for resolution or self-discipline. We have already pointed out that a morality of hypothetical imperatives is not a morality of inclination; resolution and self-discipline being at least as necessary to achieve moral ends as to achieve anything else. So let us consider the other suggestion, that the supporter of the hypothetical imperative is failing to recognise that the desires of even the most moral of men could always change. This charge should be denied. One who supports the hypothetical imperative does not forget that desires might change; he has simply given up trying to deal, in advance, with such a contingency by saying to himself that he would still be under command. That this seems hard to accept is the fact that lies, I think, at the heart of Kantianism in ethics, and to the neo-Kantianism of those who accept his strictures on the hypothetical imperative though rejecting the rest of his theory. It will seem to many impossible that one should have nothing to say about the case where moral concerns have vanished, except, of course, to note the character of the man concerned, and in the case of other people, to take what measures one can to stop them from doing harm. Perhaps the greatest fear is of a change in oneself; one wants as it were to make sure one is stuck with the idea of acting morally whatever one's concerns have become. The move betrays a lack of confidence which oddly does not often trouble people when their devotion is to causes other than those of morality.

These suggestions are, of course, directly relevant to Kant's arguments against the hypothetical imperative, for the same problems arise about the meaning of the things that he says. What, for instance, does it mean to say that moral rules are categorical commands? In the first place they are not commands at all, neither commands of men nor commands of God; or rather if they are commands of God it is not as commanded by God that they are in Kant's sense categorical commands. (This he says explicitly.) What we actually have are rules of conduct adopted by certain societies, and individuals within these societies; and Kant is saying that these rules are universally valid. But when we put it this way, in terms of rules, the difficulty of understanding the notion of universal validity is apparent. (It can no longer mean that everyone is commanded, which shows that there is some point in denying Kant the picturesque language of commands.) Kant's thought seems to be that moral rules are universally valid in that they are inescapable, that no one can contract out of morality, and above all that no one can say that as he does not happen to care about the ends of morality, morality does not apply to him. This thought about inescapability is very important, and we should pause to consider it. It is perhaps Kant's most compelling argument against the hypothetical imperative, and the one that may make Kantians of us all.

There is, of course, a sense in which morality is inescapable. Consider, for instance, moral epithets such as 'dishonest', 'unjust', 'uncharitable'; these do not cease to apply to a man because he is indifferent to the ends of morality: they may indeed apply to him because of his indifference. He is judged by the criteria of morality when moral character is in question, and Kant is indeed right in saying that these criteria are independent of his desires. (*Contrast* a word such as 'rash'). No one can escape the application of the moral terms by pleading his indifference. Nor can he escape them by turning to ways of life in which he can be counted as being neither morally good or morally bad, as he can escape being a good or a bad husband by simply not marrying, or a good or bad carpenter by refusing to take up the tools. In this sense, then, morality is inescapable, but this can be accepted, and insisted on, by Kant's opponent, the defender of the hypothetical imperative. The latter may also agree that the application of such epithets will often be the vehicle for the expression of opposition, disgust or hatred. It has already been agreed that with our present 'non-hypothetical' use of 'should' in moral contexts the application of the moral 'should' is also inescapable. But someone who thinks that significant concessions have now been made to Kant must answer the following question. Has anything been said about the inescapability of morality which could not also be said about the inescapability of etiquette? For just as a man is immoral if he does certain things, despite his indifference to the nature and result of his actions, so he is rude or unmannerly, or one who does what is 'not done', whatever his views about etiquette. Since no one says that the rules of etiquette are categorical imperatives the task must be to explain the additional inescapability belonging to morality.

We must return, therefore, to the difficulty of discovering what Kant can have meant by saying that moral rules have objective necessity, are categorical commands, are universally valid, or are binding upon the will of every free agent. Nothing that we have yet considered has given Kant what he wants, and one cannot, I think, avoid the following conclusion. Kant's argument that moral rules have a peculiar and dignified status depends wholly upon his attempt to link moral action with rationality through the mere concept of the form of law and the principle of universalizability, as interpreted by him. In acting morally Kant thinks that we do as reason dictates. In acting immorally we are acting irrationally, and if this is not how Kant puts it, it is what he must show in order to make his point; if it could be proved, then any man, whatever his desires, could be shown to have reason to act morally, since one has reason to do what it is rational to do. The difficulty, as everyone knows, is to accept Kant's arguments purporting to show that morally bad actions are those whose maxim could not belong to a universally legislative will, and moreover that action according to such maxims is irrational action. These difficulties have been argued *ad nauseam*, and I shall not repeat the arguments here. All I would claim to have shown is that no one who rejects Kant's attempts to derive morality from reason has been given any reason to reject the hypothetical imperative in morals. It is commonly believed that even if Kant has not shown the connexion between reason and morality he has at least destroyed the hypothetical imperative. I have urged that, on the contrary, there is no valid argument against the hypothetical imperative to be found in Kant should the argument from reason fail. (Footnote added in 1977.)

XII

A Reply to Professor Frankena*

Professor Frankena finds himself in a state of bewilderment about my opinions, particularly about those expressed in two recent articles, 'Morality and Art'[1] and 'Morality as a System of Hypothetical Imperatives',[2] which he discusses in an article pointedly entitled 'The Philosopher's Attack on Morality'.[3] To say, as he himself does, that he finds these articles 'somewhat unclear' seems on the internal evidence to be something of an understatement; he finds them full of uncertainties, contradictions, ambiguities and qualifications, and I do not know how he thinks anyone could have written such stuff.

I will try to be very plain in my reply. First as to the question of whether I was attacking morality itself, or a certain view of morality: it was definitely the latter. I have on occasions suggested that morality should be indicted for its ineffectiveness, and I suppose it was something of this kind that Professor Hare heard, and from which he concluded that I wanted to reject morality itself. But in the published articles it was the fictions surrounding morality that I wanted to expose; if Professor Frankena thinks that a morality such as I describe—a defictionalised morality—is no morality, this is an issue between us.

That Professor Frankena signally failed to understand me is obvious, and it is not surprising that he did. In the first place he ran together the things I said in 'Morality and Art' about the relativity of some moral judgements with the things I said there and in the later article against the doctrine of the Categorical Imperative. In 'Morality and Art' I remarked that while we were ready to admit that some judgements of artistic merit were relative to the taste of an age, we were inclined to deny relativity to any of the judgements of morality; whereas my own view is that while some moral judgements may even be strictly provable, from the definition of morality and from the facts, others at the other end of the spectrum depend on assumptions which we are free to make or not to make. (I gave as an example the assumption that the human foetus is a human being from the moment of conception.) After discussing this issue I went on to what was explicitly stated to be a further point in the contrast of our attitudes to art and morality, namely that we tend to think of morality as having an authority over our actions that artistic doctrines do not; it was the idea of moral judgements as authoritative or necessarily binding that I took up, and attacked, in 'Morality as a System of Hypothetical Imperatives', where nothing was said about the earlier point.

Professor Frankena must have failed to notice that the two points were different, or he could not have written, in a purported summary of my views, 'we pretend that moral principles and judgments are non-hypothetical, objective, absolute, fixed, universally applicable, inescapable, categorical, rational, and authoritative in ways or to degrees that we are not warranted in doing'[4] and then gone on to say that I 'qualify' this view when I say that some moral judgements are strictly provable. In the first place he has thrown the two different theses of mine together in concocting the list; and in the second he finds qualification where there is none. To say that some moral judgements are provable, from the concepts of morality and from certain facts, is not to qualify the judgement that some are not so provable. At this point I was contrasting some moral judgements with others—for instance a judgement about the wickedness of Hitler's treatment of the Jews with a judgement about abortion. But when I attacked the doctrine of the Categorical Imperative I was talking about moral judgements in general; in my view none of them have the kind of authority or binding force that is claimed for them, and I did not qualify this by saying that some of them do have it. No wonder Professor Frankena found my articles 'somewhat unclear' when he treated the two separate discussions as discussions of a single point.

This confusion is one source of Professor Frankena's bewilderment. Another and more important reason why he failed to

understand me is that he seems not to have noticed the distinction, made on pp. 160–1 of 'Morality as a System of Hypothetical Imperatives', between a non-hypothetical use of 'ought'
(Henceforth NHU) and a non-hypothetical imperative (NHI).
I used the convenient example of etiquette to illustrate the observation that one may have the first without the second. For we
say 'You ought to do *x*' to make a point of etiquette even if the
subject convinces us that it is in no way ancillary to his desires
and interests to do so. Thus we do not withdraw the 'ought'
statement as we would withdraw a statement, e.g. about the
train a man should take, or the food he ought to eat, in the
range of examples which are typically cases of advice. In my
terminology the 'ought' of etiquette should therefore be labelled a non-hypothetical use (NHU). Nevertheless we would
hardly deny that judgements of etiquette express hypothetical
imperatives, in the sense that they have no automatic reason-
giving force independent of the agent's interests or desires. My
challenge, which Professor Frankena has done nothing to
meet, is that morality should be shown to be different from
etiquette *in this respect*. Of course the two are different in many
ways; for one thing etiquette is conventional as morality is not.
But what I want to hear of is a difference relevant to my
particular problem about why we should think that judgements of etiquette are hypothetical imperatives while judgements of morality are not.

I am sure that my terminology, and particularly my invention of the expression 'non-hypothetical use of "ought"' was
not happy, and I will think up some other name for it. What I
must insist, however, is that no one can convict me of unclar-
ity by saying that it is not clear what I want to do with
'non-hypothetical "oughts"' (whether to retain or reject
them) when he himself puts the question in this form. For in
terms of my distinction between non-hypothetical uses of
'ought' and 'oughts' used to express imperatives that are not
hypothetical there are two questions here not one. Does Professor Frankena want to know if I think we should abolish the
non-hypothetical use (NHU) in morals, or does he want to
know if I think we should abolish the non-hypothetical
imperative in morals (NHI)? He should of course mean the
former, for if my thesis is correct the latter does not exist.

Moral judgements are, I say, hypothetical imperatives in the sense that they give reasons for acting only in conjunction with interests and desires. We cannot change that, though we could keep up the pretence that it is otherwise. To hang on to the illusion, and treat moral judgements as necessarily reason-giving, is something I would compare to a similar choice in the matter of etiquette; and indeed we do find some who treat the consideration that something is 'bad form' or 'not done' as if it had a magical reason-giving force. We may suppose such persons harmless, but can hardly hold them up as models of rationality. Yet this is just what Professor Frankena does think rational in the case of moral judgements. He also thinks that morality itself depends on it, to which I should reply that if this were true, as I do not believe it is, then so much the worse for morality. What Professor Frankena must do if he is to make a point against me is to show that it is not an illusion to think morality different in this respect from etiquette. All he does, however, is to *assert* that to take moral imperatives as non-hypothetical is the more rational course, and that the man who does so is morally better than the one who does not. Unless we are to think that moral goodness depends on philosophical error, the second point must wait upon proof of the first, and once more I would point out that none has been offered.

There is, if I am right, no question of choosing whether moral judgements shall be hypothetical imperatives. They are hypothetical imperatives, and a decision to obey them blindly will not alter the fact. What we can, however, choose is whether to change our linguistic usage by dropping the non-hypothetical use of 'ought' or whether to leave things as they are. This does not seem to me a very important matter, so long as we understand the consequences of each choice. Let us set them out.

1. If we make no change we are left with some uses of 'ought' which do not carry with them the implication of reasons for acting. When we say of some particular individual that he ought to do something, we may consistently add 'But he has no reason to do it'. And this we may find objectionable, once it is brought out into the open.

There are, however, ways of weakening the force of a

non-hypothetical use of 'ought'. We may, for instance, qualify 'You ought to do *a*' by adding 'from the point of view of etiquette', 'morally speaking', and so on. This qualification is, it should be noticed, stronger than the one that merely removes the implication of *conclusive* reasons for acting. The expression 'By the rules of etiquette' unambiguously makes the stronger qualification, as 'from the point of view of etiquette' does not.

2. If we decide to give up the non-hypothetical use of 'ought' in such areas as etiquette and morality, in order to preserve the strong connexion between 'ought' and reasons for action, a different connexion will be broken—a connexion between two types of moral judgement and between two types of judgements about etiquette. As things are we are inclined to infer some ought-type statements from some statements of the 'good F' 'good G' form; for instance to move from 'He will act badly if he does *a*' to 'he ought not to do *a*'. Will it matter if we can no longer do this? I think not for the following reason. Moral judgements of the '*x* is a good man' form ought to be interpreted as showing the same pattern, so far as the connexion with reasons for action are concerned, as judgements about good doctors, good friends, good daughters, good citizens, and the rest; and as I have elsewhere tried to show, propositions of the 'good F' 'good G' form do not, in general, have a direct connexion with reasons for choice.[5] One cannot, except in special cases, infer 'NM has a reason to do *a*' from 'NM must do *a* if he is to be a good such and such', since this particular individual may have no reason to be a good such and such. Outside areas such as etiquette and morality there is, therefore, a gap between judgements of the 'good F' type and the reason-bearing judgements about what an individual ought to do. If judgements about good men, good actions, etc., and judgements about what a man ought to do morally speaking are seen in their natural alliances one does not expect a simple entailment relation between one type of judgement and the other. This, I think, is the true gap that can open between 'is' and 'ought', but it comes within what has been called 'evaluation', and a different account is to be given of the distinction between, e.g. 'is a red F' and 'is a good F'.

As to the provability of certain moral judgements; what

becomes of that if we choose the second alternative and jetti-
son the non-hypothetical use of 'ought'? Obviously the provability of *ought* judgements would be affected, at least if one
were thinking, as I was, of a proof from facts such as the
intention of killing millions of innocent persons, and not from
facts among which were included the agent's interests and
desires. But even if we decided to throw out the non-
hypothetical use of 'ought' in order to keep the strong connexion between 'ought' and reasons we would not have reason to
do the same in the case of other forms of moral judgement. As
I have insisted in several articles, no one can deny that he is a
wicked or otherwise morally bad man on the ground that his
immorality is not contrary to his interests and desires. And
given the pattern on which these judgements of goodness or
badness are to be interpreted there is no difficulty about this.
Professor Frankena is, therefore, wrong in saying that on her
own views 'Mrs Foot is wrong in thinking that some moral
propositions can be proved from the facts to all men',[6] even on
a restricted interpretation of 'the facts'. But I think that Professor Frankena's mistake may here be partly due to my lack of
explicitness; I should have spelled out the difference between
judgements of different forms.

Finally I should state, for the record, that I do not hold the
view of reasons that Professor Frankena attributes to me, and I
do not think I have ever said anything to imply that I did. I do
not use 'reason' for 'something that tends to move to action' as
he postulates on p. 351. I believe that a reason for acting must
relate the action directly or indirectly to something the agent
wants or which it is in his interest to have, but an agent may fail
to be moved by a reason, even when he is aware of it, and he
may also be moved by something that is not a reason at all, as
e.g. by the consideration that something is contrary to etiquette. Being moved is therefore neither a necessary nor a
sufficient condition of having a reason.

NOTES

* 'A Reply to Professor Frankena' originally in *Philosophy*,
Volume 50, 1975.

[1] *Proc. Brit. Acad.*, LVI (1970). Reprinted in Burnyeat and Honderich (eds.) *Philosophy As It Is* (Penguin, 1978).
[2] Reprinted in this volume.
[3] *Philosophy* 49, 1974, pp. 345–56.
[4] Op. cit. p. 347.
[5] 'Goodness and Choice', reprinted here.
[6] Frankena, op. cit., p. 349.

XIII

Are Moral Considerations Overriding?

It is often said that in practical reasoning moral considerations must be overriding considerations; but I do not myself know of any good defence of this proposition, or even an exposition which makes the thesis clear. In my article 'Morality as a System of Hypothetical Imperatives' (reprinted in this volume) I said that there was nothing in this idea that could be used in defence of the doctrine of the categorical imperative, and that seems to me as true now as it seemed to me then. But I remember at the time thinking that there was something interesting in the idea that moral considerations are overriding, and that one should at least explain the pervasiveness of the thought.

I shall therefore consider two passages from a recent article by Professor D. Z. Phillips,[1] which present a weak version of the thesis, by which I mean of course not one that is weakly defended but one whose claims are modest, and which should, therefore, be defensible if any version is. Professor Phillips wants to show that to anyone who cares about morality moral considerations must be 'the most important of all considerations'.

In one passage Professor Phillips writes:

. . . moral considerations are, for the man who cares for them, the most important of all considerations . . . we *do* say that moral considerations are all-important, that not hurting a person or humiliating him in public, for example, is more important than the formalities of greeting. (p. 150)

In another he says:

A man may, of course, succumb to temptation and put other matters before his moral obligations. In that case, however, he feels remorse for what he has done. The demands of etiquette are . . . conditional in so far as morality may ask us to put them aside. The demands of morality, however, are unconditional, in that they cannot be put aside for considerations of another kind. (p. 150)

Since the theses of these two passages differ, in a way that Professor Phillips has not, perhaps, noticed, one must discuss them separately. The question to ask is what, in each of the passages, is meant by 'a moral consideration'? In the first passage we are given the following examples of moral considerations: it is a moral consideration that if a certain thing is done a man will be hurt, or again that he will be humiliated in public. In the second passage, however, it is a 'demand' of morality that is a moral consideration, so the kind of consideration that Professor Phillips now has in mind is, presumably, that it would be immoral to do a certain thing, or morally permissible, or required. Thus in the first case it was a piece of evidence that was in question, but here it is a verdict or moral judgement. Now we can speak quite naturally of a moral consideration in either case; but it is important that we know which we are talking about at any given point in the argument, and I shall therefore invent a piece of terminology, calling the first kind of moral consideration *evidential* and the second *verdictive*. That a promise is being broken, or a man killed or injured, is an evidential moral consideration; that something immoral is being done is a verdictive moral consideration.

Let us now use this terminology in discussing the passages from Professor Phillips's article. The first passage quite clearly has to do with evidential moral considerations, since he illustrates the assertion that 'moral considerations are, for the man who cares about them, the most important of all considerations . . .' with the example of the hand, offered where handshaking is not (by the rules of etiquette) appropriate. Someone who cares about morality takes this hand in order to avoid hurting the other's feelings, or humiliating him in public. The consideration that he would be hurt or humiliated if his hand were not shaken is, by implication, picked out as a 'moral consideration'; and if it is a moral consideration it is obviously a moral consideration of the evidential sort.

So now we must ask whether it is true that evidential moral considerations are, as Professor Phillips thinks, *always* seen as more important (by anyone who cares about morality) than considerations of any other kind. It seems to me clearly false, and I will bring examples to show this. But it should first be remarked that the subject could be treated with any rigour only if we first said a good deal about the distinction between evidential moral considerations and 'other' considerations. It is clear for instance that the fact that something is contrary to the rules of etiquette is not itself supposed to be a moral consideration. And yet it could be relevant to a moral judgement; and in the right context almost anything could be: as for instance that what was done was done on a Friday or by a man whose name began with 'S'. Yet we do have an intuitive idea of a moral consideration which corresponds to the notion Professor Phillips seems to have in mind. For while it is *directly* relevant to the morality of an action that it would break a promise or bring death or injury to another, it is only *indirectly* relevant that it is done on a Friday. It could, for instance, be indirectly relevant in that that action done on a Friday was apt to create a traffic hazard, and so bring death or injury.[2] Thus a moral consideration is, roughly, a consideration through which those considerations not called moral considerations get their relevance to moral judgements. But it would take a good deal of apparatus before this could be made precise, and perhaps Professor Phillips would not agree that it caught his idea of a moral consideration. So what I shall do in bringing counter-examples to his thesis so far as it concerns evidential moral considerations is simply to take his example of a moral consideration, or to use considerations which I am sure he must think of as such.

Let us concoct a variant of Professor Phillips's own example about the handshaking. Once again, we shall say, someone is in danger of suffering hurt feelings or humiliation, but this time the price at which the hurt may be avoided is not the breaking of a rule of etiquette but rather the spending of a rather large sum of money; perhaps thousands of dollars or pounds. We may further suppose that the man who would spend the money doesn't need it, and is going to spend it on something for himself, not on some morally good cause.

We have, therefore, on one side the moral consideration about the hurt the other man will suffer, and on the other the non-moral consideration about the financial loss. If Professor Phillips's thesis were correct, anyone who 'cared about' morality would have to spend the money if he were so placed. But of course no one expects him to. In face of a sizeable financial consideration a small moral consideration often slips quietly out of sight.

To find another case serving as a counter-example to this part of Professor Phillips's thesis we may think of a rule of etiquette which operates on most people so strongly that it takes precedence even over a rather weighty moral considera-tion. There is, for instance, a distinct resistance to the idea that a host or hostess might refuse to serve any more drinks when the guests have had as much as is good for them given that they must drive home. In spite of the fact that they might kill or injure someone, which is surely a moral consideration, the host is not expected to close the bar and refuse to serve more alcohol as soon as this point has been reached. A strong rule of etiquette forbids such a course of action, and it is the rule of etiquette that takes precedence in ninety-nine cases out of a hundred in circles familiar to many of us. But to say that no one in these circles 'cares about' morality would be a bit stiff.

It seems, therefore, that when a moral consideration is understood in this way, as an evidential moral consideration, the thesis that no one who cares about morality ever gives considerations of etiquette precedence over moral considera-tions (or that he feel remorse if he does so) is quite implausible. So let us turn to the other version of the thesis. Perhaps what Professor Phillips and others like him are really thinking about is what I have called verdictive moral considerations. Let us see whether these must be the most important considerations for anyone who cares about morality.

The first thing to notice is that there have been very many communities in which a strict code of behaviour incompatible with the moral judgements of that community has existed and been strictly followed. I am thinking, for instance, of societies in which duelling codes were taught, and followed, without being reconciled with the prevailing morality. Dostoevski describes such a situation in the chapter of *The Brothers*

Karamazov which treats of the life of Father Zosima. As a young man Zosima had provoked another officer, simply because he was jealous of him, and forced him to issue a challenge. However, realising that his conduct has been disgraceful he waits until the other man has shot at him and then, when it is his turn to shoot, throws away his pistol and apologises. The seconds are furious about this breach of the rules, and the following exchange takes place:

I stood facing them and now I addressed them all seriously:
'Gentlemen,' I said, 'is it really so surprising these days to meet a man who can admit he has done something stupid and apologise publicly for the wrong he has done?'
'But you cannot apologise in the middle of a duel' my second shouted at me angrily.

Now it may be suggested that the outraged second *couldn't* have recognised that an apology rather than a shot was what morality called for, or that he *couldn't* have 'cared about' morality. Are not these things being said simply to rescue the thesis, which is now in danger of becoming trivial? Suppose the second did know perfectly well that, morally speaking, Zosima was right to apologise and refuse to shoot? And supposing he did care about morality? After all duelling rules impinge rather little on most men's time and leave plenty over for the pursuit of the moral life.

Perhaps it will be insisted that at least no one could actually *say* that an action was immoral and yet that it should be done. But why not? People do say this kind of thing, and it is only a preoccupation with the 'should' of moral judgement that makes anyone deny it. In fact a stronger word than 'should' is often used: a man will say that although it is wrong to do a certain thing he 'has to' or 'must' do it in order to stave off disaster to himself, or his family, or his country. And many people are ready to do what they know and admit to be wrong for far less than this, as for instance in spending money on frivolities while other people starve. Professor Phillips will have to say either that such a man cannot *ipso facto* 'care about' morality, in which case his thesis will once more become uninterestingly trivial. Or else he will have to say that such men are succumbing to temptation and are bound to feel remorse. But has he not noticed that it is quite common for people who do care about morality to admit that some of the things they do are morally indefensible and never lose a wink of sleep over it? Only a philosopher could say the kinds of things that Professor Phillips says; and if the Martians take the writings of moral philosophers as a guide to what goes on on this planet they will get a shock when they arrive.

In view of all this one may wonder why the proposition that moral considerations are overriding considerations has received so much support. What is it that makes the thought so persuasive? This is, I think, quite easy to explain. Let us go back to the contrast between morality and etiquette, which seems to be what most people have in mind when they argue that moral considerations are overriding. The fact is that there *is* a difference between the way the two codes are taught which is of just the right kind to explain why morality is supposed to be overriding in some significant way.

To make the difference apparent we may think again of Professor Phillips's example about the handshaking. We all agree, let us suppose, that his view of matter reflects the prevailing code of conduct about such a case and that the hand is to be shaken not refused. So the official teaching is that something we describe as contrary to etiquette is nevertheless to be done; and it is to this way of teaching the prevailing code of behaviour that we should attend. For what we then notice is that etiquette, unlike morality, is taught as a rigid set of rules that are on occasion to be broken. We do not, as we might have done, incorporate the exceptions to rules about handshaking and so on into the code of etiquette, when it would have appeared as *not* contrary to etiquette to shake the hand, where we are taught to do so. And this is why children find the whole thing so confusing. They are taught that some things are 'not done' and then expected to *understand* that (of course) such rules may be ignored in an emergency, or even in the kind of case that Professor Phillips describes. We could have incorporated the exceptions into the rule of etiquette, but we do not do so. But morality we teach differently. Moral rules are not taught as rigid rules that it is sometimes right to ignore; rather we teach that it is sometimes *morally permissible* to tell lies (social lies), break promises (as e.g. when ill on the day of an appointment) and refuse help (where the cost of giving it would be, as we say, disproportionate). So we tend, in our teaching, to accommodate the exceptions *within* morality, and with this flexibility it is not surprising that morality can seem 'unconditional' and 'absolute'. In the official code of behaviour morality appears as strong because it takes care never to be on the losing side.

And now we may ask whether *this* kind of 'absoluteness' and *this* difference between etiquette and morality, can be used to meet the challenge thrown down in my article 'Morality as a System of Hypothetical Imperatives' to the doctrine of the categorical imperative? That it cannot be used is obvious from the fact that any code of conduct could be taught in the 'flexible' rather than the 'rigid' way. And as a matter of fact one can point to a rather surprising example of a non-moral code that is taught in this way. I am thinking of the way in which it is taught that some things are not to be done because the doing of them is imprudent. For in spite of the fact that philosophers commonly talk about prudential judgements as if these merely weighed the interests of the subject, we do not actually speak of imprudence in this way. That something is foreseeably contrary to the agent's interests, is not in fact enough to make it imprudent. For if it were so a man would act imprudently whenever he went against his own interests, even if the sacrifice were strictly required by virtue or honesty. And we might indeed have taught that on occasions a man must act imprudently, as we teach that on occasions he must do what is contrary to etiquette. But since we do not do so we preach against imprudence as we preach against morality, and not as we preach against etiquette. But once again this is simply because the exceptions are incorporated into the code, not because judgements about what is imprudent are 'absolute' or 'unconditional' in any other way.

It seems then that the thesis that *evidential* moral considerations are invariably taken (by anyone who cares about morality) as more important than other considerations is simply false. The thesis that *verdictive* moral considerations are invariably taken as more important than other considerations is also false. This version of the thesis that moral considerations are overriding is, however, given the appearance of truth by a genuine difference in the way in which a moral code and many other codes are taught. The exceptions to moral rules are built in to the verdictive moral system and so it is *taught* that morality is always to be obeyed. With etiquette it is different, and therefore the rules of etiquette appear as a set of 'conditional' commands.[3]

NOTES

[1] 'In Search of the Moral Must', *Philosophical Quarterly*: vol. 27, no. 107 (April 1977).

[2] I am here indebted to an unpublished article by Robert Brandom, of the University of Pittsburgh, which is the best thing I have seen on the subject of the supposed overridingness of moral considerations.

[3] I am particularly grateful to Rosalind Hursthouse and John Giuliano, for their help with this paper.

XIV
Approval and Disapproval*

When anthropologists or sociologists look at contemporary moral philosophy they must be struck by a fact about it which is indeed remarkable: that morality is not treated as essentially a social phenomenon. Where they themselves would think of morals first of all in connexion with moral teaching, and with the regulation of behaviour in and by society, philosophers commonly take a different starting-point. What the philosopher does is ask himself what it is to make a moral judgement, or take up a moral attitude, and he tries to give the analysis in terms of elements such as feeling, action, and thought, which are found in a single individual. Controversy persists between emotivists, prescriptivists, and those who have been labelled 'neo-naturalists' as to just which elements are needed and how they must be combined; all are agreed, however, in looking to the individual for their location. We are first to find out how it must be with him if he is to think something right or wrong, or to have an attitude such as that of moral approval; then we may go on, if we choose, to talk of shared moral beliefs and of the mechanism by which morality is taught. The essentials are found in the individual; social practices come in at a later stage in the story.

In a way it is strange that so few people question the methodological assumption just described, since we are well aware that many concepts cannot be analysed without the mention of social facts. For example it is a commonplace that writing a cheque, or going bankrupt, is impossible without the existence of particular social institutions such as banks and debts; no one would think that he could say what it is to write a cheque without giving an account of the social practices which give these marks on these bits of paper their significance.

Examples may easily be multiplied. One recognises at once, for instance, that voting is something that a man can do only in the right social setting. Other people come in to the matter not just as being voted for, but also as the creators or perpetuators of the arrangements which make voting possible. Voting requires conventions about what counts as voting, and voting on a certain side; and a special piece of social stage-setting is needed for each election in so far as lists of candidates must be drawn up, or the possible choices established in some other way.

We are, therefore, well aware that the analysis of certain concepts cannot proceed without the description of social institutions and conventions. Why is it thought that we can ignore such things in analysing the fundamental concepts of ethics? One answer is that it is the attitude, not the act, of approval that we speak about in our moral philosophy, and that it is easier to believe that acts may require an appropriate social setting than that attitudes may do so. Another answer is that we have in mind the analysis of emotions such as fear, and that for these concepts the individualistic assumption seems to be justified. Whatever precisely is to be said about fear, however such elements as feelings, desires, actions, and thoughts are involved in *being afraid*, it does not seem necessary to look beyond the individual in order to understand the concept. Other people come in as the possible objects of fear, and conventions are needed for its verbal expression; but there seems to be no reason why a single individual should not feel fear whatever the social setting in which he finds himself. In this instance it is, therefore, right to start with the individual, going on, if one chooses, to shared fears and fears that can be attributed to social groups. No fact about society is implied by the attribution of fear to an individual as facts about society are implied by saying that he voted or signed a cheque. There are, therefore, mental concepts for which the individualist assumption is correct. The question is whether it is also right for the case of approval and disapproval. Are approving and disapproving more like voting in this respect, or more like feeling afraid?

The thesis to be put forward in this paper is that it is no more possible for a single individual, without a special social setting, to approve or disapprove than it is for him to vote. This will be argued for non-moral approval and disapproval; moral attitudes will be considered briefly later on.

It is evident that there is one case of approval which is more like voting than feeling fear so far as the relation to a specific social setting is concerned; this is the case of approval by an inspector passing e.g. plans for buildings in a city. The distinguishing mark of this kind of approval (apart from the fact that it is opposed to rejection rather than disapproval) is that the approving is something done, whether by a performative use of 'I approve' or by some other recognised device; if told that the inspector has approved the plans we can ask 'When did he do so?', asking not for the period during which he had an attitude (which perhaps he never did) but rather for the time at which the act of approval was performed. For such an act of approval a special social setting is obviously required. In the first place anyone who approves plans must be appointed to do so; the appointment may be formal or informal, but it must exist. Someone not designated as competent in the matter cannot be said to approve the plans; if he imagines himself to be doing so he must also imagine himself to occupy the relevant position. Moreover to each inspecting position belong not only conditions of appointment but also the standards which are to be used by the inspector. He is required to see if certain standards are met, and this is one of the things that makes his act one of approving rather than merely giving permission. In some cases he will be given the tests that he must apply; in others he will rather judge, in his own way, how far particular ends are served, as a school inspector may license a school on the basis of his judgement, however arrived at, that the pupils are well educated and cared for.

It is clear that we cannot describe this kind of approving without mentioning the social practices which create and maintain the position of inspector. There is, it seems, no need to prove the thesis of this paper so far as the acts of approval are concerned; the debatable proposition concerns the attitudes not the acts. It does not, however, seem right to argue from the features of one to the features of the other. No doubt it is not an accident that we use the same word 'approval' in both cases; but who can say just where the similarities lie?

We must, then, start afresh and ask whether the attitudes of approval and disapproval can exist only in a determinate social setting? Why is it commonly supposed that nothing of the kind is required? The main reason is, I think, that approving and disapproving are thought to be rather like wanting and not wanting. The chief element in their composition is supposed to be a readiness to work towards or away from some result, or perhaps from some *kind* of result. When one approves of the thing one is thought to favour it, which means working towards it, and the ill-defined term of art 'pro-attitude' is used to slide between wanting and approving.

I shall first try to show that such things as promoting and wanting are quite different from approving, and that wanting and promoting may exist without the possibility of approving; the same going for the opposites. For this I shall use a number of examples, all of approval and disapproval on non-moral grounds. Let us consider, for instance, parents who approve or disapprove of the marriage of one of their children; it is common for parents to do so, and we understand very well what this means. We notice, however, that a stranger cannot approve or disapprove of the marriage as the parents can, and we must ask why this is so. Why is it that I can approve of my own daughter's marriage, or disapprove of it, but not of the marriage of some girl who is not a relative, or even a friend? (Perhaps I have read of her in the local paper, or heard of her from a gossiping neighbour.) No doubt it will be objected that approval and disapproval of a marriage is not in fact confined to parents or even relatives and friends. For surely many white men in South Africa disapprove of the marriage of any white man's daughter to any black man, and surely there are grounds on which even reasonable people might disapprove of the marriage of some girl with whom they had no special connexion, for instance because it was a case of child marriage, or a marriage that was forced upon the girl. This is true, but it should be noticed that these examples all come within the sphere of public manners and morals. The fact that anyone can approve or disapprove on such grounds is something we will discuss later on. It is enough for the present argument, which confines itself to other areas, that there are grounds on which a parent can disapprove and a stranger cannot. Parents may disapprove of their daughter's marriage because the man is too old for her, or not rich enough, or not well enough connected; they may disapprove because they think that the marriage will not work out well, or because the family's honour or pride is at stake. Now the very same opinions may be held by someone unconnected with the family. Why is it that this other person cannot disapprove? One might think that it is because the stranger will not care about the girl's fortunes, or the fortunes of the family. But this may not be true. One may very well care about what happens to a stranger, either through a kindly disposition, or because there is some other factor at work. Then one will hope that the marriage will not take place and be sorry if it does; but it will still be wrong to say that one approves or disapproves. Nor is it a matter of having or not having actual power. Perhaps the parents are not able to influence what happens, and perhaps the stranger has this power; he decides to prevent the marriage, and by some means or other, perhaps by an anonymous letter to one of the parties, he is able to do so.

Nor does this appear to be an isolated case, which might be thought to depend on some ancient ritual aspect of parental approval. One can find other examples with the greatest of ease. Suppose, for instance, that an elderly couple are thinking of retiring to some seaside resort, and the evidence is against the success of the venture. A relative or close friend who knows how things are likely to turn out may therefore disapprove of the idea. But what about a stranger? Or what about one who though a neighbour is not a friend? He too is of the opinion that if they go they will regret it, and being of a kindly disposition he cares, and may actually care more than the friends and relations, about whether they are unhappy or not. Moreover, he may, by chance, be in a better position than the others to make a difference to what the old people do. Perhaps there is only one bungalow in the seaside town, and he can buy it himself; or perhaps he can send an anonymous letter that will frighten them off. Even with the caring, and the power, we still cannot say of him that he disapproves of their idea unless, surreptitiously, we introduce some new rôle for him, such as that of the family doctor or the social worker in charge of elderly persons' welfare. If, not having such a position, he went and offered them *advice* he would merely be impertinent or officious; if, however, he said that he disapproved he would be saying something that could not, in the circumstances, be true.

Exactly the same point, about some people being able to approve or disapprove where others cannot, is illustrated by examples in which some but not others are involved in a particular enterprise, like giving a dinner party, or robbing a bank, or where some but not others belong to a particular institution like a college, or support an organisation such as a sporting club. If my team captain chooses a certain player I may approve or disapprove of his choice; if your team captain chooses a player I may be glad or sorry, but barring a special circumstance such as bribery or blackmail I cannot approve or disapprove.[1]

It seems, therefore, that there is this first difference between approval and disapproval and, e.g., wanting and liking. What anyone can want or like is not restricted, logically speaking, by facts about his relationship to other people, as for instance that he is the parent or friend of one, and engaged in a joint enterprise with another. Such facts can, however, create possibilities of approving and disapproving that would otherwise not exist.

Another contrast lies in the fact that approval and disapproval are logically connected with specific opinions as wanting and liking are not. It would be, at most, a requirement of rationality that one wanted or liked things for a reason, whereas attitudes of approval and disapproval are impossible without grounds. One could not say that one disapproved of the marriage, the retirement plans, the nomination of a player, or the choice of guests, but that one had no reason for doing so. And only some considerations will count as grounds for approval or disapproval in each case. A parent cannot disapprove of the marriage of one of his children on the grounds that a neighbour, with no particular standing in the matter, will be annoyed by it, or that his, the parent's, income will be somewhat reduced. If he disapproves he must hold an opinion about the way the marriage will work out for his son or daughter, or about the way the family fortunes will be affected by it. Similarly, the relatives or friends of the elderly couple can disapprove of their projected move on the ground that they will be unhappy, but not because a neighbour will be put out by the sale of their house. With special assumptions these, too, could be grounds of disapproval of a moral kind, but for the moment we are putting morality aside. In the case of the joint enterprise the grounds of approval and disapproval are similarly limited but now the restriction is that they must have to do with the success or failure of the enterprise or with other shared ends of the participants. If we are giving a joint dinner party I may disapprove of your choice of guests or food or wine if I maintain that these are unfavourable to the success of the party, or, e.g., that they will ruin us financially. I may, however, have some reason of my own for disliking and working against some idea of yours for the dinner party which is nevertheless not a ground of disapproval. Perhaps some friend of mine in another town will be annoyed by the fact that we did not take his advice about where to eat, and I do not want to offend him. It does not follow that I can disapprove of what you have in mind.

Incidentally, examples such as these help one to get away from the idea that the grounds of disapproval must be lofty, or at least respectable. If two men are engaged together in some murderous project one may disapprove of the other's choice of assassins because the man chosen is not ruthless enough for the job.

The immediately preceding paragraphs have shown that approval and disapproval are possible attitudes only in one who has an opinion from a determinate range. The opinion itself is not, however, enough any more than the right position or relationship would be. Everyone has opinions about what is and is not a good idea in the matter of marrying, house-buying, the choosing of players, the running of dinner parties, and a thousand other matters of everyday life. And each could be a ground of approval or disapproval given the right context. We do not, however, say that everyone has thousands of approvals and disapprovals, one to each of his everyday maxims. The alone should give pause to anyone who wants to insist that he does *disapprove* of retirement to the seaside, of putting a long and a short man in a team together, of inviting to a dinner party guests who see each other every day, or whatever it may be that he thinks not a good idea.

Having seen something of the part played by opinion in making approval and disapproval possible, we may now add another to our list of the special positions which may enable someone to approve or disapprove. So far we have said nothing about the position of experts, but this is obviously one which can allow one to approve and disapprove where others cannot. I am thinking, naturally, of expertise in some practical field such as the curing of illnesses or mending of motor cars. The doctor can approve and disapprove of treatments as the layman cannot, and the mechanic is in a similar position *vis à vis* the design of an engine or the mending of a car. Anyone can, of course, disapprove of a particular form of medical treatment if moral or other social issues are involved: for instance of the treatment of a patient against his will. And anyone can disapprove of the practice of dishonest mechanics who 'mend' a car in such a way that it is temporarily in running order but liable to break down at any moment. But as before we are leaving such considerations aside. What a person without medical expertise cannot do is to disapprove of a form of treatment on purely medical grounds, any more than one who knows little or nothing about car engines can approve or disapprove of something done to mend a car on the grounds that the mechanic can. And the point is not that he cannot have the opinion which they have; even if he happens to have it that it is not enough to allow him to approve or disapprove.

It may be objected that one sometimes says to someone not in fact expert on motors 'Do you approve of my new car?' or to one not versed in fashion or dress designing 'Do you approve of my outfit?' But when we notice the point of doing so the examples turn out to be ones which support the 'special position' thesis. 'Do you approve?' is, in such circumstances, a complimentary and friendly thing to say, and the reason it is so is the pretence that the conditions for approval are fulfilled. We are treating the person as if he were an expert, or alternatively as a close friend to whose scrutiny purchases would naturally be brought.

It seems, then, that the position of an expert is one of those giving the standing necessary for approving or disapproving in non-moral matters. If a doctor thinks a form of treatment a bad form of treatment he can be said to disapprove of it. *His* disapproval is general, and can be applied to any case without the need for a special relationship. The position of an expert is like that of close friend or relation, or partner in a joint enterprise, in that it is enabling with regard to approval and disapproval. It is unlike the other positions in giving standing for approvals and disapprovals of a general kind. To illustrate the difference we may use an example in which expertise but also public policy is involved. An economist may, for instance, disapprove of certain kinds of taxes both in general and in any particular case. I, on the other hand, can disapprove of a measure of taxation only in my country. Nor is it hard to see why I should be able to do so if we notice that public policy in my community is like policy in a joint enterprise in which I am taking part.

Let us now ask how all this is related to the thesis that approval and disapproval is dependent on a specific social setting? Has this been proved, at least for the range of approvals and disapprovals to which we have so far confined our attention? In fact *that* thesis has not yet been argued even for this set of cases. We have indeed seen that the possibility of approval and disapproval may depend on what could, I suppose, be called a social fact, as that *A* and *B* are engaged together in a joint enterprise. But this was not the kind of thing that I had in mind in suggesting this thesis. I was thinking of social practices that might underlie this and all other forms of approval and disapproval.

To broach this topic let us consider again what it is to approve or disapprove, still thinking of the non-moral cases, but mostly because they seem to present less difficulty than the others. So far we have said something about the occasions for possible approval or disapproval, but nothing of its consequences. It is as if we had said who is appointed inspector, and what standards he must use in his inspection, but nothing about the fact that, by and large, it is only the plans that he approves that are put into effect. It is obvious that in the case of the inspector and his acts of approval it doesn't just happen that approval has these consequences. Without the agreement that gives his words or other actions these consequences, acts of approval would not exist. What I want to consider is whether something of the same kind may not be true for the attitudes of approval and disapproval? Obviously the same consequences are not in question for the attitudes and the act. The inspector disallows plans which he refuses to approve, and no one would suggest that this kind of command is the general rule where the attitude is concerned. What is the general rule is rather some kind of influence. Even this may be too strong a word; we should rather say that those able to approve or disapprove are as a general rule taken account of or listened to. And we must notice that 'as a general rule' is not put in for caution's sake, but rather to imply that there may well be instances of the attitude which do not have any such feature, either because it is both unexpressed and unnoticed, or for some other reason. Parents, we said can approve or disapprove of their offspring's marriage; it does not follow that some parents are not totally disregarded in decisions of this kind. Going back to inspectors and acts of approval we see that there is nothing nonsensical about the idea of an individual inspector so personally feeble or badly situated that none of his acts of approval made any difference to what was done. Nevertheless it is impossible to describe the concept of an inspector, or an act of approval, without talking about the practice of building the buildings he approves rather than those he turns down.

Nobody will deny that when other people approve or disapprove of what we are thinking of doing, or have done, we do take account of it. The question is whether it is a contingent fact that we do so, or whether it is not. On one view of the matter we could have had approval or disapproval—the attitudes—without any presumption that this would make any difference to what happened, rather as we could in theory have wanting which no one else took any account of. On the other view, which is the one for which I am arguing, the attitudes of approval and disapproval would not be what they are without the existence of tacit agreement on the question of who listens to whom and about what. On this view, where we have approval or disapproval we necessarily have such agreements, though it may not be necessary that we have just the agreements that we do. Thus it may not be a necessary fact about approval and disapproval that, e.g., relations are able to

approve where others are not. It could be that different classes
of persons were able to approve and disapprove, or even that
anyone could approve or disapprove of anyone in respect of
anything. But the society just described would necessarily
have very different social practices from ours. For if it is true
that where there is approval and disapproval there must
be the understanding that as a general rule other people's
views are taken account of there would have to be a lot more
taking account of other people's views in that society than
there is in ours.

That approval and disapproval can, logically speaking, exist
only against a background of agreement about the part that
other people's views shall be given in decision making, seems
to me to be correct. It seems that it is anomalous to join a
supposition about approval and disapproval with statements
such as 'no one is expected to take any notice of that'. And if
this is not obvious it is because the presumption that account
will be taken is only a presumption, and may be destroyed in an
individual case. What may destroy it is for instance the fact that
some individual forfeits our respect by his habitually foolish
opinions.

It will not be surprising if many find this thesis unacceptable
on account of a picture that they have of what an attitude is. An
attitude, they say, is something mental, and who can rule out
in advance the possibility of any mental occurrence or state in
any social setting? Suppose that in the 'wrong' social setting,
where there was no understanding that others were to be
listened to, some individual just did have the attitude of
approval or disapproval? (The 'wrong' social setting is either
that in which there is no presumption that anyone will listen to
anyone about anything, or else one which does not accord the
right standing to someone placed as he is placed.) The idea is
that whatever the social background this might be *how it was
with him*. The proper reply for one who agrees with my thesis
is that the hypothesis is impossible: that that couldn't be how it
was with him. If they say that approving and disapproving are
states of mind, and states of mind may logically exist in an
individual whatever social setting he is in, one would reply
that on that definition of 'state of mind' (which does not
particularly recommend itself) what is at issue is whether

approving or disapproving of something is a state of mind.

More powerful, perhaps, is the thought that approving is being *for* something, and disapproving *against* it. Surely it cannot be argued that these attitudes too require a tacitly recognised position? Curiously enough this is just what can be argued. If we go back, once more, to our old examples, we find that the stranger can no more be against the elderly couple's move to the seaside than he can disapprove of their going. If a relative or close friend says that he is against their going we understand him. To say to them 'I am against your going' may be ineffective, ill judged, or impertinent, but we understand the attribution of the attitude as conceptually in order. He is against their going. But what could it mean to say that the stranger was against their going, or to say it even of the neighbour who does not want new tenants next door? Either could want the old people to stay, but wanting–that–not is not the same as being against.[2] They could hope that the old people would not go, and could work against the project, but without some addition to the story we could not describe them as being against it. If the stranger, or the neighbour not a friend, went up to them and said 'I'm against your going', this would not be merely impertinent, like offering them advice; it would be presumptuous because presuming a relationship which did not in fact exist. Nor is the rule simply a social rule against expressing an attitude impertinently: 'he is against it' is just as bad as 'I'm against it', said to the people concerned. If this is not obvious it is because what is said at a distance, and not to their faces, leaves more room for fantasies of a special relationship.

What, then, is the relation between approving and disapproving on the one hand and on the other being for and against? It seems that approving and disapproving are special cases of being for and against, and that the two are practically indistinguishable in cases like the one described above. There are, however, examples of being for or against something which are not also instances of approval or disapproval.

Let us consider the following example. A group of people are deciding how to spend the evening together. Should they go to a cinema? Should they go into town? If they go to a cinema, which one should it be? Some are in favour of one thing. some of another. And this need not be a matter of approval or disapproval; they may simply be for or against.

The characteristic of this class of examples is that here we do not always have shared ends, as with the joint enterprise, but ends that may conflict. And here each man may, though he need not, favour a course of action on the ground that it suits himself. Each has in theory a voice in the decision even if in practice some particularly ineffective or unpopular individual may be ignored. What we now want to ask, as in our question about approval and disapproval, is whether the tacit agreement about how such questions are to be settled is necessary if the attitudes of being for or against different courses of action are to exist? It seems to me clear that it is so. That the agreement is necessary for one use of the expressions 'I'm in favour of X' or 'I'm against X' is obvious. For these expressions sometimes function rather like a device for registering a vote, and it seems clear that if you are going to register a vote you must have it, and that if you have it the relevance of what you say to the decision cannot be denied. Of course even formal votes can be miscounted, falsified, wasted, etc. Nevertheless where the words 'I'm in favour of X' are used in this way there must be some presumption that what the speaker wants is to be taken into account. Now it may be said that this is all very well when we are considering the use of expression 'I'm in favour of X' as if it were the casting of a vote. Perhaps it is a different matter when an attitude is involved. This seems a strange position because it drives a large wedge between two things apparently so closely connected. One would have thought that the expression of the attitude required rather more in the way of conditions than the 'voting' use. But on the present hypothesis a social background would be presupposed by the latter but not by the former.

If being for or against, in favour of or opposed to, are attitudes that do require a particular social background, then even where approval and disapproval are not themselves in question we have social conditions which are required for the attitudes. It is not, however, to be suggested that the agreement behind each is the same. When one approves or disapproves of something it seems to be one's opinions which are to be taken into account, and hence it is right to speak of being listened to. In the cases of being for or against just discussed the understanding is rather that one's wishes are to be taken into account.

The thesis that being for and against are attitudes which, like approval and disapproval, presuppose a determinate social background is strengthened by consideration of the following example. There is a prison camp in which the prisoners have no say whatsoever in the running of the place. The camp commandant takes decisions to suit himself or his superiors, and the prisoners' wishes are considered irrelevant. Now it is easy to suppose that some ruling, as e.g. about the work they are to do, affects the prisoners adversely. They do not like the new rule; perhaps they even hate it. Nevertheless in the circumstances imagined we cannot say that they are opposed to it or against it. This might seem to be because there is no such way in which they can work against it, but actually this might not be so. They might, for instance, scheme to kill the commandant in the hope that his successor would change the rule, and might actually have more effect on things than the members of some group, in a different setting, whose wishes were supposed to be taken into account. Nevertheless, since the position of being against something is one that only society can create, it is the former, not the prisoners, to whom it is available.[3]

Turning back to approval and disapproval we may at last raise the question of approving or disapproving of something on moral grounds. Does this, too, presuppose particular social practices? My intuition is strongly that it does, and that the practices and expectations necessary for moral approval and disapproval share at least some of the features of those which other kinds of approval and disapproval require. It is not, of course, that customs about who is to be listened to here establish classes of persons able to approve or disapprove where others cannot. In matters of morality we do not need experts, and such things as relationships are irrelevant to moral approval and disapproval. If anyone can approve or disapprove on moral grounds, then everyone can do so, or any sane person over a certain age. What is understood is that anyone is to listen to anyone when considerations are brought forward which are moral considerations.

There is, therefore, no difficulty in the idea that although no exclusive position is needed for moral approval or disapproval determinate social practices are nevertheless presupposed, and one might ask at this point why it is supposed that the possibility of moral approval and disapproval must be independent of social facts? It is not, after all, that *all* moral concepts must have such independence. Obviously, promising and owing are things that require a particular social background, and it has been argued by H. L. A. Hart that obligations are in the same boat so far as this is concerned.[4] Without the institutions that give these concepts application a man could not truly think that he had promised this, was owed that, or had a certain obligation. And if he, on his own, dreamed up the ideas, he would have to dream up the social practices as well.

One cannot say that just because moral approval and disapproval are *moral* we can see, ahead of any investigation, that they cannot require a determinate social setting. But does anything, apart from the analogy with the inspector's act of approval and (if the preceding arguments have been right) with non-moral attitudes of approval and disapproval, suggest this link between social practices and moral attitudes? The crucial experiment is to suppose a world in which the practices are different in the relevant respects, and then to see what would be possible for an individual in a world such as that.

What is it then, that we have, which may make moral approval and disapproval possible? What we have, which we might not have had, and perhaps will not always have, is a certain assumption about the determination of conduct within a certain area. It is our custom, and for all I know the custom of every society in the world, to take matters such as killing, stealing, and lying as a concern of the community. Everyone has a voice in the matter of whether or not these things are to be done; actions within this range are up for scrutiny, and by and large men take account of what others say about such matters. The actions are 'passed' or 'not passed', and moreover people are accepted or not accepted on the ground that they do or do not do them. This is, of course, so familiar to us that it is hard even to see it as a particular social setting which might be necessary for moral approval and disapproval. Perhaps this will be easier if we try to think the familiar setting away.

Suppose, for instance, that no one took much notice of what anyone else did, except when it affected him, or him and his family. Cows and horses behave like this. Suppose that human beings did so as well? Or suppose that people were interested in each others' actions but only aesthetically. They liked to watch rescues and not murders, or murders and not rescues, but this had no effect on the number of murders or rescues that were performed. In such settings people would not have a 'say' in what other people did as they do in a society such as ours. No one would be taught not to murder or ostracised for stealing; these things would be treated as the affair of the agent and his victim.

Now let us place in this world an individual of universal benevolence, hating the suffering that these people inflict on each other. And suppose that he sets out to try to prevent murders and to get other people to hate them too, and to refrain from such acts. Can we now say that his attitude to murder is one of moral disapproval? It seems to me that we cannot; and that the reason is that we cannot think of him, situated as he is, as refusing to 'pass' acts of murder. In this situation, where by hypothesis there is no social regulation of behaviour, and no one cares what anyone else thinks of what he does, no one has any authority to speak against murder. Then does a man who disapproves of something on moral grounds necessarily speak with the authority of society? In one way, of course, he need not do so, or else it would be impossible for anyone to come out against established moral opinions. But it matters here what our moral theory allows. If we think that there are no limits, logically speaking, to the considerations that may be argued by a moral dissenter, that is a would-be reformer, then his moral opinions need relate to no standards or goals accepted by others who have a morality. If, however, this seems on other grounds implausible, we shall think that even the most radical moral reformer must, if he is to keep within morality, refer to more or less determinate standards or ends. He and others must have common ground, and it is this that allows him to speak with authority even when he is criticising those among whom he lives.

What, however, are we to say about those who altogether reject morality? Surely we think it possible to disapprove of their actions, although they do not agree to take any account of what we say? This is true, and it is an important fact about the phenomenon we call 'morality' that we are ready to bring pressure to bear against those who reject it. But this no more shows that moral attitudes do not depend on agreement within human society than the possibility of asserting other kinds of authority against those who do not accept it shows that authority requires no agreement. The position of the one man described in the last paragraph is not at all like our position, given that we are able to bring the pressure and authority of society against those who reject the ends of morality. Nor do we get a position like his if we think of discovering some tribe whose members behave in the way we described earlier, having no morality and not, initially at least, caring whether we accept or reject them. For it matters that if we do find such a tribe we will confront them with the confidence that we have the world with us—the world that pays at least lip service to morality. Perhaps we would coerce them; perhaps whatever might be their cruelties, we would not. In neither case would it be nonsense to speak of disapproving of what they did.

Finally, I want to consider whether what was said earlier about the need for reasons for attitudes of approval and disapproval could be true also in the moral case. Must there not be some basic moral approvals and disapprovals for which no reasons are given?[5] To see how we should answer this question it will be useful to go back to our earlier examples of non-moral approval and disapproval. We were talking, for instance, of friends and relations who disapproved of an elderly couple's plan of retiring to the seaside, and of partners in joint enterprises who disapproved of choices of dinner guests. In one case the reason for the disapproval was the thought that the couple would be unhappy; in the other cases what was in question was the success of the joint enterprise, or some other shared end, these being the standards dictated by the particular context. And we see that indeed we cannot suppose the question 'Why do you disapprove?' applied to the objects specified in the standard. It is not that we could not understand questions such as 'Why do you disapprove when your partner makes a choice disastrous to the enterprise in

which you are both engaged?' or 'Why do you disapprove
when there is a plan afoot that will probably turn out badly for
one of your friends or relatives?' But we would have to understand these questions differently from 'Why do you disapprove of their moving to the seaside?' or 'Why do you disapprove of the choice of so and so?' Perhaps what is being asked
is why we go in for this kind of disapproving, which is not
something that everyone does. But to *this* question we could
answer that we didn't know and perhaps had no reason at all.
Similarly, in the case of moral approval and disapproval the
question 'Why do you disapprove?' requires an answer so long
as the standard itself has not been reached. Here even those
who have not decided on prescriptivist or emotivist grounds
that there could not be such a standard will agree that it is
much harder to say where it is reached. Perhaps there is more
than one 'good' to which moral standards relate, as for
instance both the common good and the liberty of the individual. But given that these are standards one does not need a
reason for applying them. The question 'Why do you disapprove of harming others?' is not to be treated like 'Why do
you disapprove of homosexuality?' One can ask whether,
and if so why, someone goes in for the approvals and disapprovals we call moral, but if there is no answer to the question
'Why?' no doubt is thrown on the attitude itself.

In conclusion, I should like to go back to the main thesis of
this paper and ask about the implications of the idea that moral
approval and disapproval can exist only in a setting in which
morality is taught and heeded. Does it imply that outside this
setting all moral judgement would be impossible? The answer
to this question must depend on the connexion we see between
moral judgement and approval and disapproval. If there are
any expressions—'right' and 'wrong' for instance—that serve
only to express these attitudes, these would obviously not be
in the language. But it is not clear that the whole of our moral
language has an essential connexion with the expression of
attitudes, even if any part does so. When, for instance, we
speak of good men and bad men, or good actions and bad
actions, we are using a form of expression ('good *A*') which is,
in general, linked to standard interests rather than speakers'
attitudes. There seems to be no reason why an individual who

observes that there is a certain interest in a given class of persons or things should not have the materials for the invention of a new expression of this form—as he might have been the first to put 'good' together with 'friend' or 'neighbour' or 'singer' or 'speaker'—and similarly he might introduce 'good man' or 'good action' even into a setting in which the attitudes of moral approval and disapproval were not possible. Whether he would then be said to have introduced 'moral judgement' is another matter, and one not easily decided given that the expression 'moral judgement' is for the most part a term of art. What is clear is that the expression of approval and disapproval is part of the complex phenomenon we call 'morality', and that if approval and disapproval are essentially social in the sense explained here, then the morality we are trying to analyse is so too.

NOTES

* 'Approval and Disapproval' originally appeared in P. M. S. Hacker, ed., *Law, Morality, and Society: Essays in Honour of H. L. A. Hart*, Oxford, 1977.

[1] Someone who resolutely denies what is said here might be asked if he really thinks that an American might disapprove of the British Government's bill giving a measure of Home Rule to Scotland.

[2] The only case I know of where to say one is for or against is the same as to say that one wants something, is in the locution 'I'm for so and so', meaning that one wants him to win. In this example, which was given me by Gilbert Harman, one is simply, perhaps in imagination, taking sides, and for that no special position or social setting is required.

[3] This way of putting it was suggested by Jerrold Katz, who has given me much help in the writing of this paper.

[4] 'Legal and Moral Obligation' in *Essays in Moral Philosophy*, ed. A. I. Melden (University of Washington Press, Seattle and London, 1958).

[5] This problem was put to me by Bernard Gert, and I am grateful to him for making me think about it in this context.

Index